Canadian Pacific Air Lines

Its History and Aircraft

by D.M. Bain

Appreciation and thanks are extended to the airline employees, aircraft enthusiasts, friends, colleagues and acquaintances who have helped to make this book possible.

ISBN 0-919487-19-X

First printing February 1987

Printed in Canada by
Cal/Oka Printing Ltd.,
Calgary, Alberta, Canada

© 1987 by Donald M. Bain,
    All rights reserved

Published by Kishorn Publications, 5124 - 33 St. N.W., Calgary, Alberta, Canada T2L 1V4
Additional copies may be obtained from the above address for $15.00 including postage.

Contents

Preface

When approached to take on the presidency of Canadian Pacific Air Lines, I was at once flattered and challenged. Although not large on a world scale, the airline had earned an enviable reputation for service across its five continent route system. In the span of 43 years it had grown from a collection of bush lines operating mostly to the Canadian north, into a highly regarded jet airline whose global system was among the few that crossed the Pole, the equator and the international dateline.

While its beginnings were firmly rooted in Canada, like those of its flamboyant first president Grant McConachie, considerable energy was devoted to the development of its international growth. Tight government control of domestic civil aviation during its formative years and well into the 1970s, was one reason to move in this direction. As a consequence, Canadian Pacific Air Lines forged important links between Canada and many key areas of the world but did not have a similar strength in its home country. Clearly, that was the major challenge immediately before me when I joined the airline as its president and chief executive officer in March 1985.

Publication of this illustrated history comes almost two years later and it is fair comment that during this time expansion of domestic operations has been unprecedented in the history of Canadian Pacific Air Lines. The stage had been set for this accelerated growth. The government was formulating its policy on the deregulation of the airline industry and it was clear to my colleagues and me that in order to be a truly effective competitor from coast to coast, Canadian Pacific Air Lines would have to become larger. It was no longer valid that by frying a better steak we could hold our own in a rapidly changing environment. We had to increase the size of our jet fleet and provide more flights on more routes so that we could claim to be a true alternative to the government airline.

While there is a great deal of work still to be done, I can state unequivocally with a pride shared by all Canadian Pacific Air Lines' employees, that Grant McConachie's dream of establishing a real private enterprise alternative is in the final stages of being achieved.

This reality has come about largely through the acquisition of Eastern Provincial Airways in Atlantic Canada and Nordair in Central Canada. Forming alliances with a number of commuter carriers across the country has also established CPAL's presence, for the first time, in smaller communities which now enjoy convenient air links with a continually growing global network. Donald Bain discusses these initiatives in this volume. It is a significant point, however, that our growth has resulted in Canadian Pacific Air Lines service to over 70 communities from the Atlantic to the Pacific to the Arctic Ocean, a substantially higher degree of coverage than any other airline including our major competitor.

Concurrent with these strategic moves was a major undertaking to develop a new look for the growing and revitalized national flag carrier. We wanted to convey unmistakably our image as a world class airline to an international clientele. Colour became the major agent of change. The new blue, white and red scheme met a requirement to be visually distinctive in our expanding global market. Retention of Canadian Pacific's well-recognized MultiMark logo but with some modification to give it more a feeling of motion added to the image which was completed with a return to the full company name — Canadian Pacific/Canadien Pacifique. Our people and our name have a great reputation and we will capitalize on that reputation as we take on new challenges.

In the early 1940s, Canadian Pacific Air Lines began taking shape and since that time, has served the air traveller in a style that has earned it a respectable place in the world aviation community. As this book will attest, the airline has played an important and increasingly important role in Canada's civil aviation history.

It is my privilege to comment here on behalf of all Canadian Pacific Air Lines employees who can justly take credit not just for the building of an airline, but for a significant contribution to the development of their country and for the regard in which Canada is held worldwide.

Donald J. Carty,
Vancouver, February 1987

Foreword

Having been on the fringes of Canadian Pacific Air Lines since its incorporation on May 16, 1942 and having served as a Director from 1943 to 1972 and Chairman from 1961 to 1968, I felt qualified to write a short Foreword to this very fine history of the Company written by my friend Donald Bain. After reading the galley proofs, I find it ranks with the excellent series of books he has written on the Canadian Pacific Railway. Moreover, it will fill a long-felt need since it provides a detailed review of the Company rather than being a biography of one person as was Ronald Keith's *Bush Pilot With A Briefcase*.

I became Senior Assistant to the Vice-President of the Canadian Pacific Railway in Montreal shortly before Grant McConachie was appointed by W.M. Neal as his assistant for Air. I was therefore in a unique position to watch the work of those two hard-nosed characters, C.D. Howe and W.M. Neal in full-flight during the formation of Canadian Pacific Air Lines. In 1943, I was sent to Toronto as an operating line officer when the railway was handling maximum wartime traffic and had a break from the airline until 1948 when I returned to Montreal.

Donald Bain has suggested that I include a few of my experiences with Grant McConachie whose part in the development of Canadian Pacific Air Lines he has covered in the ensuing text. Having known Grant from 1942 until his unfortunate death in 1965 and having flown hundreds of thousands of miles to many parts of the world with him, it is difficult to choose what to relate. I really do think that "the mould was broken" when Grant died.

His ebullient nature, salesmanship, technical knowledge and perspicacity combined to make him an ideal travelling companion. When we first saw the Parthenon in Athens, he commented that it must have been a fine building but that its maintenance had been awful! Two of our trips together stand out in my memory. In 1955, we made an eight day sweep over northwestern Canada, along the DEW line and over the Arctic Islands to above 75 degrees North. We had several of the directors and senior officers on board our DC-4 which was equipped with long-range tanks. Then, in 1959, Grant and I flew on a test flight of a Boeing 707. This was the first non-stop passenger jet flight from Seattle to Tokyo. On both flights, Grant blew up, with a mixture of hot-air and cigar smoke, the plastic world globe he always carried in his brief case and then proceeded to use a piece of string to demonstrate his Great Circle Theory of intercontinental routes centered on Vancouver. With the lesson over, he would then sit on the globe to expel the air!

Perhaps the low point in Grant's career was the Trans-Continental hearings held in Ottawa in 1958 where, because of inadequate preparation to meet the highly adversarial courtroom approach by the opposition, Canadian Pacific Air Lines' witnesses and Grant himself were cut to pieces. Reports were so bad that I went to Ottawa and sat in on the hearings on the third day with our General Solicitor, Ian Sinclair. On the fourth day, Ian was in complete charge and subsequently Canadian Pacific Air Lines was granted a licence for the transcontinental service. Later, of course, Ian followed me as Chairman of Canadian Pacific Limited and as Chairman of CP Air.

Grant also had remarkable foresight as evidenced by his action on the first jet airliner, the Comet, in 1949. It is too bad that the plane had not been thoroughly wrung out by the British as we figured that they had a five to seven year lead over other nations in jet propulsion. It must be fully 25 years since Grant lectured me on both supersonic and even hypersonic aircraft. He had worked out a flight plan for a hypersonic aircraft which would operate from San Francisco to Tokyo in 27 minutes, the passengers being strapped in in the horizontal position! Grant was ahead of his time for in his recent State of the Union Address, immediately after the Challenger disaster, President Reagan stated that "We are going forward with research on a new Orient Express that could, by the end of the next decade, take off from Dulles Airport, accelerate up to 25 times the speed of sound and obtain a low-earth orbit or fly to Tokyo within two hours." I am not sure that I would be happy in such a space vehicle knowing that each part had been built by the lowest bidder!

Donald Bain also requested that I write something on the differences in thinking in the 1940s and 50s between railwaymen and the airline personnel. Succinctly stated, we expected to keep the railway operating profitably and were skeptical of the airline ever contributing much to the parent company's profits. Time has proven this assumption to be correct. With the benefit of hindsight, had we to do it all over again, many of our decisions would have been different.

It is too easy to be critical of decisions made in the past and it must be remembered that the 20th century has been a period of the most rapid technological development in history. Perhaps the scope of this change is best illustrated by Sam McLaughlin of General Motors and one of my directors at Canadian Pacific. Sam was born at Oshawa in 1871 and served his apprenticeship as a carriage maker at his father's shop. Yet, he lived to watch, on a coloured television in 1969, man's first steps on the Moon. With such developments in one man's lifetime, is it not reasonable that some mistakes were made? Unlike the social, political and economic fields, where change has been less dynamic, we engineers have been in the vanguard of development. This makes choosing the right course of action difficult, but I am sure that, with luck, Canadian Pacific Air Lines' new owners have the ability to achieve profitability. Under the present policy of deregulation, airlines have had to adapt to changing situations. This may be the answer to obtaining profitability but I note that Canada is following the American lead in this area. Some thirty years ago, Kenneth Galbraith conducted an overall study of Canadian Pacific and I find it interesting that in a speech to the Press Club in Washington on June 9, 1986 he said, "Canada will never be able to escape the influence (of the United States). The Canadian and Polish situations are similar: they are both major errors of location."

N.R. Crump, C.C., D.Eng.
Calgary, February 1987

5

Introduction

Canadian Pacific has always been one of my "favourite" companies and one of my earliest memories is being lifted up by my uncle to look in the window of CP's offices in Trafalgar Square, London to see the models of the ships that were on display there. He had served on several Canadian Pacific vessels and enthralled me with stories of the sea. As a result, I grew up with warm feelings towards Canadian Pacific. This might sound strange as the company is not always held in such high regard by some Canadians. Nevertheless, in wartime Britain Canadian Pacific had an excellent reputation and this continues to the present day. From my own experience both as an adult customer of Canadian Pacific and for six years as an employee of a Canadian Pacific subsidiary, I can only say that I have always been treated courteously and well.

During 1977, while working for Canadian Pacific's subsidiary PanCanadian Petroleum, I spent some months coordinating the company's annual report and in the course of this work met Canadian Pacific's Special Photographer, Nicholas Morant. All my life I have been interested in transportation, with railways being my primary interest, and Nick and I had many discussions about the Canadian Pacific Railway or, as it was by then, CP Rail. He had taken photographs all over the system and I urged him to publish a work of his excellent shots. Unfortunately, I could not persuade him to do this and, as a result, decided to prepare it myself. As no company was interested in publishing the work, two railway enthusiast friends, Martin Booth, Bill Cruickshanks and I

determined to do it ourselves and on April 1, 1978 the first volume of *Canadian Pacific in the Rockies* was published. Because of the cost involved, we could only afford a 26 page booklet but with a map, an introduction and 25 large photographs, complete with extensive captions, it proved to be a popular format. Volume One has been kept in print since it was first published and, to date, approximately 15,000 copies have been sold. Not wishing to tamper with success, we have not altered the original format and the *Canadian Pacific in the Rockies* series extended to ten volumes. Other authors have prepared *Canadian National in the West, Canadian National in the East, Canadian Pacific in the East, Canadian Pacific's Big Hill,* and *Canadian Pacific in the Selkirks,* etc. There seems to be no shortage of areas to be covered and we now intend eventually to issue books on all aspects of Canada's railways. So far, we have published 30 railway works.

In 1979, I left PanCanadian to work for the Canadian Imperial Bank of Commerce, looking after the technical and business development areas of the Bank's international oil and gas interests. This involved extensive overseas travel and I have become quite an "expert" on the world's airlines. To pass the time in lonely hotel rooms around the world, I began reading anything I could on airlines, including CP Air. As was the case with CP Rail, I soon found that there had been relatively little published about the airline. True, there were numerous articles in magazines but nowhere could one find a single complete story detailing the history and aircraft of CP Air. So, in the summer of 1983 I decided to write this work which

would be considerably longer than our previous publications as it was felt that the complete story should be contained in a single volume.

Unfortunately, many of the airline's early records have not survived. This is probably the result of a number of factors. Possibly the constituent companies may not have kept complete records or, if they did, they may have been lost or destroyed. In addition, World War Two was at its height when Canadian Pacific Air Lines was formed and presumably there were more important things to do than ensure that old and sometimes trivial records were preserved. Furthermore, in 1949, the airline's headquarters were moved from Montreal to Vancouver and possibly all existing records were not transferred. Where gaps or conflicting reports exist, I have tried to determine the most likely information. If any errors have crept into my work, I alone am responsible and apologize for them. Where possible, events have been described chronologically although this has not been adhered to strictly where clarity and continuity have indicated otherwise.

While writing the work I have tried to be objective though I have no doubt that the Mackenzie King government tried its hardest to place Canadian Pacific in a subordinate position on the board of Trans-Canada Air Lines because of its distrust in the private enterprise system. During World War Two, when wartime conditions and intense competition had produced chaos among the many minor airline companies of northern and western Canada, the same government encouraged Canadian Pacific to purchase these companies and

soon after this announced that the railway companies would have to divest themselves of airline operations within a year of the end of the European war. That Canadian Pacific managed to weather these storms is a measure of the parent company's strength and determination to operate an airline successfully. That it succeeded in this is due in no small part to the character and business acumen of Sir Edward Beatty, L.B. Unwin, W.M. Neal, D.C. Coleman, Grant McConachie and the other senior executives who followed them.

As a result of the change from the regulatory atmosphere of the 1940s to the "open skies" policy of the 1980s, Canadian Pacific had an entirely different series of problems to overcome. With the acquisition of Eastern Provincial Airways and Nordair, together with the commercial agreements with commuter airlines, the new Canadian Pacific Air Lines offered a serious challenge to Air Canada in the home market. Now that Pacific Western Airlines Corporation has purchased CPAL, this challenge will become even more serious for the government airline and there is little doubt that the PWA/CPAL combination will be an important world airline.

Donald Bain
Calgary, February 1987

Canadian Pacific

The Canadian Pacific Railway Company was formed by Act of Parliament on February 15, 1881 and was incorporated formally under the laws of the Dominion of Canada the following day. The new company was charged with constructing a railway line linking Canada's west coast with central Canada and providing a railway service in perpetuity. Construction had already been commenced in several areas by the Canadian government and the newly formed company took over these projects. William C. Van Horne of Chelsea, Illinois was appointed General Manager on December 31, 1881 and began his duties the following day with the responsibility for building the line between Calendar, Ontario and Winnipeg, Manitoba (1,078 miles) and between Oak Lake, Manitoba and Savona's Ferry, British Columbia (1,090 miles). Originally, ten years had been allocated for this task and it is a tribute to Van Horne's drive and initiative that the final link between Calendar and Winnipeg was completed in May 1885 at Jack Fish Bay, 150 miles east of Fort William (now Thunder Bay). The last spike of the entire 2,891 mile line between Montreal and Port Moody, British Columbia was driven home by Sir Donald Smith at Craigellachie, 27 miles west of Revelstoke, British Columbia, on November 7, 1885.

However, although the physical link was complete, the government-built sections of the line had not been constructed to Canadian Pacific's standards and it was not until June 28, 1886 that the first through passenger train left Montreal for the west coast, arriving at Port Moody on July 4th. With this important event, Van Horne began to develop business for the newly completed line, encouraging immigrants to settle in the prairies and tempting tourists to visit Banff, Lake Louise, Glacier, and other mountain resorts. With financial acumen which must have brought pride to the hearts of the canny Scots who had played such an important part in the founding of Canadian Pacific, Van Horne elected not to solicit the outside assistance of companies such as Western Union or Pullman, instead opting for company controlled operations of telegraphs, sleeping cars and hotels. Hotels were established in the 1880s at Banff and Lake Louise in Alberta and Field, Glacier, and North Bend in British Columbia. Admittedly, the last three were constructed primarily to provide eating facilities for passengers on the transcontinental trains, dining cars being too heavy for the then relatively small steam locomotives to haul through the Coast, Selkirk and Rocky Mountains. Nevertheless, Canadian Pacific's ancillary services prospered and very soon the company had developed considerable tourist business together with through passenger traffic from Europe to the Far East. As early as July 27, 1886, the *W.B. Flint* sailed into Port Moody on charter to Canadian Pacific with a cargo of tea from Yokohama, Japan. Recognizing the potential of trans-Pacific traffic, Van Horne, made plans for regular services from the west coast to the Orient and on October 12, 1889, an order was placed with a British yard for three 6,000 ton vessels. During the construction of the ships by the Naval Construction and Armament Company at Barrow in northwestern England, R.B. Angus, who had been a member of the original railway syndicate,

suggested that they should be named after India, Japan and China, a suggestion adopted by Van Horne. Accordingly, the first of the ships the *Empress of India* arrived in Vancouver on April 28, 1891 at the end of its maiden voyage from Liverpool by way of the Suez Canal and Hong Kong. The *Empress of Japan* arrived in Victoria on June 22, 1891 and the *Empress of China* came into Vancouver on September 23, 1891. Very quickly, these vessels established an excellent reputation for comfort and service and Canadian Pacific ships plied the Pacific until the outbreak of World War Two.

Van Horne resigned as President of Canadian Pacific in June 1899 and was succeeded by Thomas Shaughnessy, another American and one who had been attracted north by the former as Chief Purchasing Agent for the Railway. Shaughnessy was equally as aggressive as his predecessor and in 1903 the company purchased the Allan Line which then operated a trans-Atlantic steamship service from Montreal to the United Kingdom. Canadian Pacific developed this service and the first Atlantic Empress, the *Empress of Britain*, was launched at Govan, Scotland on November 11, 1905. During World War One, Canadian Pacific vessels, which were registered in the United Kingdom, were requisitioned for war service and following the end of hostilities a very depleted fleet was returned to the company. But although the Great War brought about the development of the submarine, which had wrought considerable damage to the company's fleet, it also ensured great advances in aviation and Canadian Pacific, which had never ignored technolgical advancement, was

quick to recognize the future potential of air travel. As a result, in 1919 Shaughnessy had the company's charter altered by the Canadian Parliament such that:

"The Canadian Pacific Railway Company may establish equip, maintain, and operate services of aircraft of all kinds, for the carriage for hire of passengers, mails, express and freight between such points and places, within or without the limits of the Dominion of Canada, as may from time to time be determined upon by the Company, and for such purposes may acquire, purchase, lease or otherwise, and hold and dispose of property real and personal, and may layout, build, erect and construct aerodromes, hangars, depots, sheds, stations, workshops, buildings and structures, and the Company may purchase, manufacture and otherwise acquire and deal in aircraft of all kinds, and machinery, appliances, equipment, accessories, implements, apparatus, and all things whatsoever, and generally may exercise and enjoy all and singular such other powers, rights and privileges as may be necessary or expedient for the full and complete carrying out of the purposes aforesaid: provided that the exercise of the powers hereby conferred shall be subject to all such legislation and regulations by competent authority, whether general or special, as may have been heretofore or may hereafter be enacted or sanctioned for regulating or prescribing the conditions of aerial navigation

◀Opened in 1886, Glacier House was one of Canadian Pacific's first hotels and was constructed initially to provide railway passengers with meals during brief stops for all passenger trains. Following the opening of the Connaught Tunnel beneath the Rogers Pass, Glacier House's importance declined and it closed on September 15, 1925. It was demolished in 1929.

Archives of the Canadian Rockies NA66-241

or carriage and the obligation incident thereto."

From this statute, Canadian Pacific Air Lines developed although no immediate advantage was taken of this addition to the company's powers. However, to prevent eastern Canadian aircraft operators being purchased by American interests, Canadian Pacific was involved in the formation of the Aviation Corporation of Canada in 1929 although the company's involvement was not publicly acknowledged at the time. It was not until 1930, with the formation of Canadian Airways, that Canadian Pacific began to play a significant role in Canadian aviation. Throughout the 1930s, under the direction of Sir Edward Beatty, the Chairman and President of Canadian Pacific, the company became increasingly interested in commercial aviation. Between 1935 and 1937, Beatty made a strenuous effort to have Canadian Pacific become a major shareholder in what was to become Trans-Canada Air Lines, the national airline. However, because Canadian Pacific was required to provide half the capital investment but gain only a third of the representation on the new organization's board of directors, Sir Edward elected not to participate under these terms. As a consequence, the act creating Trans-Canada Air Lines as a wholly government owned company was passed by Parliament on April 10, 1937.

Undaunted, Sir Edward continued to support Canadian Airways and to make every effort to ensure that Canadian Pacific became more deeply involved in aircraft operations. By the end of the 1930s, competition was intense and, in many cases, routes were being flown at rates where profits were almost impossible to achieve even when aircraft were full. Frequently, several small companies were licensed to operate over the same route and, with the outbreak of World War Two, traffic declined rapidly and many aircraft operators found themselves in financial difficulties. In 1939, James A. Richardson, the President of Canadian Airways, died and Sir Edward subsequently was appointed as President of the company. In this position, the chaos of the airline industry caused by over-competition was readily apparent to him and the company decided to try to bring some order to this situation by acquiring various small airlines. During 1940 and 1941, Canadian Pacific purchased:

Canadian Airways Limited
Arrow Airways Limited
Dominion Skyways Limited
Ginger Coote Airways Limited
Mackenzie Air Services Limited
Prairie Airways Limited
Quebec Airways Limited
Starratt Airways and Transportation Limited
Wings Limited
Yukon Southern Air Transport Limited

Initially, the individual companies continued to operate under their own names but gradually services were co-ordinated and Canadian Pacific Air Lines Limited, which was formed on May 16, 1942, commenced operations on July 1, 1942.

The most important constituent companies of Canadian Pacific Air Lines were, without question, Canadian Airways and Yukon Southern Air Transport. Canadian Airways received its charter on June 27, 1930 and commenced operations on November 25, 1930. It was the result of a merger of two other important early Canadian air transport companies — Western Canada Airways and Aviation Corporation of Canada and to understand the formation and importance of Canadian Airways, it is necessary to review briefly these two predecessor organizations.

Western Canada Airways was formed by James Richardson of Winnipeg on December 10, 1926. Richardson has quite rightly been referred to as the "Father of Canadian Aviation" and, had it not been for his drive and determination to have Canadian companies provide Canadian air services, the nation's aviation scene might have been very different from what it now is. Richardson was born in Kingston, Ontario on August 21, 1885, and, after graduation from Queen's University, joined the family business of James A. Richardson and Sons. In 1912, he took charge of the company's western Canadian business in Winnipeg and developed the organization into one of Canada's largest grain exporters. In addition, he organized the diversification of the company into the operation of commercial radio stations and formed the Securities Division of the company. He had always had the desire to bring about the development of the mineral resources of the Canadian Shield and, following his abortive formation of Central Canada Air Lines in August 1926, he invested $200,000 of his own money to form Western Canada Airways. The company's first aircraft, Fokker Universal G-CAFU *City of Winnipeg*, was flown into its base at Hudson, Ontario on December 25, 1926 and made its first revenue flight two days later. The second aircraft, another Fokker Universal G-CAGD *City of Toronto* arrived at Hudson on February 26, 1927 and the new company soon developed a considerable amount of business, including airmail service, in northwestern Ontario and southeastern Manitoba.

Operations expanded to the coast of British Columbia in 1928 and an airmail service across the prairies was established. On May 1st, Pacific Airways of Vancouver was taken over and the company then operated the west coast fishery patrols. Late in the year, the Post Office authorized an experimental airmail service between Winnipeg and Calgary via Regina, Saskatchewan from December 10 to 29th and during this short period over 3,000 lbs. of mail was carried although it was only possible to complete the entire schedule on ten of the 20 days. By year end, the fleet had expanded to 27 aircraft, comprising primarily Fokker Universals and Super Universals.

In 1929, Western Canada Airways expanded its service northward along the Mackenzie River to Aklavik, North West Territories and in mid-year the company was awarded the contract for a prairie airmail route. The Post Office had started issuing airmail contracts in 1927 and the aviation industry welcomed this move as it provided companies with some additional revenue which ensured that otherwise uneconomic routes could continue to operate. In fact, in the case of the prairie airmail route, the govern-

ment had approached Western Canada Airways to determine if it would be interested in this contract. As a result, the company obtained a four year contract at the rate of 75 cents a mile, though at this time contracts at up to $1.25 a mile were being awarded in eastern Canada. The Mackenzie River airmail contract went to Commercial Airways but, on the basis of the four year prairie contract, Western Canadian Airways purchased six Fokker F.14 and three Boeing 40B aircraft to operate the service which commenced on March 3, 1930. Under this contract, mail was flown between Winnipeg, Regina, Moose Jaw, Medicine Hat, Lethbridge and Calgary with a branch route to Saskatoon, North Battleford, and Edmonton.

In eastern Canada, the late 1920s proved to be a period of consolidation for a number of small aircraft operators primarily because these companies lacked the necessary funds for successful continued operation — an all too common occurrence in early Canadian aviation. In spite of receiving higher rates for carrying airmail, these companies were in imminent danger of collapse and during 1929, to prevent them being sold to American interests, Canadian Transcontinental Airways, Canadian Airways, International Airways, and Interprovincial Airways came under the umbrella of the Aviation Corporation of Canada. There were six shareholders in this latter organization including James Richardson and the Canadian Pacific Railway. Two aircraft operating companies now controlled the bulk of flying services throughout Canada and the story of their combination into one organization is probably best told in James A. Richardson's own words:

"During 1929, Sir Henry Thornton, (President of CNR) called on me in Winnipeg and told me he felt the Canadian National Railways should have an interest in aviation, that they had to keep up with the times by giving all the services given in the United States, but that he realized that a pioneering enterprise was full of grief and trouble and he had no desire to assume the responsibility of setting up an airways company if he could acquire the services in any other way. He said he was impressed with everything he heard about Western Canada Airways, and he wanted to acquire an interest in it for the Canadian National Railways. I told him to avoid the possibility of competition, the two railways should be consulted.

When in Montreal, I took up the matter with Mr. Beatty and mentioned to him that I thought it would be very unfortunate indeed if any action of the Canadian National were to force the Canadian Pacific to spend money in aviation, as I did not need to assure him there was no room for two large aviation companies in Canada. I told him I believed there was no country in the world where aviation could make the same contribution to our national wealth as in Canada . . . that our Air Mail contracts would enable us to function satisfactorily, and while we would not be in a position to make any money in the strict sense of the word, we should be able to earn enough . . . to replace old equipment with new and continue to provide a highly desirable service, that, insofar, as we might be helpful in the opening up of mines, we would make a direct and valuable contribution to the railways, and that this appeared to be a matter in which the two railroads might co-operate instead of compete.

Mr. Beatty stated that he was most anxious to do everything he could to prevent anything in the form of wasteful competition and that he felt the Airways were in every way worthy of support and that it would be agreeable for the Canadian Pacific Railway to come in with a small investment along with the Canadian National."

Early in 1930, Richardson was approached to ascertain if he were willing to sell Western Canada Airways to the Aviation Corporation of Canada but no agreement could be reached. Subsequently, American interests offered to purchase his aircraft company from him but were unsuccessful. Aviation Corporation of Canada then agreed to dispose of its assets to a new company to be called Canadian Airways Limited which received its charter on June 27, 1930. The stock for this new organization was owned partly by James Richardson, who received 60,000 Canadian Airways shares in exchange for his Western Canadian Airways stock, and by the Canadian Pacific Railway and the Canadian National Railway each of which invested $250,000 in the new venture. Richardson became President and Sir Henry Thornton and Edward Beatty became Vice-Presidents. Montreal was the location of the head office but Richardson controlled the organization from his home office in Winnipeg. Like Canada's two major railways, the com-

pany comprised two divisions, Eastern Lines and Western Lines.

Crew training flights for the Post Office commenced on February 12, 1930 and contract flights were inaugurated on March 3rd. However, in broad terms, business was not good during the year. The 1929 stock market debacle resulted in little money being available for mineral exploration and the Royal Canadian Air Force, Civil Operations Branch made further inroads to the available traffic by performing much of the work for non-military government departments. At the end of the year, the only item to invite optimism was Canadian Airways being awarded the Winnipeg to Pembina, Manitoba Post Office contract. Service on this 66 mile route commenced on February 3, 1931. However, this optimism proved to be short-lived for in early 1931 the newly elected Conservative government of R.B. Bennett began cancelling airmail contracts as a money-saving measure. First to go were the Moncton, New Brunswick to Montreal and Moncton to Charlottetown, Prince Edward Island contracts. In May, Canadian Airways acquired the assets of Commercial Airways and thus obtained the Mackenzie River airmail contract but, although the prairie airmail run continued, as of June 1st, operations were reduced to six days a week. On August 15th the Regina to Edmonton route through Saskatoon was cancelled but the extension of the Lethbridge - Calgary run to Edmonton reduced the effect of the lower mileage. On the same date, the Montreal to Toronto airmail contract was cancelled although the company retained the Toronto to Windsor service. A new service between Vancouver and Victoria was opened on July 1st and the following month the route was extended to Seattle, Washington. Two Boeing C-204 flying boats were used on this service but receipts were disappointing as seat

occupancy for the summer season averaged only 21.5 percent.

The following year, 1932, brought even worse results for Canadian Airways as the prairie airmail service was cancelled at the end of March and the Toronto to Windsor contract was terminated at the end of the following month. Despite stringent economies, heavy losses could not be avoided. Much of these losses were the result of expenditures incurred in fulfilling the Post Office airmail contracts and, in spite of persistent lobbying, the government took no action to alleviate Canadian Airways' acute financial plight. However, on July 11, 1933 James Richardson attended an Inter-Departmental Committee meeting on the government's proposed trans-Canada airline system and was asked if Canadian Airways wished to be considered to operate this service. He replied in the affirmative to the effect that:

"... we are prepared to co-operate to the fullest extent possible with whatever may be the policy of the government."

At a further meeting on October 18, 1933, the company was asked to prepare operating schedules and cost estimates for the proposed national service and this was completed by November 28th.

Some bright spots developed during the year, although returns were insufficient to offset losses. Charter flying continued to improve and traffic on the Vancouver to Victoria summer service more than doubled. Canadian Airways was able to renew the Mackenzie airmail contract and also was successful in retaining the contract for the north shore of the St. Lawrence. Nevertheless, 1933 was another disaster financially with a net loss of $431,000 and plans were made in early 1934 for the complete shutdown of operations. Later in the year, bush

flying increased as mining exploration picked up but during 1934, it became apparent that Canadian Airways was not being considered by the government to operate the national airline. Indeed, James Richardson was unable to obtain a copy of the government's Trans Canada Airway Committee Report of January 18, 1934 until the following year, and the assumption that Canadian Airways would be unsuccessful subsequently proved to be correct. Possible competition on the north shore of the St. Lawrence materialized during the year but it was finally agreed that a joint venture company, Quebec Airways, would be formed utilizing up to four Canadian Airways aircraft and staffed by Canadian Airways personnel. It was agreed that Canadian Airways would hold 75% of the new company's stock with the remainder being held by Quebec interests. Operations commenced in January 1935 and the two companies worked alongside each other within the north shore area.

By the end of 1934, it was apparent that the economics introduced to keep Canadian Airways operating had been successful and a small profit was returned in the second half of the year. In 1935, the Winnipeg to Pembina mail contract was awarded to Northwest Airlines and Canadian Airways was granted the Vancouver to Seattle service. As yet, no international agreements existed to control the awarding of routes to operators and in the Vancouver to Seattle case the Post Office merely took the contract from United Airlines and awarded it to Canadian Airways. As a result, United continued flying the route with a Boeing 247 while Canadian Airways assigned a newly acquired de Havilland Dragon Rapide to the route which commenced service on October 1, 1935 although passenger service did not begin until March 7, 1936.

R.B. Bennett's government was replaced by Mackenzie King's Liberals in 1935 and it was hoped that this change would improve Canadian Airway's chances of being involved in the trans-Canada system. Competition was anticipated from a Toronto based syndicate but Canadian Airways was the only company with air service operations across the country and Richardson and the company's senior staff spent much of 1936 attempting to participate in the new venture. These efforts ultimately were unsuccessful but following the passage of the Trans Canada Air Lines Act, C.D. Howe approached Richardson and invited him to accept a seat on the board of directors of the newly formed national airline. In addition, Howe offered to allow Canadian Airways to subscribe to shares of Trans-Canada Air Lines and, as a further inducement, cooperation with the granting of feeder lines was also suggested. Richardson refused these offers and shortly after this Canadian Airways decided to give up the Vancouver to Seattle service as it could not be operated economically. The route was then awarded to the newly formed Trans-Canada Air Lines which purchased three aircraft from Canadian Airways for this route and commenced operating the service as its first route on September 1, 1937.

Post Office contracts continued to cause problems in 1937. Mackenzie Air Service underbid the contracts for the Mackenzie River route and the service into Lake Athabasca. In the Red Lake area of Ontario, a contract was turned over to Starrat Airways & Transportation by the Post Office for what appeared to be political considerations. In western Canada, United Air Transport was awarded the Edmonton to Whitehorse airmail contract without tenders being called for. However, Canadian Airways was successful in renewing its west coast fishery patrols for a further three years in March 1937 and the following

month it was announced that the RCAF would no longer undertake airlift commitments for other government departments. This meant that aircraft operators would now get the government's business but, even with this apparent incentive, 1937 and 1938 were not good years for Canadian Airways and the company withdrew from the Vancouver to Victoria service and concentrated almost exclusively on bush flying to isolated communities.

In late 1938, the company started weekly services between Vancouver and Zeballos and Seymour Inlet in British Columbia. An airmail contract for the Zeballos service began on November 28th and early the following year Canadian Airways was awarded the Vancouver to Victoria airmail contract because there were no adequate airport facilities in Victoria to allow Trans-Canada Air Lines to provide the service. Canadian Airways used a float equipped Fairchild 71 for the service which began on March 1, 1939. This was soon replaced by a Dragon Rapide and three round trips daily were being flown by the middle of the summer.

On June 26, 1939, James A. Richardson suffered a fatal heart attack in Winnipeg. Although Canadian Airways continued without its president and founder, extremely difficult times were ahead. The war effort led to the requisitioning of aircraft and business declined rapidly as exploration and trapping slowed down. In 1940, Sir Edward Beatty became president and the company acquired four new contracts to carry mail in the Maritimes. Two new Beechcraft 18As were purchased to provide this service but on April 15, 1941 the Post Office turned over these contracts to Trans-Canada Air Lines. Mrs. Richardson had owned the controlling interest in Canadian Airways since her husband's death and at first it was decided to amalgamate her inter-

▲ Lockheed Vega CF-AAL was one of the oldest aircraft in Canadian Airways' fleet. In this photograph, it is seen at Calgary in 1929 when it was imported by Commercial Airways of Edmonton. It was registered by Canadian Airways on May 22, 1931 and, because of its speed, was a popular aircraft with the pilots. It was taken over by CPAL and sold to International Aviation Enterprises of New York in 1944.

▲ The best known aircraft in Canadian Airways' fleet was the Junkers 52 CF-ARM which, when imported from Germany in October 1931, was the largest aircraft in Canada. After being re-engined with a Rolls-Royce Buzzard engine in 1937 it proved to be more reliable but it continued to crab through the air with the left wing slightly forward at a sedate 97 mph. Canadian Airways' pilots learned to live with this and CF-ARM was the natural choice whenever a bulky load had to be hauled to a remote location.

Public Archives Canada PA88902

Aircraft Type	Number Acquired	In Service July 1, 1942
Avro Avian III	1	—
Beechcraft A-18A	3	3
Bellanca Pacemaker	9	—
Bellanca Aircruiser	1	1
Boeing A-213 Totem	1	—
Boeing B-1E	3	
Boeing C-204 Thunderbird	1	—
de Havilland DH60 Moth	4	—
de Havilland DH80 Puss Moth	1	—
de Havilland DH83 Fox Moth	2	1
de Havilland DH84 Dragon	2	2
de Havilland DH89 Rapide	5	1
Fairchild FC-2	4	—
Fairchild FC-2W2	10	1
Fairchild 71	17	6
Fairchild 82	3	1
Fokker FVIIb	1	—
Fokker Universal	9	—
Fokker Super Universal	8	—
Junker W33	3	1
Junker W34	5	3
Junker JU52	1	1
Laird 200	4	—
Loening Amphibian	1	—
Lockheed Vega 1	1	1
Lockheed 10A Electra	2	—
Noorduyn Norseman	5	4
Pitcairn PA-6 Super Mailwing	2	—
Sikorsky S-38C	1	—
Stearman C3B	1	—
Stearman Junior Speedmail	4	—
Stinson Reliant	5	3
Travel Air 2000	1	—
Travel Air BM 4000	2	—
Total	123	29

▲ Canadian Airways' de Havilland D.H.89A Rapide CF-BBH is seen at Whitehorse, Yukon Territory in September 1939 as the Sternwheeler Casca thunders past. CF-BBH was purchased by Canadian Airways in May 1939 from Consolidated Mining & Smelting and was damaged beyond repair at Pentecost, Quebec in March 1947 when it stalled while attempting to take off on sticky snow. The Casca was the third vessel of this name and was built by the British Yukon Navigation Company in Whitehorse in 1936. This 1,300 ton vessel served through World War Two but was then beached at Whitehorse and accidentally burned out on June 21, 1974.

ests in Canadian Airways, Arrow Airways, and Dominion Skyways with the aircraft interests of Canadian Pacific but, before this was done, Sir Edward Beatty indicated that his company wished to purchase Mrs. Richardson's interests. This deal, concluded in December 1941, gave Canadian Pacific controlling interests in Canadian Airways and Quebec Airways with complete control of Arrow Airways and Dominion Skyways. At the time of the takeover, Canadian Airways was operating the following scheduled services:

Sioux Lookout — Uchi Lake
Ilford — Sechigo
Kenora — Red Lake
Kenora — Populus Lake
Winnipeg — Mackenzie Island
Winnipeg — Bisset
Winnipeg — Little Grand Rapids
Edmonton — Aklavik
Edmonton — Coppermine
Fort St. James — Prince George
Vancouver — Victoria
Vancouver — Zeballos
Big River — Sulphide Lake

Although in existence for only slightly more than 11 years, Canadian Airways acquired over 120 aircraft of 34 types from 17 different manufacturers. Clearly, standardization was not an important factor in the 1920s and 30s when operators purchased aircraft at the lowest possible price and considered the replacement of parts only as and when this became necessary. Nevertheless, Canadian Airways was the country's largest airline and the following list outlines its total fleet, together with the number of aircraft of each type which

With increasing airline business in the United States in the mid-1930s, Canadian's began thinking of a long distance airline service and the first proposal by Mackenzie King's Liberal government for a trans-Canada airline company was put forward by an interdepartmental government committee in September 1936. This committee recommended that a joint government/private enterprise company be formed to operate the national airline. Ownership was to be shared between private aviation interests with a 45 percent share in the company, the government in the form of a 25 percent interest and the remaining 30 percent to be shared equally by the Canadian Pacific Railway and the Canadian National Railway. It was further proposed that the private aviation interests would appoint three directors, the government two and each of the railways one.

C.D. Howe, the Minister of Transport, loaned a copy of the committee's report to Sir Edward Beatty on September 17, 1936 and Sir Edward returned this on September 28th proposing that the new company should be owned 25% by Canadian Airways with the remainder being split between the Canadian Pacific Railway and the Canadian National Railway. Canadian Airway's share would be represented primarily by its existing assets while the two railways would provide $3,400,000 of new capital. Sir Edward made no reference to the composition of the board but he did express reservations about private individuals becoming stockholders of the new company. On November 10th, Sir Edward again wrote to the minister asking for confirmation that the proposed allocation of the stock was acceptable to the government because, if so, it would be necessary to proceed with the formation of the new company and to appoint the necessary staff. C.D. Howe replied the following day stating that he personally thought the proposed share of the stock was equitable if Canadian Airways were prepared to subscribe for the full amount of its share and if it were prepared to accept fair market value only for items turned over to the new company. He added, "I presume that each of the three shareholders should have the privilege of appointing directors proportionately with its own interest."

Sir Edward replied on November 18th agreeing with the proposed division of the stock and Howe's stipulation for Canadian Airways to pay for its share of $500,000 either in cash or with assets at agreed valuations. He suggested that between seven and eleven directors should comprise the board but was "prepared to accept any number which seems wise to you." On November 20th, Howe wrote to Sir Edward explaining he had arranged for a Select Committee to examine the structure of the airline as proposed and when this had been done, a memorandum would be submitted to Council. He stated:

"It seems to be generally agreed between us that the setup will be arranged so that the company is guaranteed against loss, and also limited to modest profit until such time as the carriage of mail can be placed on a parity with the United States for similar service."

The Minister next wrote to Sir Edward on December 22nd stating:

"At a meeting yesterday, the Government considered the setup of Trans-Canada Airways and passed it in a form considerably distorted from the one I placed before you. However, I think that we can work out a situation in the light of the Goverment's decision."

On December 30th, Sir Edward and Mr. Howe had a lengthy discussion concerning the new airline company and the Minister gave Sir Edward a memorandum outlining the terms which he thought the Cabinet would be prepared to accept. The stock of Trans-Canada was to be owned equally by Canadian Pacific and Canadian National and such private aviation interests as each might nominate. The board would comprise nine directors of whom one would be appointed by the Minister. Howe again wrote to Sir Edward on January 5, 1937 indicating that, because of an oversight, an important condition had been omitted from the memorandum given to Sir Edward on the previous December 30th. This provided that the, "Stock of the company may be purchased by the Dominion Government at any time after notice and upon payment of its book value."

Sir Edward replied on January 11th stating that the Canadian Pacific directors, after careful considerations, suggested that no action by the airline's board should become effective unless it were approved by a majority of directors of the two railways. He also suggested that the airline's stock could be purchased at any time by the Dominion Government on payment of a *fair* value, which should not be less than its *book* value. Sir Edward indicated he was not in favour of having as shareholders, "various individuals who do not represent aviation interests."

Howe replied on January 12th that he was:

"still of the opinion that, for political reasons if for no other, it is very desirable that a meeting of others desirous of participating in the service be arranged. In that way I think their opposition to the bill when it reaches Parliament can be rather effectively removed."

On February 4th, Sir Edward was given a draft of the bill to incorporate Trans-Canada Air Lines. This draft also provided for a board of nine directors, four to be appointed by the Canadian National, four by the Canadian Pacific, and one by the Minister. Sir Edward wrote to the Minister on February 8th indicating he thought part of Section 6, providing for the appointment of directors, should be redrafted to ensure that in:

"all mattters coming before the directors the affirmative vote of at least a majority of the directors elected by the holders of the Canadian National and Canadian Pacific shares shall be required."

In his reply of February 9th, Howe stated he felt that this was a matter that should be provided for in the by-laws of the company. Thus, it would not be necessary to introduce the clause into the bill especially "as a suggestion is expected that the Railways will use control to throttle competition." Sir Edward wrote to Howe on February 10th indicating that if it were the understanding between him and the two

CPAL

railways that the by-laws would contain the necessary provision he would be agreeable. However, he could not agree to the control of the directors being in the hands of four Canadian National appointees and one appointed by the Minister. This "would put the Canadian Pacific, with a fifty percent interest in the stock, in a minority on the Board, which, of course, is unthinkable."

On March 6th, Howe forwarded Sir Edward a copy of the Trans-Canada Air Lines Bill for his confidential perusal. This provided for a board of nine directors, three to be appointed by the Canadian National, three to represent the Canadian Pacific, and three to be appointed by the Governor-in-Council. On March 10th, in a letter to James Richardson of Canadian Airways, Sir Edward said Howe, "told me yesterday it (the Bill) had passed the Cabinet after a great deal of opposition." On March 12th, Sir Edward informed the Minister that the bill had been discussed with the members of Canadian Pacific's executive committee and, "their view is that it would be hard to justify to our stockholders the provision of two and a half million dollars . . . in the Air Lines, when we would only have a minority voice in its administration." The two and a half million dollars was half the new company's capital and Canadian Pacific was not prepared to participate with only one third of the votes on the board of directors. He added, "we are more than willing to be associated with the enterprise and to contribute in any way possible to its success, and we hope that you will find a way to provide for our participation on an equitable basis."

Howe's reply five days later stated that Cabinet took the view that as the government was accepting responsibility for all deficits in operations, as well as providing airports, radio services, and meteorological services, its responsibility for the effective operation of the company was as great as, or perhaps even greater than, Canadian Pacific and Canadian National which were to provide the capital under conditions that would at least guarantee reasonable interest returns. Sir Edward's suggestion requiring a majority of the railway appointed directors to agree was not a proper arrangement. He could not agree with Sir Edward that Canadian National was to all intents and purposes a department of the government and concluded with the hope that "further consideration will lead you to believe the recent changes will not seriously interfere with participation by the Canadian Pacific Railway." Sir Edward replied to the Minister on March 16th saying:

"It is not, in the circumstances, necessary to continue our correspondence, and I should appreciate it if, in the Bill as introduced, you would omit any reference to this company. I hope that your company will realize your highest hopes."

Thus, Canadian Pacific elected not to participate in Trans-Canada Air Lines on the basis that Sir Edward could not justify the "assumption of one-half the financial responsibility for the Company without a corresponding representation on the directorate." It should be noted that in spite of the Minister's claims about the government accepting the responsibility for "all deficits in operations", the bill then under discussion and the act as passed by the House of Commons provided for the assumption of deficits for only a two year period. Subsequently, this was extended from time to time though as an undated Canadian Pacific memorandum dryly notes, "it may well be doubted if this would have been done had the Company been jointly owned by the two Railways."

On April 10, 1937, the passing of the Trans-Canada Air Lines Act finally presented the country with its long-awaited national airline. This foster child, under the guardianship of the Canadian National Railways, commenced service with a flight between Vancouver and Seattle on September 1, 1937. As a ward of the Crown, it is perhaps understandable that the new company expanded rapidly and on May 1, 1947, only a few weeks after the company celebrated its tenth anniversary, Trans-Canada Air Lines operated its inaugural flight on the trans-Atlantic route. On January 1, 1965, the company's name was changed to Air Canada to indicate more properly the company's international as well as domestic services. Today it has more than 100 aircraft and in addition to the services within Canada, operates routes to the United States, the Caribbean, Europe, and Singapore.

In the late 1930s and the early 1940s, the majority of Canada's private airline companies were in financial difficulties. Too many operators were vying for too little business. Unwise licensing practices by the Canadian Transport Commission and the Department of Transport had allowed more than one operator to provide service on many routes and on the Kenora - Red Lake route Canadian Airways, Starratt Airways & Transportation, and Wings all had permission to operate. Indeed, of Canadian Airways' 13 routes on June 30, 1942 other operators were licensed to provide flights on no less than six of these services. Under these conditions it was difficult, if not impossible, to break even and problems were not confined to routes facing competition. Yukon Southern, in the apparently happy position of having no competitors on its six licensed routes, consistently operated at a loss. By 1940, most of the private airline companies found themselves in a critical financial position and many of these under-capitalized companies were in danger of bankruptcy primarily because of increasingly destructive competition.

Coupled with this was the fact that by September 1939, Canada was embroiled in World War Two and very soon it was realized that any aircraft and personnel not essential to the war effort would have to be released from commercial activities for war service. It therefore came as no surprise when the federal government requested hearings to be held throughout western Canada by the Board of Transport Commissioners in June and July 1940 in an attempt to solve these problems. In the following October, Canadian

Pacific learned that the Board had submitted a report to C.D. Howe, Minister of Munitions and Supply, recommending the cancellation of all existing licences and the creation of a zoning system under which new licences would have to be applied for. Canadian Pacific, as already mentioned, had a considerable investment in Canadian Airways and because this was the largest company with the most extensive operations, it could be expected to suffer most under the Board's proposals. Accordingly, Sir Edward Beatty, who had maintained a keen interest in aviation matters, acquired a copy of the report. Howe, in acknowledging the return of the report by Sir Edward, wrote:

"I think you should review the matter from the position that something must be done to place the northern flying on a war footing, having in mind the growing demands of the Air Training Plan makes on flying personnel and equipment and the unsatisfactory position of the private airline companies."

Subsequently, Canadian Pacific decided to acquire some of the independent companies and Sir Edward informed Howe of this. The latter, according to Sir Edward:

"expresses himself as in entire accord and said that he had always realized that if proper groupings of the companies could be made by mutual arrangement it would constitute a correct answer to the whole question . . . Mr. Howe assured me that he would give me some weeks to see if I could make progress on the plans we

discussed, and I then promised to keep him advised."

In November, the Chief Commissioner of the Board of Transport Commissioners invited discussion with the Board and towards the end of the month Sir Edward discussed the matter with two of the commissioners. He then wrote to Howe saying:

"they very much favour proceeding as we are doing in connection with Western Air Services, and thus, if possible, eliminating the necessity of drastic orders by the Board and obtaining the results desired in full agreement with the operating companies."

As a result, the Order-In-Council cancelling all the existing licences was not issued and Canadian Pacific undertook to purchase and co-ordinate the services of the "Northern Lines", as the feeder routes to Trans-Canada Air Lines' trunk services were referred to.

Between October 1940 and August 1941, Canadian Pacific gained control of Mackenzie Air Services, Yukon Southern Air Transport, Ginger Coote Airways, and Starratt Airways & Transportation. On August 11, 1941, Sir Edward wrote to the Minister proposing that Trans-Canada and Canadian Pacific jointly operate a co-ordinated airline but the plan was too ambitious for the existing political climate and nothing came of it.

In the latter half of 1941, Canadian Pacific acquired Prairie Airways and Wings and on December 3rd Sir Edward wrote to the Minister outlining how CP could obtain Mrs. Richardson's shares of Canadian Airways. Howe

replied: "I see no objections to your proposal" and in mid-December 1941 Canadian Pacific acquired control of Canadian Airways together with Arrow Airways, Dominion Skyways, and Quebec Airways. Canadian Pacific did not exert pressure on the various companies to sell their interests. Fair market prices were paid and it seems quite probable that most owners were not reluctant to have a well financed, competently organized company take over what were becoming increasing liabilities. It is interesting to note that of the total purchase price of $4,201,000, over $704,000 went to pay outstanding liabilities incurred by the constituent companies. It is likely that much of this debt might never have been paid had Canadian Pacific not acquired these organizations.

Canadian Pacific now had ten subsidiaries operating a total of 48 licensed routes and although many of the companies continued to function very much as before, retaining the original company names for some years, Canadian Pacific Air Lines, Limited commenced operations on July 1, 1942. L.B. Unwin was appointed president of the new company. He was born and educated in England, joining the Canadian Pacific Railway in 1908 at Chapleau, Ontario as a clerk. In 1932, he was appointed Vice President and Treasurer of the railway and in 1939 Sir Edward Beatty assigned him the task of scrutinizing bush airlines to determine the condition of these organizations. It was Unwin's report that persuaded Sir Edward to proceed with the acquisition of the independent operators.

Unwin appointed C.H. "Punch" Dickins, formerly of Canadian Airways

but by this time with Canadian Pacific Air Services as vice president and general manager. W.M. Neal, Vice President Western Lines of the railway, and based in Winnipeg, was also ap-

pointed a vice president of the airline and he selected G.W. McConachie of Yukon Southern Air Transport as his assistant to operate the air services in the west.

▲ An example of Grant McConachie's foresight is this publicity shot taken in 1941. At a time when air transport was still an exciting and relatively risky venture, two models are posed nonchalantly beside a 1939 Packhard convertible. In the background is Lockheed 18-40 Lodestar CF-BTY which was ob-

tained from Pacific Alaska Airways of Portland, Oregon in April 1941 and returned to the United States in September 1941. While the other constituent companies were running bush operations, Yukon Southern was an airline.

Although Canadian Airways was the largest single constituent company of Canadian Pacific Air Lines and has been dealt with separately because of its importance in developing Canadian Pacific's interest in aviation, the remaining nine constituent companies also played their part in the formation and evolution of the new organization. Indeed, it could be argued that Yukon Southern Air Transport had more effect on Canadian Pacific Air Lines than the much larger Canadian Airways principally because at the time of its acquisition it was already being operated primarily as a trunk airline and also because of the influence of Yukon Southern's president, Grant McConachie.

Yukon Southern Air Transport

The company was incorporated on January 16, 1938 by Grant McConachie, who was later to be instrumental in the development of Canadian Pacific Air Lines from a bush flying operation to an international airline. McConachie was born in Hamilton, Ontario in 1909 and grew up in Edmonton. After working as a locomotive fireman and at other similar jobs to finance his flying lessons, he formed Independent Airways in 1931 with himself serving as the pilot, engineer, mechanic, treasurer, etc. and his uncle providing the capital. His first charter flight was to fly 200 crows to Drumheller as part of an experiment to determine whether light rather than temperature controls the migratory instincts of birds. This unlikely beginning was followed by charters to haul frozen fish from Cold Lake to Bonnyville,

Alberta whenever snow blocked the roads. More permanent contracts were obtained to haul fish from Peter Pond Lake, Saskatchewan to Cheecham, Alberta during the winter months. In 1932, he was contracted to haul equipment and supplies to the Two Brothers gold mine in British Columbia but this work terminated in early 1933 when the mine was worked out. Joining forces with R.B. Phillips, the mine owner's son, McConachie formed United Air Transport in 1933 with one Fokker Universal which was quickly followed by a second similar machine and a third Fokker in 1934. In 1936, a Ford Trimotor was acquired and, equipped with skis in winter and floats in summer, this aircraft operated charter flights from Edmonton to the Yukon. The 1,200 mile flight took an average of 16 hours, 40 minutes. About the same time, United Air Transport also obtained an air mail contract for the route between Fort St. John and Fort Nelson. Business continued to develop and in 1937 the company obtained the mail contract between Edmonton and Whitehorse. McConachie personally inaugurated the scheduled service on July 5th when he piloted the float-equipped Ford Trimotor CF-BEP between the two cities. The route was extended to Dawson City the following month.

In 1938, United Air Transport was re-organized into Yukon Southern Air Transport and McConachie proceeded to develop the trunk line routes between Vancouver and Edmonton and the Yukon. Recognizing that his airline could only become truly effective if it could operate on wheels all year round rather than on floats in summer and skis in winter, McConachie constructed rudi-

mentary airstrips at Fort St. John and Fort Nelson during 1938. The following year Yukon Southern became the first Canadian bush airline to operate a twin engine all-metal airliner when the company's first Barkley-Grow arrived. In addition, Yukon Southern was the first Canadian airline to use two-way voice radio communication. The same year it was awarded the Vancouver to Fort St. John weekly mail contract. In 1940, Yukon Southern was authorized to purchase two of eight Lockheed Lodestars assigned to the Canadian market and a second weekly system-wide mail contract was awarded. At about this time, Canada and the United States signed a joint defence agreement. This called for the construction of airports along the western Canadian routes already pioneered by Yukon Southern. Improved facilities were constructed by the Canadian government at Edmonton and Whitehorse and new airports were provided at Prince George, Grande Prairie, Watson Lake, Fort Nelson, and Fort St. John. These improved facilities allowed Yukon Southern to become an "all wheels" airline and with the provision of navigational aids and well lit approaches and runways, night flying was possible,—an important factor where winter days are extremely short.

As war traffic built up in 1941, two Lockheed Lodestars were obtained from Pacific Alaska Airways of Seattle but these were released to the Canadian government in September 1941 and were replaced by two Lockheed 14s from Trans-Canada Air Lines. As this meant the company lost almost 30% of its seating capacity, a third weekly system-wide postal contract was awarded. By this time the mail contracts accounted for

40% of the airline's summer revenue and for 50% in winter but even this additional revenue could not keep Yukon Southern solvent and operating independently. In 1938, the company had lost $70,000. This was reduced to $40,000 in 1939 and $20,000 in 1940 but McConachie could not quite manage to get Yukon Southern into the black. Accordingly, it was made known that the company was available for acquisition and Canadian Pacific purchased it for $1,057,000 which included $181,000 of liabilities.

At the time of the handover in early 1941, Yukon Southern had a total workforce of 70 including nine pilots, four stewardesses, and 12 ground crew. It was operating the following routes:

Vancouver — Whitehorse
Edmonton — Whitehorse
Prince George — Two Brothers Lake
Fort St. John — Fort Simpson
Prince George — Watson Lake
Whitehorse — Dawson City

McConachie joined Canadian Pacific along with most of his company's personnel and in 1947 he became president of the airline, a position he held until his untimely death in 1965. Readers wishing further details of Grant McConachie's story are referred to the excellent biography *Bush Pilot With A Briefcase* by the late Ronald A. Keith, published in 1972 by Doubleday Canada Limited.

Yukon Southern Air Transport owned a total of 13 aircraft including an American Pilgrim 100B, a Boeing 247D, a Curtis Wright D-3 Kingbird and a Curtis Wright T-32-C Condor acquired from British Yukon Navigation of Vancouver on August 7, 1942, after Canadian Pacific

Air Lines commenced service. The airline's fleet was:

Aircraft Type	Number Acquired	In Service July 1, 1942
American Pilgrim 100B	1	—
Barkley-Grow T8P-1	3	3
Beechcraft D-17S	1	1
Boeing 247D	1	—
Curtiss-Wright D-3 Kingbird	1	—
Curtiss-Wright T-32-C Condor	1	—
Fairchild FC-2W2	1	—
Fairchild 82	1	1
Ford 6-ATS Special Trimotor	1	—
Lockheed 18-40 Lodestar	2	—
Total	13	5

In addition to the above, Yukon Southern Air Transport received the two Lockheed 14-H2s from Trans-Canada Air Lines. In January and February 1942, two Boeing 247Ds were loaned to the company by the RCAF. The two Lockheeds were not registered by Canadian Pacific Air Lines until November 17, 1942 and the two Boeing 247Ds were bought on October 1, 1943.

Arrow Airways

In 1929, J. Hone who operated three stores in Flin Flon, Herb Lake, and Wabowden, Manitoba, decided to take a refresher pilot's course at Regina. He sold his stores, obtained his commercial pilot's licence and purchased an Avro Avian. With these limited resources he commenced commercial flying out of Flin Flon, Manitoba. He incorporated his company on June 7, 1932 and served as president until May 1934 when financial difficulties forced him to sell a large interest in his company to H.L. Weber of The Pas, Manitoba. Weber, associated with surface transportation in the area since 1929, became the new president and Hone served as vice-president and operations manager.

The Company was acquired by James A. Richardson in 1938 through his wholly owned Airways Limited, which had been formed at the time it was thought Canadian Airways might be involved in the national airline. At this time, Arrow Airways had contracts to carry mail between Flin Flon and The Pas and from The Pas to Sturgeon Landing. Other routes being flown were:

The Pas — Cumberland House
Flin Flon — Puketawagan
Flin Flon — Island Falls
Flin Flon — Brochet

Probably because of licensing arrangements which were being introduced by the Department of Transport, Arrow Airways was not merged with Canadian Airways although cooperation between the two companies was extensive with Canadian Airways servicing and maintaining the Arrow aircraft at Winnipeg. Canadian Pacific purchased Arrow Airways in December 1941 for $76,000. At this time, only two of the airline's fleet remained in service.

Aircraft Type	Number Acquired	In Service July 1, 1942
Fairchild FC-2W2	1	—
Fairchild 82	1	—
Fokker Universal	2	—
Noorduyn Norseman	1	1
Waco UKC	2	—
Waco YKC-S	1	1
Total	8	2

Dominion Skyways

This company was incorporated on February 5, 1935 and on May 23, 1937 commenced a scheduled service between Montreal and Rouyn. Initially this was operated twice weekly using a Waco. Later, this was increased to three times weekly using a Noorduyn Norseman.

In 1938, Dominion Skyways was acquired by James A. Richardson for an undisclosed amount of cash and 3,681 shares of Canadian Airways. Although this purchase was by Richardson personally and not by Canadian Airways, the two companies operated in close cooperation. The Senneterre bases of both companies were combined and Canadian Airways conditions and rates of pay were applied to Dominion Skyways personnel. It is probable that the two companies were not merged because of proposed licensing arrangements to be introduced by the Department of Transport. It was thought that the original operator of a route would stand the best chance of receiving the official licence for that service and probably this was responsible for Dominion Skyway retaining its name until its acquisition by Canadian Pacific in December 1941 for $142,000. At the time of this acquisition, Dominion Skyways was licensed to operate the Senneterre to Waswanipi Lake and the Roberval to Wakonichi Lake services. Its total fleet comprised eight aircraft of which five survived to be registered by Canadian Pacific Air Lines:

Aircraft Type	Number Acquired	In Service July 1, 1942
Bellanca Pacemaker	1	—
Fairchild FC-2W2	1	1
Fairchild 71	2	1
Fairchild 82	1	—
Noorduyn Norseman	1	1
Waco YKC-S	1	1
Waco ZQC-6 Custom	1	1
Total	8	5

Dominion Skyways single Noorduyn Norseman was the prototype aircraft. This was acquired in 1935 and was sold by Canadian Pacific Air Lines on October 8, 1947 to Cap Airways of Cap de la Madeline, Quebec.

Ginger Coote Airways

On October 27, 1938 Ginger Coote Airways was incorporated and provided services between Vancouver and Zeballos and Vancouver and Port Alice. Canadian Pacific acquired the company for $63,000 on February 1, 1941, and the services of Ginger Coote Airways and Canadian Airways in southern British Columbia were integrated almost immediately. The airline operated the following aircraft:

Aircraft Type	Number Acquired	In Service July 1, 1942
de Havilland DH83 Fox Moth	1	—
de Havilland DH89A Rapide	1	1
de Havilland DH90 Dragonfly	1	1
Noorduyn Norseman	1	—
Waco YKC-S	1	1
Waco YKS-6	1	—
Waco AQC-6 Custom	1	—
Total	7	3

MacKenzie Air Services

W. Leigh Brintnell incorporated Mackenzie Air Service to provide air services in the Mackenzie district of the Northwest Territories on January 30, 1932. Prior to this, he had been Assistant General Manager of Canadian Airways. He had joined Western Canada Airways in early 1927 and stayed with the organization when it was incorporated into Canadian Airways in 1930. In 1931, he was placed in charge of air services between Sault Ste. Marie and the Pacific and Arctic coasts. He then left to form Mackenzie Air Services. When this company was acquired by Canadian Pacific in 1940 for $658,000, it was operating the following routes:

Edmonton — Stony Rapids
Edmonton — Aklavik
Goldfields — Yellowknife
Edmonton — Coppermine
Peace River — Yellowknife

In order to overcome the problems that the various bush airlines were experiencing, Brintnell had suggested in July 1939 that Canada should be split up into a number of areas and the various companies operating in each area should be amalgamated into one organization. Canadian Airways personnel did not support this concept and subsequently Canadian Pacific was able to purchase Mackenzie Air Services in late 1940. Canadian Airways and Mackenzie Air Services' flights in northwestern Canada were then co-ordinated. The company owned a total of 19 aircraft of which six were taken over by Canadian Pacific Air Lines:

Aircraft Type	Number Acquired	In Service July 1, 1942
Barkley-Grow T8P-1	2	2
Beechcraft C-17R	1	—
Bellanca Aircruiser	2	2
Curtiss C-1 Robin	1	—
Fairchild 71	2	—
Fairchild 82	3	2
Fokker Super Universal	2	—
Fokker AF-14A	1	—
Noorduyn Norseman	4	—
Stinson Reliant	1	—
Total	19	6

Prairie Airways

This Moose Jaw based organization was incorporated on March 15, 1934 and was acquired by Canadian Pacific in late 1941 for $528,000. At that time, the company was operating the Regina - North Battleford service. It had owned a total of nine aircraft, of which five were taken over by Canadian Pacific Air lines.

Aircraft Type	Number Acquired	In Service July 1, 1942
Barkley-Grow T8P-1	1	1
Beechcraft 18D	2	2
Cessna C-34 Airmaster	1	—
Cessna C-37 Airmaster	1	1
de Havilland DH60 Moth	1	—
de Havilland DH80 Puss Moth	1	—
Waco RNF	1	—
Waco ZQC-6 Custom	1	1
Total	9	5

Quebec Airways

In the winter of 1932 - 1933, Canadian Airways air-lifted a large number of lumberjacks across the St. Lawrence. Previously, the Clarke Steamship Company of Quebec City had provided this service and, as a result of Canadian Airways' competition, the shipping company made plans to create its own aircraft operations along the St. Lawrence. Even though Canadian Airways indicated that there was insufficient business for two companies, Desmond Clarke seemed anxious to proceed and it was eventually agreed that Quebec Airways would be formed with Canadian Airways holding a 51 percent interest and the remainder to be held by Clarke or his nominees. In the event, Clarke did not take up his full allotment of shares and Canadian Airways' share was increased to 75 percent. The new company was expected to handle only the mail contracts east of Quebec City while Canadian Airways conducted the bulk of the bush flying and aerial surveys in the rest of Quebec. Three Fairchild 71s were sold to the newly-formed company which was incorporated on December 28, 1934 and commenced operations in January 1935. Canadian Pacific acquired the controlling interest in the company in December 1941 with the purchase of Canadian Airways. At that time, Quebec Airways had licences to operate from Montreal to Saugenay and from Rimouski to Blanc Sablon. The outstanding stock was not acquired until 1951 when Quebec Airways was merged into Canadian Pacific Air Lines. The airline's fleet totalled 13 aircraft and six were taken over by Canadian Pacific Air Lines. Unlike the other companies which were acquired by Canadian Pacific, Quebec Airways showed a high degree of standardization operating no less than eight de Havilland DH89/89A Rapides.

Aircraft Type	Number Acquired	In Service July 1, 1942
Bellanca Pacemaker	1	1
de Havilland DH84 Dragon	1	—
de Havilland DH89/89A Rapide	8	5
Fairchild 71C	3	—
Total	13	6

In addition to the above, Quebec Airways operated three Boeing 247Ds which were obtained on loan from the RCAF in the first half of 1942. These aircraft were registered by Canadian Pacific Air Lines on October 1, 1943.

Starratt Airways & Transportation

On February 4, 1938 R.W. Starratt incorporated this company to consolidate his business and private flying interests. In 1927, Starratt had started a freighting business carrying equipment and supplies by ground transport to mines in the Red Lake area of Ontario. In 1932, he purchased a de Havilland Moth to maintain contact with his ground detachments and subsequently formed Starratt Airways & Transportation offering service and air transportation from Hudson, Ontario. Canadian Pacific acquired the company in 1941 for $425,000. At this time, the following licensed routes were being operated:

Hudson — Lac du Bonnet
Hudson — Pickle Lake
Kenora — Red Lake

The company's fleet totalled 17 aircraft and, of these, seven were registered by Canadian Pacific Air Lines:

Aircraft Type	Number Acquired	In Service July 1, 1942
Bellanca Pacemaker	1	—
Beechcraft C-17R	1	1
Beechcraft 18A	1	—
de Havilland DH60M Moth	1	1
de Havilland DH83 Fox Moth	1	—
Fairchild 71	1	—
Fairchild 82	3	2
Fokker Super Universal	2	1
Noorduyn Norseman	2	—
Stinson SM-1D-3000	1	—
Stinson Reliant	1	1
Travel Air B-6000	1	—
Travel Air SA-6000A	1	1
Total	17	7

Wings

This company was incorporated in Winnipeg on July 11, 1934 by R. Brown, E.W. Stull, M.E. Ashton, and J. Moar, all of whom had been staff pilots with Canadian Airways. Brown, who served as president, and Ashton, who served as general manager, had both served as pilots in World War One and had joined Western Canada Airways in February 1928 and July 1929, respectively. Wings was bought by Canadian Pacific in late 1941 for $190,000 and at that time was operating the following routes:

Sioux Lookout — Red Lake
Sioux Lookout — Pickle Lake
Ilford — Gods Lake
Winnipeg — Red Lake
Winnipeg — Bissett
Winnipeg — Little Grand Rapids
Kenora — Red Lake

19

Kenora — Straw Lake
Flin Flon — Halfway Island

A total of 24 aircraft was owned by Wings and of these, nine were registered by Canadian Pacific Air Lines. As in the case of Quebec Airways, the company showed an unusual degree of standardization with the bulk of the company's fleet comprising Fairchild and Waco aircraft.

Aircraft Type	Number Acquired	In Service July 1, 1942
Bellanca Pacemaker	1	1
Fairchild 71	6	3
Fairchild 82	3	1
Fokker Universal	1	—
Noorduyn Norseman	1	—
Travel Air B-6000	1	—
Waco UKC	4	—
Waco YKC	1	—
Waco YKS-6	1	1
Waco ZQC-6	4	2
Waco ZKS-6	1	1
Total	24	9

By the end of 1941, Canadian Pacific had acquired all ten companies and Canadian Pacific Air Lines was incorporated on May 16, 1942. It commenced operations under its own name on July 1, 1942 with a varied collection of 77 aircraft of 27 types which had been constructed by 13 manufacturers:

Aircraft Type	In Service July 1, 1942
Barkley Grow	6
Beechcraft C-17R	1
Beechcraft D-17S	1
Beechcraft 18	5
Bellanca Pacemaker	2
Bellanca Aircruiser	3
Cessna C-37	1
de Havilland DH60 Moth	1
de Havilland DH83 Fox Moth	1
de Havilland DH84 Dragon	2
de Havilland DH89 Rapide	7
de Havilland DH90 Dragonfly	1
Fairchild FC-2W2	2
Fairchild 71	10
Fairchild 82	7
Fokker Super Universal	1
Junker W33	1
Junker W34	3
Junker JU52	1
Lockheed Vega 1	1
Noorduyn Norseman	6
Stinson Reliant	4
Waco YKC-S	3
Waco YKS-6	1
Waco ZQC-6	4
Waco ZKS-6	1
Travel Air SA-6000A	1
Total	77

It also operated two Lockheed 14-H2s on loan from Trans-Canada Air Lines and five Boeing 247Ds loaned by the RCAF, giving an overall total of 84 aircraft of 29 different types.

Consolidating such a diverse collection of aircraft and coordinating staff from companies which had, until recently, been intense rivals took time. At first, many of the companies continued to operate in their own names. Gradually, Canadian Pacific eliminated the old identities and although rivalries amongst the staff were to continue for many years, Canadian Pacific Air Lines standardized service throughout the system, issuing its first timetable on November 1, 1943.

Public Archives Canada C-36252

▲ Fairchild 82A CF-AXF of Wings Limited seen at Lac du Bonnet, Manitoba. Note the skis which are equipped with oleos to absorb some of the unevenness of the snow packed and ice runways used in winter. Most of the other ski-equipped aircraft illustrated in this work have solid pedestal skis where any unevenness on the runway was transmitted directly into the aircraft.

Public Archives Canada PA103358

▲ Fairchild 71C CF-AWX of Wings Limited serves a lodge in the Manitoba/Ontario lake country in the period 1935 -1937. The aircraft was taken over by CPAL but was damaged beyond repair at Deschambault Lake, Saskatchewan in July 1943 when, after engine failure, the floats collapsed on landing.

Although Canadian Pacific withdrew from Trans-Canada Air Lines in March 1937 and subsequently built up an independent and extensive route system by acquiring the ten companies outlined in the previous chapter, Sir Edward Beatty maintained the hope that eventually Canadian Pacific and Trans-Canada could amalgamate under suitable conditions. On October 2, 1940 he and G.E. Woods-Humphery, the Vice-Chairman, of Canadian Pacific Air Services, wrote to C.D. Howe, by then Minister of Munitions and Supply, outlining a plan for instituting a trans-Atlantic airline service. Long before aircraft were capable of flying the Atlantic on a regular commercial basis, forward thinking aircraft operators and designers were discussing the possibility of how this dream might become a reality. In 1935, the United Kingdom government together with the governments of Canada and Ireland had agreed to form a company to "develop British Atlantic services." Under this agreement the United Kingdom would hold 51% of the capital stock with the remaining portion being shared equally between Canada and Ireland, However, nothing developed from this plan and Woods-Humphery and Beatty suggested:

"that the 1935 inter-Government agreement should be cancelled and that Canada should take over the responsibility for the development of British Atlantic air services, leaving in abeyance until the war is over the question of United Kingdom and Eire participation . . . We suggest that, under your direction as the Minister in charge of aviation, the Canadian Pacific Railway and Trans-Canada Air Lines should jointly accept the responsibility for initiating the development of this vital enterprise."

They went on to state that only landplanes should be used and that the service should operate non-stop between Montreal and London. Canadian Pacific had brought R.H. Mayo, a British aeronautical engineer, to Canada to act as an advisor. Mayo had long advocated a trans-Atlantic airline service and on July 21 - 22, 1938, had pioneered non-stop airmail service across the North Atlantic when his Short S20 float plane *Mercury* had operated from Foynes, Ireland to Montreal with a payload of 1,000 lbs. Because the four engined *Mercury* had insufficient power to take off with the amount of fuel required for the 2,930 mile journey, Mayo had developed a composite system with the long range aircraft being hauled aloft on the back of a Short S21 flying boat *Maia*. At altitude the two aircraft separated and the *Mercury* flew to Montreal in 20 hours and 20 minutes at an average of 140 mph.

Woods-Humphery and Sir Edward indicated that as the scheme they were suggesting:

"requires the design and construction of new aircraft, about a year must elapse before it can be put into operation, and this, in our view, makes it all the more important that no further time should be lost. We have searched the American market for suitable planes and are satisfied that there are none that could satisfactorily perform this service. There are, however, two types of military aircraft, a few of which could probably be obtained quickly, that could operate a temporary service while the planes for the permanent service are being constructed . . . With a 'long range' plan of this kind under your Ministerial sponsorship and direction, and managed jointly by the Canadian Pacific Railway and Trans-Canada Air Lines, through a separate company jointly controlled and bearing a distinctive name such, for example, as 'Canadian Atlantic Air Lines', Canada would be making a very important contribution to the prosecution of the war . . .

The Minister replied on October 7, 1940 that he had:

"expressed to the officers of British Airways Limited (sic) and to the Ministry of Air for the United Kingdom . . . that Canada is dissatisfied with the way our partnership agreement is being administered, and have stated to them both that Canada would like to take over Britain's share of the partnership . . ."

Howe had discussed this with Captain Balfour, the United Kingdom's Secretary for Air, and Sir John Reith, then Chairman of Imperial Airways. "Neither of these gentlemen seemed to be at all willing to relinquish their share of the agreement or to permit Canada to undertake the operation. Whether anything can induce them to change their position is doubtful." Britain had recently negotiated the purchase of six bombers from the United States and subsequently, modified Avro Lancaster bombers, known as Lancastrians, were used on the service. Trans-Canada's Lancastrian CF-CMS operated the first Canadian Government Trans-Atlantic Air Service flight on July 22, 1943. Canadian Pacific's first attempt to participate in the international airlines business thus ended in failure.

Nevertheless, Sir Edward maintained his interest in aviation and in the spring of 1941 he and the Minister discussed the air service situation in Canada. Howe asked Sir Edward to submit his suggestions to him in writing but because of pressure of work and his worsening health, Sir Edward did not write to the Minister until August 11, 1941. In his letter he indicated that:

"the Canadian Pacific (holds) a minority interest in Canadian Airways since the inception of that organization (and) could, I believe, now secure the controlling interest held by the Richardson Estate on favourable terms, as well as other minority shares."

He continued:

"as you have been kept advised, we have attempted to do something to remedy the chaotic situation in connection with smaller companies, particularly in Western Canada, and we now have acquired control, amounting to almost complete ownership, of Mackenzie Air Service, Yukon Southern Air Transport, Ginger Coote Airways and Starratt Airways."

Sir Edward pointed out that between them:

"the Government and Canadian

Pacific Railway own, control, or could easily acquire control of, all the established air services which are necessary to furnish the Dominion with a completely co-ordinated system of air transport, which could readily be linked with Trans-Atlantic and Trans-Pacific services, to provide a complete Empire service from Britain to Asia and; if necessary, to Australia."

Canadian Pacific had pioneered trans-Pacific steamship services and had, for long, had a dominant position on the St. Lawrence route to Europe. In support of its services, the Company had developed an extensive overseas network of offices and agents and had generated considerable goodwill both for itself and for Canada. In view of this experience and expertise, Sir Edward suggested that:

"1) The Canadian Pacific should be permitted to acquire the 24,900 shares (49.8%) of the stock of Trans-Canada Air Lines, which, under the present statute, the Canadian National railways are permitted to sell;

2) The Government should purchase 50% of this company's interest in Mackenzie Air Service, Yukon Southern Air Transport, Ginger Coote Airways and Starratt Airways;

3) The Richardson Estate holdings in Canadian Airways should be purchased jointly and equally, by the Government and the Canadian Pacific, with the Government purchasing 50% of the shares in this enterprise now held by the Canadian Pacific;

4) The Government and the Canadian Pacific should subscribe, in equal shares, the capital which may be required for Canadian participation in Trans-Atlantic

and/or Trans-Pacific ocean air services as they may be developed."

Sir Edward was suggesting the creation of one airline, to be jointly owned by the government and Canadian Pacific and combining the mainline services of Trans-Canada Air Lines with the feeder services owned by Canadian Pacific. There is no doubt that such a company would have eliminated costly competition. In addition, the Canadian air traveller might have benefited from the combination of Canadian Pacific's experience and operating acumen with the Government of Canada's control of aviation within the Dominion and its strength in dealing with foreign governments for negotiating international routes. It was, however, not to be as the Minister replied on September 15th stating that:

"While I see advantages in your proposal, I have come to the conclusion that the move you suggest is one that should be considered after the war. At the present time, Trans-Canada Air Lines is losing ground both in the matter of equipment and personnel. I have no doubt that you are having a similar experience with your airline properties. All that either of us can hope to do is to keep air transportation alive and be ready for the sharp expansion that will occur after the war. When equipment can be purchased and with the return of our pilots from overseas, the undertaking of a number of new services will be inevitable, and I hope before that to have a well co-ordinated plan for financing and controlling these services . . . I suggest that no steps be taken to work out a permanent solution of Canada's air transportation under present circumstances."

Howe thus stated that nothing was going to be done until after the war and that the status quo would continue until hostilities ceased. Sir Edward, understandably, believed that the government was prepared to allow Canadian Pacific to expand its airline operations and on December 3, 1941 he wrote to the Minister again:

"I should like to advise you that we approached the Canadian Airways Limited, which is controlled by the Richardson Estate, with the idea of acquiring control of the Company, and they have made us an offer. The number of shares will be a little over 50%, and the price is a little higher than I expected to have to pay. However, we think it is wise to do this as a method of carrying out the larger plans which I discussed with you, and we would like to have your approval of the arrangement."

Howe replied on December 6th:

". . . as Minister of Munitions and Supply responsible for administration of Air Services, Department of Transport, I see no objection to your proposal."

However, in parliament the attitude was not quite the same and Canadian Pacific's actions in acquiring the constituent companies was referred to as "obtaining by the end of 1941 a monopoly in the field of transportation by air, except for Trans-Canada Air Lines." Clearly, not everyone saw Sir Edward's actions as being of benefit to Canada and Canadians. In restoring order from the previous chaos when severe competition caused most operators to lose money, Canadian Pacific was seen by some as benefitting only itself.

Because of persistent ill health, Sir Edward Beatty resigned as President of the Canadian Pacific Railway in May

1942, just before Canadian Pacific Air Lines commenced operations. He never returned to full time work and died in May 1943. Soon after the newly formed company took over operations, it was decided that the 48 operating licences of the constituent companies should be secured in the name of Canadian Pacific Air Lines. At this stage, the Board of Transport Commissioners advised the airline that it believed that the licences were not transferable and that new licences should be applied for together with an undertaking that the old licences would be suspended as new ones were issued. Canadian Pacific Air Lines replied that if new licences were to be issued, duplication of routes could be eliminated by consolidating the various services. Accordingly, in January 1943 Canadian Pacific Air Lines applied for 15 licences which would cover the services operated under the existing 48 licences. No new or additional points were to be served and none of the new licences would have resulted in any change to the routes already operated. However, in a number of cases, the consolidation resulted in a different grouping of the places to be served. Accordingly, the Board of Transport Commissioners recommended to the Governor-in-Council that the grouping of the points be renamed so that new licences could be issued in a consolidated form. However, the Council refused to do this and announced its decision on June 28, 1943. On August 5th, Howe told L. Unwin, the President of Canadian Pacific Air Lines, that the government wished to look into the legal ramifications of those companies where Canadian Pacific had not acquired the entire company — Quebec Airways being a case in point. The government did not want to take away the principal assets of these companies and replace them with assets only in Canadian Pacific Air Lines' name. Gradually, this problem was solved and by the end of the war Canadian Pacific Air Lines had obtained the following licences in its own name:

Vancouver — Victoria
Vancouver — Zeballos
Vancouver — Port Alice
Regina — North Battleford
Prince George — Watson Lake
Big River — Sulphide Lake
Seneterre — Waswanappi Lake
Roberval — Wakonichi Lake

At the same time as it began its attempt to acquire the licences of the constituent companies in its own name, Canadian Pacific Air Lines also made an effort to expand its services and in 1943 applied for licences from the Board of Transport Commissioners which would have placed the company in direct competition with Trans-Canada Air Lines. As a consequence, on April 2, 1943 Prime Minister Mackenzie King made a policy statement in the House of Commons on Canada's post-war airline industry. He concluded:

"a) The Government sees no good reason for changing its policy that Trans-Canada Air Lines is the sole Canadian agency which may operate international air services.

b) Within Canada, Trans-Canada Air Lines will continue to operate all trans-continental systems and such other services of a main line character as may from time to time be designated by the government.

c) Competition between air services over the same route will not be permitted, whether between a publicly owned service and privately owned service or between two privately owned services."

This was obviously an open rebuke to Canadian Pacific Air Lines' overtures. Stung into action which, with the benefit of hindsight might at best be termed unwise, D.C. Coleman, Canadian Pacific's President, wrote to the Prime Minister with the support of his Board of Directors on April 13, 1943. He reminded the government of Canadian Pacific's contribution to Canada's development and the Dominion's international trade. He stated:

"by the Act of 1919, the Company was specifically empowered to operate aircraft for the carriage of passengers and goods within or without the limits of the Dominion of Canada. Your statement of government policy would not only deny the exercise of these powers but would limit the opportunities of expansion in the field of world transportation which this Company has developed over so many years."

Worse was to follow. In 1944, the Aeronautics Act was amended to create the Air Transport Board. The act stated:

"No licence shall be issued in respect of a commercial air service owned, leased, controlled or operated by any person who is engaged in the transport of goods or passengers for hire or reward

by means other than aircraft unless the Governor-in-Council is of the opinion that it is in the public interest for such a licence to be issued . . . after full consideration the government has decided that the railways shall not exercise any monopoly of air services. Steps will be taken to require our railways to divest themselves of ownership of airlines to the end that, within a period of one year from the ending of the European war, transport by air will be entirely separate from surface transportation. In the meantime, no new air routes other than government-operated routes, will be allocated to airlines owned by any railway or other operator of surface transportation . . ."

Considering the country was in the fifth year of a war which had stretched the nation's resources to the limit, and in view of Canadian Pacific's considerable war effort, the efficacy of this policy certainly seems to have left something to be desired. Subsequent legislation required the railway company to divest itself of the airline by May 1946 but this was later changed to May 1947. W.M. Neal succeeded L.B. Unwin as President of Canadian Pacific Air Lines in April 1946 and to him fell the task of presenting Canadian Pacific's case to Prime Minister Mackenzie King. Neal's well thought out and eloquently presented arguments led to a change of heart on the government's part and in August 1946, Howe announced that the company would not be required to dispose of the airline.

Mr. Howe stated that when the legislation was introduced in 1944:

". . . Canadian Pacific Air Lines were very ambitious to extend their territory over other parts of Canada. Today they find they have a sufficient task to develop the parts of Canada for which they were then and are now responsible for giving service, with the result that any new airlines that care to enter the business and are able to finance their operation can find a scope for their activities in parts of Canada not at present served."

This was the official reason for the change in the government's plans but the real reason was probably the fact that Trans-Canada Air Lines had more than it could handle in replacing outdated aircraft, expanding its domestic route network and taking over the government's trans-Atlantic service. These tasks made it virtually impossible for Trans-Canada Air Lines to contemplate absorbing the Canadian Pacific Air Lines system and, as no other company had the expertise, resources and financial capability to do this, Canadian Pacific was permitted to retain its airline service. However, Canadian Pacific Air Lines was strictly controlled and no direct competition with Trans-Canada Air Lines was allowed. Indeed, Canadian Pacific Air Lines obtained its first international routes to Sydney, Australia and Tokyo, Japan only after they had been offered to Trans-Canada Air Lines which rejected them as being impossible to operate economically.

Nicholas Morant for the Director of Public Information, Ottawa

▲ Lockheed Venturas, the military equivalent of the Lodestar, seen at Dorval, Montreal in 1943 being serviced prior to departure for Newfoundland and then Britain. By this time, Canadian Pacific Air Services had long turned over its responsibility for the trans-Atlantic delivery to the Ministry of Aircraft Production and the Royal Air Force's Ferry Command, but scenes like this with Lockheed Hudsons being prepared for their ocean crossing were common in the winter of 1940/1941 when the railway company organized the service. Canadian Pacific pioneered regular inter-continental air transport under unusual conditions and had delivered over 300 aircraft by the time the service was handed over to government control.

Canadian Pacific has served Canada and the allied nations with all its resources in two world wars and during World War Two it made a considerable contribution to the war effort through its involvement in aviation even though its direct interest in the air transport industry in 1939 was confined to its share of Canadian Airways. Nevertheless, in early 1940 Canadian Pacific approached the government to discuss the possibility of the company contributing to the war effort by helping to establish a trans-Atlantic air service principally to carry priority mail and secondly to lay the groundwork for an aircraft ferrying operation from Canada to Britain. At that time, Britain urgently required all the aircraft that could be obtained and the only immediate source was the United States. If assembled aircraft could be flown across the Atlantic, valuable time would be saved as partial disassembling for the sea voyage would be unnecessary, manpower required for reassembly in Britain could be put to other uses, the danger from losses as a result of U Boat action could be avoided and valuable cargo space would be freed for other supplies. However, it must be remembered that trans-Atlantic air travel was very much in its infancy and even as late as 1940 relatively few aircraft had made the journey. Much would depend on Canadian Pacific's ability to create the necessary administration to perform the job. Sir Edward Beatty was named chairman of the newly created Canadian Pacific Air Services and G.E. Woods-Humphery, who had previously served as managing director of Britain's Imperial Airways, joined the organization as vice-

chairman. The administrative staff was obtained mainly from Canadian Pacific and the pilots were primarily Imperial Airways personnel although subsequently volunteers came from all over the western world. Many of the radio operators came from the Canadian Department of Transport's Radio Branch. Colonel H. Burchall, ex-General Manager of Imperial Airways became general manager.

The agreement between the British Government and the Canadian Pacific Railway was initialled on August 16, 1940 and plans were made to commence operations late in the year. There was an immediate need to develop facilities at the western terminal of the ocean crossing. In the mid-1930s Hattie's Camp, 113 miles from St. John's, Newfoundland had been chosen as the western base for future North Atlantic land plane service and a rudimentary airport had been constructed beside the narrow gauge railway line. Subsequently, this airport was renamed Gander and became an important trans-Atlantic refuelling point in the postwar propeller aircraft era, Hattie's Camp required considerable development to enable the ferry service to operate and at first overnight accommodation for the pilots was provided by railway sleeping cars stationed on a spur beside the main line. With its considerable organizational resources, Canadian Pacific was able to arrange for living quarters, maintenance hangars and storage facilities to be constructed. Dorval, Montreal was selected as the headquarters of the ferry service and aircraft were delivered there for onward transport to the United Kingdom. Air-

craft were flown individually to Gander and from there they flew in groups across the Atlantic.

On the evening of November 10, 1940 the first flight of seven Lockheed Hudsons left Gander and landed in the United Kingdom just under 10½ hours later. The second flight crossed the Atlantic on the night of November 29th and the third group left Gander on December 17th. On February 1, 1941, C.H. Dickins of Canadian Airways became Vice-Chairman of Canadian Pacific Air Services and the following month took over as General Manager of Ferry Operations. With Dickins' knowledge of aircraft operations and his organizational skills, the pace of deliveries picked up. However, political pressure, primarily from President Roosevelt, was growing to have the ferry operations completely under military control and on May 27, 1941 the British Ministry of Aircraft Production requested termination of the original contract. A letter to Sir Edward Beatty stated:

"I regret to inform you that owing to conditions over which we have no control it is necessary to give you formal notice of termination of the agreement dated August 16, 1940, between yourself, Mr. G. Woods-Humphery and His Majesty the King, as represented by M.W. Wilson acting on behalf of the Ministry of Aircraft Production, of His Majesty's Government, under which you performed certain services in connection with the ferrying of airplanes across the Atlantic. The exigences of the war have made it necessary that

this service be operated in future direct by the British Ministry of Aircraft Production in close collaboration with the Government of the United States and Canada.

I take this opportunity of expressing on behalf of the Ministry of Aircraft Production and myself, personally, deep appreciation of the valuable service rendered by your company in inaugurating these activities. The services performed by your company have been a notable contribution to the war effort."

In essence, this letter called for the termination of the contract on June 30, 1941, but, because of personnel and accounting details, it was mutually agreed that Canadian Pacific Air Services would legally transfer the project to the Ministry of Aircraft Production on July 15, 1941. In turn, Royal Air Force Ferry Command took over the Atlantic Ferry duties on August 1, 1941. In fact, although Canadian Pacific Air Services was the legal operator of the service until July 15th, the Ministry of Aircraft Production exercised *de facto* control from March 1941 until Ferry Command assumed the responsibility. Nevertheless in the short period before Canadian Pacific relinquished the Atlantic Ferry Service, over 300 aircraft had been delivered to Britain. Because of wartime censorship, the company received no publicity. From the experience gained in this sustained operation, subsequent trans-Atlantic flights became a reality.

In addition to ferrying aircraft, Canadian Pacific became closely involved in training pilots and navigators through the British Commonwealth Air Training

Plan. In late 1939, after a series of conferences involving the Canadian Government and a British mission headed by Air Chief Marshal Sir Robert Brooke-Popham, it was decided to have civilian airline companies operate the Air Observer Schools to train the aircraft navigators who would be required to mount the European bomber offensive. Tenders for the first school were requested from six companies and Dominion Skyways was the successful applicant. No. 1 Air Observer's School (A.O.S.) came into being at Toronto Island Airport in April 1940 and moved to Malton on May 27, 1940. Another eight such schools were opened and, of the total, six were operated by companies which eventually became part of Canadian Pacific Air Lines. The other Canadian Pacific schools were:

No. 2 A.O.S. Edmonton
— opened August 5, 1940
— operated by Canadian Airways

No. 5 A.O.S. Winnipeg
— opened January 6, 1941
— operated jointly by Wings and Starratt Airways & Transportation

No. 7 A.O.S. Portage la Prairie
— opened April 28, 1941
— operated by Yukon Southern Air Transport

No. 8 A.O.S. Ancienne Lorette, Quebec
— opened September 29, 1941
— operated by Quebec Airways

No. 9 A.O.S. St. Johns, Quebec
— opened July 7, 1941
— operated by Dominion Skyways

In addition, No. 11 Elementary Flying Training School, at Cap de la Madeleine, Quebec, was opened on October 14, 1940 and provided initial pilot training. At first, it was operated by Quebec Airways. Canadian Pacific Air Lines became responsible for the schools from July 1, 1942. All schools were operated on a non-profit basis and, at the end of

the program, $945,000 was refunded voluntarily to the government. No. 11 E.F.T.S. closed on February 1, 1944 and No. 2 A.O.S. ceased operations on July 16, 1944. The other schools ceased training on March 31, 1945 by which time Canadian Pacific had trained more than 29,000 aircrew.

Canadian Pacific Air Lines also undertook the management of five repair depots which overhauled aircraft and engines used in the British Commonwealth Air Training Plan. Two depots were located in Winnipeg and were originally the responsiblity of Canadian Airways and Wings. Canadian Airways also managed the Cap de la Madeleine depot when it was opened and Prairie Airways was in charge of the Moose Jaw, Saskatchewan depot. The fifth overhaul facility was in Vancouver. Buildings were provided by the Department of Munitions and Supply and the depots were opened in 1942. Aircraft overhauled included Tiger Moths, Cessnas, Norsemen, Bolingbrokes, Cansos, Stranraers, Hurricanes, Hampdens and Kittyhawks. Modifications were also carried out on various types including the winterizing of Ansons, modifying the wings and tails of Cessnas, and making modifications to Hampdens.

Another area where Canadian Pacific Air Lines made an appreciable contribution to the war effort was in the construction of the Alaska Highway and the Canol pipeline. Following the attack on Pearl Harbour on December 7, 1941, the vulnerability of Alaska to enemy attack was cause for alarm and, in order to provide a land route to Fairbanks, a 1,523 mile all-weather road was built from the Northern Alberta Railways terminus at Dawson Creek, British Columbia to Fairbanks, Alaska. As already indicated, Yukon Southern Air Transport had pioneered air service from this southern area to Whitehorse. From March to November 1942, the

company was heavily committed to aerial surveying of potenial routes, flying-in ground surveyors to locate the right of way, transporting men and equipment for the actual construction and then supporting the operations until the road was completed. USAAF and RCAF aircraft were also used but Canadian Pacific Air Lines, working out of both Dawson Creek and Whitehorse handled the bulk of the airlift.

At the same time, the Canol pipeline and its service road were constructed from Norman Wells to Whitehorse to ensure that the Alaska Highway and the State of Alaska would have a source of petroleum safe from enemy attack. The 500 mile pipeline was constructed through extremely mountainous country and proved to be an immense project. Heavy equipment and pipes were barged down the Mackenzie River during the five months it was ice-free. Construction proceeded from the Norman Wells end. Canadian Airways and Mackenzie Air Service had both pioneered air service in this area and thus the bulk of the men and supplies were flown in by Canadian Pacific Air Lines from Edmonton. The pipeline was completed but, as the project came on stream, hostilities ceased and the pipeline and the refinery at Whitehorse were abandoned because cheaper oil from again secure sources became available. Nevertheless, throughout the construction of both the Alaska Highway and the Canol pipeline, Canadian Pacific Air Lines had provided essential support and had developed rapidly from a group of separate companies into a cohesive, unified company offering both airline and charter services throughout northern Canada. Some of its services were conducted using wheeled aircraft but skis in winter and floats in summer were essential for many of the flights in northern Ontario, Manitoba, and the Northwest Territories. With the de-

velopment of airports along the Yukon and Mackenzie routes, much of the Alaska Highway and Canol project work had been flown by wheel-equipped aircraft whereas the Vancouver-Victoria, Vancouver - Zeballos and some of the Quebec Airways scheduled services used float planes.

During the war, obtaining aircraft was a severe problem. As already noted, on July 1, 1942 the airline had commenced operations with the 77 planes detailed in Table No. 1 plus a few aircraft operated by Yukon Southern Air Transport and Quebec Airways and not officially registered by Canadian Pacific Air Lines until after the airline commenced operations. Even in times of peace, standardizing such a fleet would have been a daunting task but during the war, the acquisition of new aircraft was more or less impossible. Canadian Pacific had to operate with what it had though some aircraft did join the fleet. Yukon Navigation's Curtiss Condor, Curtiss Kingbird, American Pilgrim, and Boeing 247D were purchased on August 7, 1942 and a few aircraft were obtained from the RCAF. At the beginning of the war many planes had been requisitioned by the RCAF as the force underwent a massive expansion. Some of the planes swept up in this program were either surplus to requirements or were unsuitable for RCAF service and because of the vital nature of many of Canadian Pacific's routes, some were made available to the new company. A de Havilland Dragonfly was acquired on December 5, 1942 from this source but it was not until 1943 and 1944 that some Noorduyn Norsemen were obtained for service with the airline.

Because the airline was involved in constructing the Alaska Highway and the Canol pipeline, a number of Lockheed Lodestars were made available to Canadian Pacific Air Lines at a time when even Trans-Canada Air Lines could not acquire new aircraft. Many years after the war, L.B. Unwin, the airline's first President, stated that President Roosevelt had to intercede to ensure that the aircraft were assigned to the company. He stated that one of the deciding factors in providing the aircraft was the company's operations in northern Saskatchewan and that Canadian Pacific aircraft carried the original raw material from Uranium City Saskatchewan which was used in the manufacture of the first atomic bombs.

Three further Lodestars were acquired in 1945 and these aircraft performed valuable trunk-line duties on both the Mackenzie and Yukon routes until the early 1950s when they were replaced by DC-3s. Barkley Grows were also used

out of Edmonton together with Norsemen, Fairchild 71s, and Bellanca Airbuses. The British Columbia coastal services were operated with de Havilland Rapides and Barkley Grows and in Saskatchewan, Beechcraft provided the scheduled services. Float-equipped, single-engined equipment comprised much of the northern Manitoba, northwestern Ontario and Quebec fleets though de Havilland Rapides were used on some Quebec services. When the war ended and surplus aircraft became available, Canadian Pacific Air Lines rapidly replaced obsolescent equipment and commencing in 1946, 17 Douglas DC-3s were obtained to augment and eventually replace the Lodestars in trunkline service. Ansons and Hudsons were acquired for freight and photo-

graphic surveying and four PBY Cansos were also obtained in 1946 to operate the British Columbia coastal services and to operate between Montreal, Rouyn and Val d'Or. By the end of 1948, Canadian Pacific Air Lines fleet comprised DC-3s, Lodestars, Norsemen, Barkley Grows, Beechcraft, Rapides, Ansons, Hudsons, and Cansos with the bulk of the passenger services being flown by the first three types.

Operation of larger aircraft was a direct result of the war effort as airports, suitable for year-round wheel operation, had been constructed throughout much of Canadian Pacific Air Lines' route system. For example, on the Mackenzie routes new airfields had been provided at Fort McMurray, Fort Smith, Yellow-

knife, Hay River, and Norman Wells and, as already mentioned, a similar development had taken place along the Yukon routes. With larger aircraft providing regular, year round scheduled services, Canada's northern population literally took to the air as scheduled flights increased rapidly and fares and freight rates were lowered voluntarily by the airline. In 1940, the Vancouver and Edmonton route to Whitehorse was operated three times a week by a six seat Barkley Grow. By 1948, this has become a daily except Sunday service flown by a DC-3 equipped for 28 passengers. Over the same period the passenger fare had fallen from $85.00 to $75.00 and 100 pounds of air cargo now cost only $21.39 compared with $43.00 in 1942. On the Mackenzie routes, similar improvements had taken place. The Edmonton to Yellowknife service had increased from tri-weekly in 1942 to daily except Sunday in 1948. Over the same period, the passenger fares were reduced from $110.00 to $80.00 and the cargo rate for 100 pounds was $14.97 compared with $50.00 in 1942. On the Montreal - Saguenay route, the three times weekly service with a de Havilland Rapide seating six passengers had improved to 12 round trips a week with a 28 passenger DC-3 and the fare had fallen from $20.00 to $15.50. Even on bush type operations, which the company now sought to relinquish, Canadian Pacific Air Lines had managed to reduce fares and the Kenora to Red Lake fare which was $20.00 in 1942, was

Nicholas Morant CPAL 1753

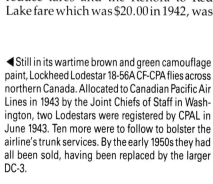

◄ Still in its wartime brown and green camouflage paint, Lockheed Lodestar 18-56A CF-CPA flies across northern Canada. Allocated to Canadian Pacific Air Lines in 1943 by the Joint Chiefs of Staff in Washington, two Lodestars were registered by CPAL in June 1943. Ten more were to follow to bolster the airline's trunk services. By the early 1950s they had all been sold, having been replaced by the larger DC-3.

only $8.00 in 1948. Although long distance flying was never likely to be considered cheap, Canadian Pacific had done much to bring down the cost of air travel to prices which the general public in many more remote locations could afford.

L.B. Unwin returned to full-time railway service in 1946 and W.M. Neal succeeded him as president of Canadian Pacific Air Lines in April 1946. N.R. Crump, former Chairman and President of Canadian Pacific Limited has described Neal as, "the most brilliant transportationist" he ever knew and, although his tenure as president of the airline was to last only until February 1947, Neal had a lasting effect on the organization as one of his first actions was to make Grant McConachie his assistant. In this appointment, McConachie was able to influence the development and operations of the airline. C.H. Dickins, who until then had been Vice President and General Manager of the airline, became Director of Northern Developments and McConachie virtually ran the airline. When D.C. Coleman retired from Canadian Pacific, Neal became President and Chairman of the parent company and he appointed the 37 year old Grant McConachie President of the airline on February 7, 1947.

Grant McConachie was one of those rare people about whom no criticism is ever heard. N.R. Crump once described him as, "a visionary, a superb salesman, a considerate manager and a truly wonderful person." He stated that, although he hated the sayings, "Grant McConachie was a prince of a man and they threw the mould away after he was created." When asked if he had no bad points at all, Mr. Crump chuckled and, with a twinkle in his eye, said "Let's say he sometimes let his entrepreneurial skills stand in the way of a sound business decision!" Nevertheless, there were few such lapses and it was Grant McConachie who developed Canadian Pacific Air Lines from a small domestic carrier into an international airline.

CPAL

◀CPAL operated two Lockheed 14-H2s which were constructed in 1939 and supplied to Trans-Canada Air Lines. In July/August 1941, CF-TCR and CF-TCS were transferred to Yukon Southern Air Transport to ensure that the company could maintain its trunk lines to the Yukon. In November 1942, the aircraft were re-registered as CF-CPC and CF-CPD by CPAL. Unfortunately, CF-CPD was written off at Mt. Cheam, B.C. on December 20, 1942 but CF-CPC continued with CPAL and in this photograph is seen at Montreal in the mid-1940s.

From the time Canadian Pacific took over the ten constituent companies, it had been the intention to form an airline rather than to continue operating a series of minor domestic routes, charter services and bush flights but, because of the war, it was not possible to do this immediately. Soon after Canadian Pacific Air Lines commenced operations, it became apparent that the merging of the constituent companies had resulted in a considerable duplication of jobs. To remedy this, many staff were made redundant in 1943 and 1944 and released to the war effort. As a result, the company's efficiency improved considerably.

Following the war, large numbers of surplus aircraft were sold off by the government and many of the single engined types found their way into the hands of newly established companies providing charter and off-line services. In 1946, Canadian Pacific Air Lines, no longer threatened with the government's requirement that it dispose of all its airline operations, approached the Air Transport Board with the proposal that it withdraw from bush operations where such services could be provided by new companies and concentrate on domestic and international routes. During 1947, Canadian Pacific Air Lines received licences to operate between:

Winnipeg — Dauphin — The Pas — Flin Flon
Vancouver — Prince Rupert
Seven Islands — Knob Lake
Vancouver — Penticton — Calgary

In accordance with the government's revised policy, C.D. Howe, the Minister of Transport had been unwilling to grant Canadian Pacific Air Lines the Van-couver - Calgary licence but, as Trans-Canada Air Lines was not prepared to serve Penticton, he eventually agreed to award the licence to the private airline. The service from Vancouver to Penticton was inaugurated by a DC-3 on September 8, 1947 and the first Vancouver - Calgary flight, again with a DC-3, was on September 22, 1947.

Even before World War Two, Grant McConachie had been planning inter-national air services from western Canada through Alaska and eastern Russia to the Far East but Yukon Southern Air Transport could not break-even flying from Vancouver and Edmonton to the Yukon and official approval of inter-national routes was beyond even Mc-Conachie's powers of persuasion at that time. But with the resources of Canadian Pacific behind him, McConachie was now in a strong position to bring his original plans to fruition. In November 1948, he led a mission to Australia to obtain a licence for the company's first overseas route and this was granted by the Prime Minister of Australia, Ben Chiffley, only after he learned that McConachie was, like himself, an ex-railwayman. Again, Trans-Canada Air Lines had been offered the route by the Canadian Department of Transport but, because of poor economic forecasts, the government airline had declined the route and Candian Pacific Air Lines was awarded the licence. Similarly, Trans-Canada Air Lines was not inter-ested in the Vancouver - Far East route and in January 1949, McConachie flew to Tokyo to obtain permission from General Douglas MacArthur for Cana-dian Pacific Air Lines to fly between Vancouver and Tokyo. After three weeks of futile efforts to see MacArthur, the Canadian ambassador to Japan arranged a meeting for McConachie with the Allied Supreme Commander who autho-rized the company to operate the North Pacific route. Because of Canadian Pacific's steamship's excellent reputation in China, no problem was experienced in obtaining Chiang Kai-Shek's per-mission to serve Shanghai and, in Hong Kong, service rights to the Crown Colony were obtained. The company was thus in a position to offer service spanning both the North and South Pacific.

At this time, none of Canadian Pacific Air Lines' aircraft was suitable for intercontinental service and a four engined plane had yet to be acquired. Perhaps at the insistence of C.D. Howe or maybe at the suggestion of McCona-chie who thought it might improve the company's chances of receiving Cana-dian permission to fly the Pacific routes, four Canadian C-4-1s had been ordered by Canadian Pacific Air Lines. But before the first of these could be delivered, the proving flight to Japan, China, and Hong Kong left from Vancouver on April 19, 1949 using Canadair DC-4M1 North Star, CF-TEP borrowed from the RCAF. With this unpressurized aircraft, an almost full load of pilots and navigators flew on a route survey flight to Anchor-age, Shemya, Tokyo, Shanghai, and Hong Kong returning to Vancouver on May 1st via Okinawa, Tokyo, Adak, and Anchorage. The most memorable occurence of the flight was the visit to Shanghai on April 25th. The aircraft was on the ground for only three hours and was the last departure from Lung-wha airport before the People's Liber-ation Army ousted the Chinese Nation-alist forces in this area. Weekly service to Tokyo and Hong Kong via Anchorage and Shemya commenced on September 19, 1949.

The company's first C-4-1, CF-CPI, was delivered in April 1949 and the second aircraft, CF-CPR, departed Van-couver on a survey flight to Australia on May 28, 1949. This flight was via San Francisco, Honolulu and Canton Island and returned to Vancouver on June 11th. A pre-inaugural flight with CF-CPI and carrying McConachie and 32 guests left Vancouver for Sydney on July 10, 1949. In Sydney, the wife of the Australian Minister of Air named the aircraft *Empress of Sydney*, reintro-ducing the Canadian Pacific tradition of naming its passenger vessels with the title of a fictitious Empress. Although naming the aircraft was merely a public relations gesture and, as can be seen in Table 2, many aircraft have carried various names during their Canadian Pacific careers, McConachie ensured that this Canadian Pacific tradition continued and other Canadair C-4-1s became the Empresses of Vancouver, Hong Kong, and Auckland. Happily, naming the aircraft continued with the Boeing 747s being named after countries, the DC-10s primarily being assigned names of provinces and cities, and the Boeing 737s receiving the names of North American cities. The 737-300s were named for Canadian provinces.

The first scheduled Vancouver - Syd-ney flight departed on July 13, 1949 and subsequently one flight was oper-ated every two weeks. With a fuelling stop at San Francisco, the flight to Honolulu took an elapsed time of 15 hours. The crew and aircraft then laid over for 36 hours and flew to Nadi, Fiji in 15 hours via Canton Island. After an overnight stop, the final 1,968 miles to Sydney were flown non-stop in approximately nine hours. Although this sounds most primitive to today's traveller who has become used to 550 mph jets, it must be remembered that the C-4-1 carried only 36 passengers in wide, fully reclining seats. In some respects, perhaps the journey was not as gruelling as today's 19 hour flight in high density seating with stops in Honolulu and Nadi. One crew stayed with the aircraft for the entire round trip which took ten days. Thus, only two crews were required for the service which was just as well as, for the first few years, passenger load factors were not encouraging. To its credit, Canadian Pacific Air Lines persevered and the service is now operated twice a week with DC-10-30s. Some indication of the difficulties can be gauged from the fact that the airline carried 125 passengers to Hawaii in the 1950 winter season. Additional traffic developed after December 1951 when the Nadi-Sydney non-stop flight was re-routed via Auckland but in the early years the South Pacific service was most unprofitable.

On the North Pacific route to Tokyo and Hong Kong, load factors were much better. A surprising amount of immigrant business developed from Hong Kong to Canada and, with the outbreak of the Korean war on June 25, 1950, air space to and from the Far East was at a premium. Canadian Pacific Air Lines also operated charter flights carrying military personnel to and from Tokyo. Primarily these were American servicemen and between August 14, 1950, and March 30, 1955, nearly 40,000 military personnel were carried on 703 charter flights. Unlike those businessmen who might have cut back on the inflight service to maximize immediate returns, McConachie stipulated that full service

was to be provided and Canadian Pacific Air Lines flights became extremely popular with the troops. In fact, junior personnel had little chance of getting on such flights when the advantages of flying with Canadian Pacific Air Lines became common knowledge. No doubt McConachie's concept of having satisfied passengers provide word of mouth advertising accounts for many of the U.S. citizens who fly from Vancouver to the Far East on Canadian Pacific Air Lines.

But even with excellent load factors on the North Pacific, Canadian Pacific Air Lines was not happy with its Canadair Fours. They were proving to be expensive to operate because of the high fuel consumption of their Rolls Royce Merlin engines which had been designed for military operations where reliability, rather than economy, is of primary importance. Furthermore, the Merlins were extremely noisy, causing uncomfortable conditions within the cabin. This problem was overcome by Trans-Canada Air Lines and British Overseas Airways which changed to crossover exhaust systems on their C-4s. However, Canadian Pacific did not equip their aircraft with this modification and when the opportunity arose to acquire five DC-4s from Pan American in 1950 and 1951, it purchased these aircraft as replacements for the three remaining C-4s. CF-CPR had been written off in February 1950 when it ran off the end of the runway after landing in heavy rain at Tokyo. The Canadian Pacific C-4s were transferred to Trans-Canada Air Lines and the refurbished DC-4s replaced them on the company's international routes. However, the DC-4 also had only a brief service life with Canadian Pacific, as the company's first DC-6, CF-CUO, was delivered on January 17, 1953 and the airline thus obtained its first true long-range aircraft. The first DC-6 proving flight operated from Van-

couver to Honolulu with CF-CUO on January 24, 1953 and the same aircraft introduced the type to passenger service on the return flight two days later. On the North Pacific, the DC-6Bs were introduced into revenue service on March 10, 1953 and CF-CUO *City of Lima* left Vancouver for Mexico City and Lima, Peru on October 24, 1953 on the inaugural South American flight. Once again, Trans-Canada Air Lines had been offered the route but, although operating the Toronto to Mexico City service, had declined and Canadian Pacific was awarded the licence.

No further expansion was undertaken until 1955 when Canadian Pacific Air Lines was authorized to operate from Vancouver to Amsterdam. Scandinavian Airline System had introduced the first so-called polar flight when it commenced a DC-6B Copenhagen - Sondestrom - Winnipeg - Los Angeles service on November 15, 1954. Although the service barely crossed the Arctic Circle, the term polar route caught the public's imagination and Canadian Pacific's first survey flight on the polar route was with a DC-4 which left Vancouver for Churchill, Sondestrom, Keflavik, and London on April 10, 1955. DC-6B, CF-CUR operated the pre-inaugural flight from Vancouver to Sondestrom and Amsterdam on June 3, 1955, returning to Vancouver the following day. Later the same year, Trans-Canada Air Lines exchanged its Toronto - Mexico City route for Canadian Pacific Air Lines' Quebec District domestic services. Canadian Pacific made its first familiarization flight from Mexico City to Toronto with CF-CUO on October 23, 1955. In return, Canadian Pacific's routes in eastern Canada were turned over to Trans-Canada Air Lines on November 1, 1955. On June 1, 1956 the company's route to Lima was extended to Buenos Airies, Argentina and Santiago, Chile was included in the route from September

21, 1957. The Montreal to Lisbon route commenced revenue service on May 30, 1957 and the company's first revenue flight into Madrid was made on June 6, 1957. DC-6B CF-CZE operated both flights. From 1958 until 1971, the southern European route also served the Azores and in April 1976 service to Madrid was suspended for economic reasons.

While the overseas routes were being developed, operations in Canada were also undergoing some changes. In 1949, McConachie transferred the headquarters of the airline from Montreal to Vancouver and the following year scheduled service was begun linking North Battleford, Lloydminster and Edmonton. When possible, charter services were transferred to smaller companies and by 1949, Canadian Pacific Air Lines had divested itself of all its bush operations with the exception of those in the Mackenzie area and along the north shore of the St. Lawrence River. Airline operations on the Prince Rupert - Terrace route began on April 28, 1952 and later the same year five Convair 240s were purchased from Continental Air Lines. These were used to improve service on domestic routes. The first proving flight with this type was operated by CF-CUU from Vancouver to Port Hardy and Sandspit on January 24, 1953. Revenue service commenced with this type over the same route on February 2, 1953 and the first Convair 240 passenger flight from Whitehorse to Vancouver was flown on March 13, 1953. Later the same year, the company applied to the Air Transport Board for a licence to operate a cargo service from Vancouver to Edmonton, The Pas, Toronto, and Montreal. So confident was the company that it would be granted authority for this service that two DC-6A freighters, CF-CUS and CF-CUT were purchased from Douglas, arriving in Vancouver in August and September

1953 respectively. It was believed that as the route was to the north of the Trans-Canada Air Lines service, the Air Transport Board would grant the necessary licence but Trans-Canada's protest was upheld and the two new freighters, were disposed of in 1954. Trans-Canada Air Lines then purchased three Bristol 170 Freighters to operate the cross-country cargo service which proved to be totally uneconomic and the Bristols were disposed of. No doubt this caused a certain amount of glee in Canadian Pacific Air Lines' Vancouver headquarters!

As a result of the tensions created by the Korean conflict and the subsequent Cold War, the Canadian and United States governments decided that North America's best defence against possible attack by Russian aircraft was a series of radar station lines across Canada which would give ample warning of an impending attack. The Pinetree Line was to be constructed along the Canadian/United States border and the Mid-Canada Line was to be built further north. The most northerly chain of stations was designated the Distant Early Warning Line which was constructed along the 70th parallel from Alaska to Labrador. Construction of this immense project was announced in March 1955 and soon many Canadian operators were airlifting supplies for the venture. Canadian Pacific acquired eight C-46F aircraft from Flying Tigers to use on charter flights, hauling in freight and equipment to the various supply bases and radar sites. The airlines' operations were confined primarily to the western Arctic and the aircraft were used exclusively in the Edmonton, Fort Nelson, Yellowknife, Norman Wells, and Cambridge Bay areas, flying a gruelling schedule which saw many pilots log their monthly limit of 95 flying hours in ten days or less. Frequently, flight conditions were terrible but Canadian Pacific acquitted itself well during this operation even though flying aids were rudimentary and the eight C-46s had at least five different flight deck layouts. In support of the construction of the DEW line, Canadian Pacific aircraft carried 36.5 million pounds of freight but after the Company completed its contracts on January 31, 1957, six of the C-46s were soon disposed of. As an interim measure, the two remaining aircraft were converted to Super 46s with accommodation for 44 passengers. On July 21, 1959 both were sold to Pacific Western Airlines.

During 1957, the DC-6Bs, which until then had been used exclusively on the international routes, began limited operations within Canada. The first domestic flight using this type flew from Vancouver to Terrace on June 28th. On July 1, 1957 the DC-6B made its first trip between Vancouver and Whitehorse and the type remained on this route until finally they were displaced by Boeing 737s in 1968. On September 30, 1957, Canadian Pacific Air Lines ceased its Central District operations covering services out of Winnipeg, and a month later the Saskatchewan District flights were also terminated. After this, Canadian Pacific's only charter and bush services were those in the Mackenzie District operating from Yellowknife. These were destined to be transferred to Pacific Western Airlines and Canadian Pacific operated the services for the last time on July 20, 1959.

▲ Douglas DC-6B CF-CUQ *Empress of Tokyo* at Auckland, New Zealand.

CPAL

31

Had McConachie's plans come to fruition, Canadian Pacific Air Lines would have been one of the first carriers in the world to operate jet aircraft. In September 1949, McConachie had attended the Farnborough Air Show in southern England and had seen the prototype de Havilland Comet in operation. He immediately saw the potential of this innovative aircraft and somehow managed to persuade the directors of Canadian Pacific to order two Comets for service on the Pacific route between Sydney and Honolulu. Like the North Star, the early Comet did not have the range to fly from Honolulu into Vancouver but even with refuelling stops at Fiji and Canton Island, it would still be possible to take some advantage from the jet's high cruising speed. Two Comets were ordered from de Havilland on December 15, 1949 and the first was ready for acceptance in late February 1953. Following a familiarization program, Captains Pentland and Sawle left England for Sydney on March 1, 1953. After stopping at Beirut and Karachi, CF-CUN crashed on take-off from Karachi on March 3rd and all aboard were killed. Many theories have been put forward for this tragedy including the pilots' limited experience with the type. Whatever the cause, Canadian Pacific Air Lines decided to cancel its plans for jet service in the South Pacific. It is quite possible that this decision enabled the airline to avoid being involved in an even worse tragedy as the original Comets later revealed a design flaw which led to metal fatigue and in some cases explosive decompression at high altitude. It was only after two British registered Comets were lost in the Mediterranean that the problem was located and the fault area was redesigned. The other Canadian Pacific Comet, CF-CUM was not accepted by the airline and was sold in Britain.

This disaster delayed the introduction of pure-jet aircraft by Canadian Pacific Air Lines for some years although three Comet 2s were ordered in 1953 but were never delivered. In early 1955, the company undertook a study for a replacement aircraft for the DC-6B on major overseas routes to be phased in between 1957 and 1960. The only aircraft which would be available for delivery in 1957 were the Douglas DC-7C, the Lockheed L-1649A Constellation and the Bristol Britannia 300LR. It was known that Canadian Pacific Air Lines' competitors were going to operate the DC-7C and the Constellation on international routes and so the company had to upgrade to an aircraft at least comparable to DC-7C standards. After considerable study of various aircraft, the company purchased the turbo-prop powered Britannia. Although the unit cost of $2.86 million for a Britannia was 17 percent more expensive than the DC-7C and operating costs were forecast to be greater by $1800 per hour, the Britannia, with its greater passenger capacity and higher operating speeds, was calculated to be the more suitable aircraft. Eight Britannias joined the fleet between April 1, 1958 and November 12, 1959 and operated on the Far East, Australia, and European routes until they were replaced by the company's DC-8s. The Britannia had been acquired purely as an interim measure until larger, faster pure-jets became available and maybe, in retrospect, it proved not to be a wise choice.

Reliability was not the type's strong point as the electrical systems gave considerable trouble and it has been said that the only way to keep a Britannia servicable was to never switch off the engines, especially in wet weather! The first proving flight with a Canadian Pacific Air Lines Britannia was by CF-CZA which departed Vancouver on May 14, 1958 to Shannon and Amsterdam, returning on May 16th via London, Goose Bay, and Calgary. On May 22nd the same aircraft operated from Vancouver to Prestwick, London, and Amsterdam and returned the following day. On August 12th, CF-CZA operated the first North Pacific proving flight to Anchorage and Tokyo and the type entered revenue service to Tokyo on August 23rd. On September 16th, the flight from Vancouver to Tokyo was covered in 11 hours 44 minutes, an average speed of 400 mph. Although the elapsed time was considerably better than any other currently available commercial aircraft, this advantage was not to last for long. The initial Britannia flight to Honolulu was by CF-CZB on November 30th and CF-CZD inaugurated passenger service on this route on December 13, 1958. D-6Bs, however, remained in charge of the rest of the South Pacific service to Sydney.

On May 4, 1959, Britannias CF-CZX and CF-CZW respectively flew the first eastbound and westbound Canadian Pacific trans-continental flights between Vancouver and Montreal. This was an important step forward for the company as it allowed the airline to break into what had, until then, been Trans-Canada's private preserve. Successive Liberal governments had consistently prevented any competition between the publicly owned airline and Canadian Pacific Air Lines, citing safety as the main reason. It was rationalized that with too many aircraft seats available for too few passengers, airlines would begin to cut corners and, as a consequence, safety might suffer. In 1957, Canadian Pacific Air Lines had applied for licences to operate five domestic routes: Winnipeg - Ottawa - Montreal; Edmonton - Regina - Toronto; Vancouver - Calgary - Saskatoon - Ottawa - Montreal; Vancouver - Edmonton - Montreal; and Vancouver - Winnipeg - Toronto - Montreal. If these routes were approved, this would have brought the country's two major carriers into direct competition contrary to the Liberal government's wishes. However, the election of the Diefenbaker Conservative government in 1958 led to Canada'a airline policy becoming less rigid. A British economist, Stephen Wheatcroft, was hired by the government to study the situation and found that Trans-Canada Air Lines was running up to 12 round trips daily between Montreal and Vancouver in summer and that some competition was justified. Wheatcroft suggested that four round trips should be granted to Canadian Pacific Air Lines but after lengthy and heated public hearings, the airline was granted one daily round trip between Vancouver and Montreal with compulsory stops at Winnipeg and Toronto. Canadian Pacific Air Lines' inaugural eastbound flight took eight hours 35 minutes and the westbound journey was completed in nine and a half hours.

In late 1959 and early 1960, Canadian Pacific Air Lines judiciously introduced its Britannias on other overseas routes.

On September 11, 1959, they took over the Tokyo - Hong Kong route and CF-CZD introduced the type to revenue service between Vancouver and Mexico City on December 16, 1959, returning north to Montreal the following day. CF-CZW was used on Canadian Pacific Air Line's first flight to Rome which departed Montreal February 20, 1960 on a flight to introduce the press to the service. The same aircraft operated the inaugural revenue flight on March 5, 1960 and CF-CZC took the first Britannia flight into Buenos Aires on May 10, 1960. However, by this time the Britannia's service with the airline was drawing to a close. The initial training flight with the company's first DC-8, CF-CPF, was made from Vancouver on February 21, 1961 and the first revenue flight with the new aircraft departed Vancouver for Honolulu on March 26, 1961. Although the Britannia was a great improvement over the DC-6 and had been popular with passengers, it could not compete with contemporary jet aircraft. CF-CPD and CF-CPE, which were leased to Canadian Pacific Air Lines, went to Cunard Eagle in February and April 1961. On February 4, 1962 Britannia CF-CZC replaced a DC-6B on the Honolulu -Sydney service for the first time and on April 2, 1962, CF-CZB introduced the Britannia to the Vancouver - Whitehorse run. However, the long-haul designed aircraft was not suitable for this relatively short sector route and apart from charter flights and substitutions, there was little work for the Britannias. Between May 1965, and January 1966, Canadian Pacific Air Line's five remaining Britannias were phased out and sold to British operators. CF-CZB had been written off in a mishap at Honolulu on July 23, 1962.

During the late 1950s, competition for sales between Boeing and Douglas was intense and for some time it appeared that Canadian Pacific Air Lines

might purchase the Boeing 707. However, at the last moment it was decided that the slow speed performance of this aircraft would not measure up to the standards Canadian Pacific considered essential. As a result, five DC-8-43 aircraft were ordered in October 1959, and the first four were delivered between February and November 1961. DC-8 CF-CPH, substituting for an unserviceable Britannia, made the first jet flight from Vancouver to Amsterdam via Edmonton on April 21, 1961. Earlier the same day, CF-CPH had operated the first Canadian Pacific Air Lines trans-continental flight by a DC-8 between Vancouver and Toronto, also substituting for a failed Britannia. From April 30, 1961, DC-8s were scheduled to operate on the Amsterdam service and as further aircraft of this type became available, they were assigned to replace the Britannias on other overseas routes. Rome was served by DC-8s from June 1, 1961; Hong Kong from October 8th; Mexico from December 16th; Buenos Aires from April 10, 1962; and the first non-stop revenue flight between Vancouver and Amsterdam departed on April 15, 1962 when CF-CPG covered the 4,786 mile route in nine hours 20 minutes, a considerable improvement over the pre-inaugural flight of June 3, 1955, when DC-6B CF-CUR had an elapsed time of 20 hours eight minutes for the same journey.

At this time, Canadian Pacific Air Lines had high hopes of being able to compete directly with Trans-Canada Air Lines and British Overseas Airways on the lucrative routes between Canada and the United Kingdom. The bilateral agreement between the two countries was ratified on August 19, 1949, and allowed each government to designate one airline to operate across the Atlantic. Not unnaturally, both governments licensed the airlines they owned to operate the various routes. With the increased range of jet aircraft, it became

apparent that direct routes from western Canada to the United Kingdom would be practicable and on September 6, 1960, the Canadian and British governments amended the agreement by an exchange of notes. This change stipulated "routes to be operated in both directions by the designated airline *or airlines* of Canada" and on February 20, 1961, Canadian Pacific Air Lines applied to operate the Vancouver - Edmonton - Gander - London route. On August 17th, an Order-in-Council granted the company permission to operate the service as well as a Vancouver - Calgary - Gander - London route and these licences were issued by the Air Transport Board on August 25th. At about the same time, the U.K. government requested further information from the Canadian government on the service Canadian Pacific Air Lines intended to operate. This information was supplied by the airline to the Canadian government on September 7th and was followed by a meeting in Ottawa on November 14th between the Canadian Minister of Transport and the British Minister of Air. At this meeting, it was agreed to defer the whole question for "further study" but, in fact, this killed Canadian Pacific Air Lines' hopes of operating into London. The licences were withdrawn, no doubt because of pressure from the British government whose own airline (now British Airways) was, like Trans-Canada Air Lines, developed with competition being strictly controlled. Probably, it was felt that the two government airlines would suffer if they faced competition. Whatever the reason, Canadian Pacific's London services never materialized and Amsterdam has remained the company's main European gateway.

The fifth DC-8-43 from the 1959 order arived in May 1963 and a sixth was ordered for delivery in 1965. Sadly, just a few months before this aircraft was due for delivery, Grant McConachie

suffered a fatal heart attack in Los Angeles on June 29, 1965. But no one would forget McConachie as his foresight, management skills and dedication to the airline he loved were reflected in the company's growing fleet of modern aircraft and a route network which connected Canada with parts of Europe, South America, Asia and Australia. Both were tributes to a man who had the skill and persistence to lift a bush airline into a place of respect among the world's commercial air carriers. McConachie was succeeded as president by J.C. Gilmer who continued to run the organization in accordance with McConachie's policies and under his administration further DC-8s were acquired.

The sixth and final DC-8-43, CF-CPK, arrived in Vancouver on October 14, 1965 and allowed the type to be introduced on the Montreal - Amsterdam - Rome service from November 2, 1965. Regrettably, this aircraft was written off at Tokyo in March 1966 when it landed short of the runway in bad weather. A DC-8-53, CF-CPM, was obtained from Douglas in May 1966 and second hand DC-8-51, CF-CPN arrived in early October 1966 enabling the airline to introduce a non-stop Toronto - Honolulu service. The first revenue flight was operated by DC-8-43 CF-CPF on October 30, 1966 in seven hours, 34 minutes. Revenue service between Vancouver and San Francisco commenced on January 30, 1967, this being the airline's first scheduled service to continental U.S.A. In 1969, the schedule was increased to two flights daily and a third was added in 1970.

The company's ninth DC-8, a 55F series, was obtained from Braniff in November 1967. At this time, until the DC-8-63s became available, the company was leasing a Boeing 707-138B, N791SA, from Standard Airways of Seattle. As Canadian Pacific Air Lines had no flight crews trained to operate this type of aircraft, Standard Airways supplied the pilot, first officer, flight engineer and navigator with Canadian Pacific Air Lines providing the cabin crew. On February 7, 1968, while landing at Vancouver at the end of a flight from Honolulu, the "pilot lost visual reference between flare-out and touch-down and the aircraft ran off the runway and collided with a small building near the south terminal." One airport employee and the aircraft's purser were killed and N791SA was written off. There was a thin ground fog at the time which could be seen through from above but at ground level was impenetrable.

The first of the five DC-8-63s, CF-CPO, arrived in Vancouver on January 1, 1968 and four of these aircraft, were in operation by mid-year. CF-CPO was introduced on the Vancouver - Tokyo - Hong Kong route on January 31, 1968 and the arrival of these higher capacity jets freed the earlier DC-8s for service on other routes. In March 1967, J.W. Pickersgill the Minister of Transport in the Pearson Liberal government announced that Canadian Pacific Air Lines would be allowed to provide 25% of the capacity on Canadian trans-continental routes and that additional stops could be made in Edmonton, Calgary, and Ottawa. However, turnaround of the aircraft was to remain restricted to the Vancouver and Montreal terminals. The initial second daily flight was operated by DC-8-43, CF-CPI on February 1, 1968, between Montreal and Vancouver with stops in Toronto, Winnipeg, and Edmonton. Total elapsed time for the flight was eight hours. The trans-continental flight through Calgary was inaugurated by CF-CPT on February 2, 1968.

During the ensuing months, the DC-8-63, or *Spacemaster* as it was called by Canadian Pacific Air Lines, was introduced on the majority of the company's overseas routes. CF-CPP made the first DC-8-63 flight to Honolulu on February 7, 1968 and two days later the same aircraft inaugurated the service to San Francisco. On February 29th, it replaced an earlier series DC-8 on the Amsterdam route and CF-CPQ operated the first *Spacemaster* flight from Montreal to Madrid on April 4th. On April 10th the same aircraft was the first of its type to fly between Toronto and Rome. CF-CPO extended the route from Rome to Athens on September 9, 1968. A further extension to Tel Aviv was made on April 2, 1971 but this was suspended in 1976 and service to Athens ceased in 1981 because of low load factors.

By the late 1960s, there is no doubt that many believed the entire Canadian Pacific organization to be both "stodgy and tradition encrusted" as the railway's in-house magazine *The Spanner* described it in the July-August 1968 issue. Canadian National had undergone an updating of its corporate image using a simplified script version of its initials which became instantly recognized though traditionalists resented the change. Under the direction of N.R. Crump, Canadian Pacific introduced a similar but more extensive program where each of the transportation subsidiaries adopted a shortened trading name together with a common logo displayed in a distinctive colour. Canadian Pacific Air Lines began trading as CP Air and the logo, comprising a triangle, a segment of a circle, and a square and termed the multimark, coloured orange. The triangle suggests motion or direction, the circle indicates global activities, and the square indicates stability. Whatever one thinks of the concept, and there were many who deplored the change, it is extremely distinctive and in any major airport it was not difficult to pick out "Big Orange." When one flew into Amsterdam, Hong Kong, or Sydney on another carrier, it was very comforting to know at a glance that the onward flight home was waiting.

CPAL

▲ Douglas DC-8-53 CF-CPM and DC-8-43 CF-CPI at Vancouver soon after the introduction of the orange livery.

CP Air's orange livery first appeared on the company's initial Boeing 737, CF-CPB, which was accepted on October 22, 1968. This colour-scheme was soon applied to the entire fleet including the sole surviving DC-3 which had been retained for pilot training. Five Boeing 737-200s, ordered in 1966 were acquired in 1968 and the first revenue flight with this type was by CF-CPC between Vancouver and Whitehorse on November 20, 1968. The 737 rapidly replaced the remaining DC-6Bs on the Whitehorse, Terrace and Prince Rupert services and two more 737-200s were delivered in March 1969 allowing the final DC-6Bs to be sold in August 1969 making CP Air an all-jet airline, except for the DC-3. The first five 737s were sold to People Express in 1982 and 1983. CF-CPE operated the first revenue transcontinental flight using this type of aircraft on April 1, 1969.

Early 1969 saw the first curtailment in CP Air's international network when the New Zealand government withdrew the company's authority to operate into Auckland. The last flight to Auckland operated on April 24, 1969 and the Honolulu-Sydney service then became either a non-stop service or also served Nadi. The loss of the Auckland flight was, however, one of the few low points in an otherwise encouraging time. Traffic was increasing and aircraft of greater capacity were required. CP Air chose the Boeing 727-117 and four aircraft of this type were delivered between March 1970 and April 1971. The first 727, CF-CPN, made its initial revenue flight on March 30, 1970 between Montreal and Toronto. Two 727-217s were obtained

in April 1975 but, unlike Air Canada, CP Air found the 727 to be unsuitable for its domestic route network. Primarily, it was found to be uneconomic in terms of fuel consumption and the four earlier models were disposed of during a cost cutting drive in 1977. The remaining 727s were sold to the British airline, Dan Air, in 1983 and 1984.

Route expansion continued in the early 1970s. As already noted, the first CP Air flight to Tel Aviv was made from Rome on April 2, 1971 with DC-8-63, CF-CPP. The following year, the company operated its first charter flight to the People's Republic of China. Canadian Pacific Air Lines' first and only previous flight to China had been in 1949 when Canadair Four CF-TEP was the last aircraft to depart from Shanghai prior to Liberation. It is therefore perhaps appropriate that CP Air's DC-8-53, CF-CPM, was one of the first jet aircraft from the western world to fly into China. This flight, the first of four charters, left Vancouver for Beijing via Anchorage, Tokyo, Hong Kong, and Guangzhou (Canton) on August 13, 1972. Between Guangzhou and Beijing (Peking), a navigator and radio operator were supplied by the Civil Aviation Administration of China. On October 18, 1972, and on the opposite side of the world, the first of ten CP Air charter flights arrived in Entebbe, Uganda to pick up Ugandans of Asian ancestry dispossessed by the regime of Idi Amin. In all, 1,476 passengers were airlifted from Entebbe and the last charter flight arrived back in Montreal on November 6, 1972.

CP Air's first Boeing 747-217B CF-CRA *Empress of Asia* was delivered on

November 16, 1973 and pilot training commenced the same day. This aircraft entered revenue service on December 16, when it operated Flight 401 from Vancouver - Tokyo and Hong Kong. Soon after it entered service, the name was changed to *Empress of Japan* and the remaining three 747s, all delivered by December 1974, were named as Empresses of countries rather than continents. As in the case of previous aircraft types in Canadian Pacific service, name exchanging among the 747s occurred. Aircraft names are only a public relations gesture and are not used to identify individual aircraft officially and names have been exchanged whenever it was expedient to do so. For example, C-FCRD* *Empress of Australia* was to be used on the inaugural 747 flight to Sydney but was under repair at the time so C-FCRE *Empress of Italy* was rapidly re-christened, and pressed into service.

The first 747 flight to Honolulu was made on April 9, 1974 by CF-CRA when it was substituted for an unserviceable DC-8. The flight was unusual in that it originated and terminated in Seattle because of a fire fighters' strike at Vancouver Airport. The following day, the second 747, CF-CRB was assigned to pilot training and entered revenue service to Tokyo on April 28th. CF-CRA operated the first CP Air 747 flight from Vancouver to Toronto on the same day. This was a non-stop flight as the company was not required to land its transcontinental flights at Edmonton or Calgary, and Winnipeg when using this type of aircraft. On July 4, 1974, CP Air's last DC-3, CF-CRX was used to fly a group of Air Cadets on a tour of

the Fraser Valley. The group landed at Abbotsford and, after taking off, the pilot was unable to get a positive indication that the landing gear had retracted. The pilot had no alternative but to return to Abbotsford and the crew and passengers were taken to Vancouver by bus. The following day CF-CRX was ferried to Vancouver with its landing gear down and on October 23, 1974 the aircraft was sold. CP Air had now become an all-jet airline.

Boeing 747, C-FCRD, entered revenue service on December 9, 1974, and C-FCRE followed on January 2, 1975. Both aircraft made their first revenue flights from Vancouver to Honolulu. Pilot training with the first of the Boeing 727-217s, C-GCPA commenced on April 15, 1975, and this aircraft was pressed into revenue service on the Vancouver - San Francisco route on April 24th when several aircraft unexpectedly went unserviceable. On April 27th the second Boeing 727-217, C-GCPB entered revenue service and on the same day DC-8-43, CF-CPF inaugurated the Vancouver - Los Angeles route which became CP Air's second route to continental United States. To date, no other U.S. routes have been awarded to Canadian Pacific.

The mid-1970s were generally a difficult period for airlines as the first oil-crisis caused a recession which affected passenger traffic throughout the world. Until the OPEC price increases, few people realized what a bargain the consumer received when purchasing fuel and jet engines of the pre-1970 era, like many automobile engines, were notoriously energy inefficient. Reacting to the increased price of fuel, CP Air took a DC-8-43 out of service in Sep-

*On January 1, 1974, Canada's aircraft registration prefix changed from CF- to C-.

CPAL

tember 1975 in an effort to cut costs and the aircraft remained grounded until August 1976. During 1976, J.C. Gilmer retired and was succeeded as president of the airline by I.A. Gray who had to enforce a strict cost cutting program. The last scheduled flight to Madrid and Tel Aviv departed Mirabel, Montreal on April 26, 1976 and between March and May 1977 the four Boeing 727-117s made their last revenue flights for CP Air. The last one, CF-CPK was delivered to its new owners on June 6, 1977. Following this, a start was made on retiring the DC-8 fleet and on February 17, 1978 DC-8-55F, CF-CPT, left Vancouver on its delivery flight to England. But it would be wrong to think that the

second half of the 1970s provided only bad news for CP Air as in 1977 the airline was given permission to increase its share of Canadian trans-continental traffic to 35 percent. Subsequently, on March 23, 1979 the Minister of Transport, Otto Lang, announced that CP Air would be subjected to no restrictions on its participation in trans-continental routes. After 37 years of restrictions, CP Air was free to compete directly with Air Canada and, in anticipation of this happening, further Boeing 737s had been ordered for the domestic routes.

Like many other carriers, CP Air has had excellent results with the Boeing

737 and it received its first two 737-217 Advanced aircraft, C-GCPM and C-GCPN, in mid-1979. Further new and used 737s have been acquired and leased. During 1985, the first three Boeing 737-317s were delivered and a further two were received in 1986. Originally, it had been intended to purchase four Boeing 767s in the 1980s but, because forecast passenger growth did not materialize, this order was changed to ten 737-300s. Subsequently, the 737-300 order was reduced to five aircraft and these have now been sold and replaced by 737-200s.

During the 1960s, both Lockheed and McDonnell Douglas designed three

engined jet aircraft with seating for a maximum of 300-350 passengers. These aircraft were to become the Lockheed L-1011 TriStar and the McDonnell Douglas DC-10 and, although both have basically the same layout with one engine at the rear and one under each wing, McDonnell Douglas announced a long range version, the DC-10-30, soon after the prototype was rolled out for flight testing on August 10, 1970. Lockheed delayed designing an intercontinental version of the L-1011 and after considering its needs for a high capacity long range aircraft to replace its ageing fleet of DC-8s, CP Air selected the DC-10-30, placing an order for four aircraft of this type with delivery scheduled to commence in 1979. The first of these, C-GCPC, was delivered on March 27, 1979 but on April 4th was leased to Varig Airlines of Brazil until April 3, 1980. Similarly, the second DC-10-30, C-GCPD, was leased to the Brazilian airline from July 20, 1979 to June 14, 1980 and it was CP Air's third DC-10-30, C-GCPE, which introduced the type to revenue service on November 17, 1979 when it operated a Vancouver -Toronto flight, substituting for a failed DC-8. The same aircraft operated the first CP Air international flight with this type on December 11, 1979 when it flew from Montreal to Milan and Rome. With the return of C-GCPC and C-GCPD from Varig in mid-1980, the type was introduced to other routes. C-GCPD made CP Air's first DC-10 flight to Sydney, leaving Vancouver on July 2, 1980.

Following the second OPEC oil crisis of 1979, which saw the price of oil triple and the world subsequently face the most serious recession encountered since the 1930s, airline passenger traffic fell significantly throughout the world. CP Air had carried 3.524 million passengers in 1981 but this was reduced to 3.29 million in 1982 and 3.27 million in 1983. Losses in 1981 were $22.781 million and almost doubled in 1982 to $39.214 million. In late 1982, D. A. Colussy was recruited as President and Chief Operating Officer with a mandate to turn the company around and make it profitable. Colussy had considerable airline experience culminating with Pan-American and no one can deny that he and his successor D.J. Carty have turned the company around. During the past five years, CP Air, or Canadian Pacific Air Lines as it is again known, has been revitalized and is to be hoped that the aggressive and innovative approach adopted by both Colussy and Carty leads to success.

Colussy began by enforcing a cost cutting program initiated before he joined CP Air and, between the beginning of 1982 and the end of 1984, the total number of employees decreased from 8,860 to 7,207. In addition, he was instrumental in arranging a novel cross-leasing of three McDonnell Douglas DC-10s with United Airlines; introducing the first hub and spoke route system in Canada; acquiring CP Hotels from Canadian Pacific Enterprises; arranging the purchase of Eastern Provincial Airways; introducing the first true business class service on domestic flights and commencing the first frequent flier program in Canada. As a result, by the end of 1983 CP Air's annual deficit

had been reduced to $16.4 million and in 1984 a profit of $13.8 million was achieved.

The cross-leasing arrangement with United Airlines was a novel approach by the two airlines to provide both companies with aircraft more suitable to each one's needs. CP Air had selected the DC-10-30 to operate the bulk of its overseas flights but was also using this model on some of its transcontinental flights where, because of its heavier all-up weight and relative fuel inefficiency, it was proving to be less than ideal. United, on the other hand had purchased a considerable number of the shorter ranged DC-10-10 and had no suitable aircraft with which to commence its Seattle-Hong Kong service. In early 1983, the two airlines agreed to exchange three aircraft of both series for a two year period which could be extended for up to another two years. CP Air received DC-10-10s N1834U, N1836U and N1837U in return for DC-10-30s C-GCPF, C-GCPG and C-GCPH. Rather surprisingly, the Canadian Ministry of Transport and the U.S. authorities agreed that the aircraft would retain their original registrations and one frequently hears passengers expressing surprise on CPAL flying U.S. registered aircraft. Equally incongruous is the sight of a Canadian registered DC-10 in United colours in Hong Kong.

Prior to inaugurating their Hong Kong service, United modified the cabin interiors of the three Canadian Pacific aircraft and installed additional fuel tanks to provide the extended range necessary for the non-stop Seattle-Hong Kong service. CP Air benefited from the exchange not only by acquiring

financial incentives from United but also in operating aircraft which require less fuel per passenger on short range flights and which attract reduced landing fees because of their lower weight. However, with the airline's late 1985 decision to standardize on the Boeing 737 for its domestic routes, the United aircraft have been operating on the shorter trans-Atlantic services and between Vancouver and Hawaii. They have thus been employed on flights from Montreal to Amsterdam, Montreal to Lisbon and Halifax to Amsterdam etc. which are all within to DC-10-10s operating capabilities. On the completion of the cross leasing agreement in 1987, the DC-10-10s will be returned to United and the DC-10-30s, will rejoin the Canadian Pacific fleet.

Colussy's introduction of the hub and spoke system in 1983 was the first application of this concept in Canada although it had been in operation in the United States for a considerable time. Under this system, hub cities become terminals through which connections must be made to reach other centres. Airlines in the United States developed this concept using hubs such as Atlanta, Houston, Dallas and Salt Lake City with great success as it ensures that considerable traffic is retained by the originating airline. As many incoming flights as possible are scheduled to arrive at the hub from the spoke cities at more or less the same time and the return flights to the spokes are arranged to depart after passengers and their baggage have transferred to their onward flights. At the time CP Air introduced the hub and spoke system, it operated relatively few domestic routes except those on the transcontinental service

and those in the interior of British Columbia. It therefore had to approach other carriers to co-operate in its hub and spoke system and timetables were co-ordinated with Eastern Provincial Airways at Toronto and Montreal on April 24, 1983. A co-operative agreement was introduced which provided through-plane service from western Canada to Halifax and allowed quick and convenient connections to be made between the two airlines. Timetable integration with U.S. carriers, which also share Terminal One at Pearson International Airport, Toronto with Canadian Pacific was also introduced and this gives U.S. bound passengers flying from both eastern and western Canada considerable motivation to fly with Canadian Pacific as connection times at Toronto are reduced to a minimum in most cases and it is not necessary to change terminals.

On October 3, 1983 a similar integration of services took place with AirBC at Vancouver. This airline was formed in 1980 when the Jim Pattison Group took over several westcoast airlines including Gulf Air Aviation, Trans Provincial Airlines, Omineca Air Services, Haida Airlines, Pacific Coastal Airlines and West Coast Air Services. Using a mixed fleet of wheel and float equipped aircraft comprising primarily de Havilland Canada Beavers and Twin Otters together with Britten Norman Islanders, Cessna Skywagons and Grumman amphibians, the company provides service to Victoria, Nanaimo, Duncan, Texada Island, Powell River, Port Hardy, Bella Bella, Bella Coola and Ocean Falls, etc. At the time of the integration, AirBC took over CP Air's Vancouver - Victoria services using its newly acquired de Havilland Canada Dash 7s. Subsequently, the carrier has developed into one of Canada's most successful commuter airlines and in 1985 handled 550,000 passengers—more than any other Canadian commuter airline. Currently, AirBC operates flights from Vancouver Airport to Campbell River, Castlegar, Comox, Kamloops, Kelowna, Port Hardy, Powell River, Quesnel, Victoria and Williams Lake. A Victoria-Seattle service provides four return flights on weekdays and Sundays. Harbour services using float-equipped aircraft link downtown Vancouver with the harbours at Victoria and Nanaimo. In 1986, AirBC introduced a Vancouver - Penticton service and also operates on the Cranbrook - Kelowna route. During 1985, CP Air and AirBC exchanged 6,000 passengers a month.

Following the purchase of Eastern Provincial Airways and Nordair, both of which use Terminal One at Toronto's Pearson International Airport, Toronto became a true hub city in the U.S. sense of the word and CPAL's spokes from here now include Halifax, Frobisher Bay, Thunder Bay and Windsor. Indicating the effectiveness of the system from the passenger's point of view is the fact that passengers from Nordair's domestic services can connect with Canadian Pacific's trunk flights with only a 30 minute stopover. Prior to the acquisition of EPA and Nordair, the hub and spoke system allowed Canadian Pacific to reduce its flight requirements by 10 percent, yet services from Vancouver and Toronto to Calgary, Edmonton and Winnipeg were increased by over 50 percent.

In December 1983, CP Hotels was transferred from Canadian Pacific Enterprises to CP Air and in January 1984 became an autonimous division of the airline. As pointed out at the beginning of this work, Canadian Pacific originally entered the hotel business in order to provide dining rooms for passengers on transcontinental trains in British Columbia. Because of the steeply graded line through the Fraser Canyon, the Selkirk Mountains and the Rockies, it was decided not to run restaurant cars west of Calgary and hotels were opened at Field, Glacier and North Bend in 1886. Subsequently, hotels were opened at Banff, Lake Louise, Calgary, Toronto and Quebec City, etc. During the railway era, the hotels were an extremely valuable adjunct to the company as railway passengers naturally were directed to Canadian Pacific's hotels whenever accommodation was required. With the decline of passenger rail traffic and Canadian Pacific's exit from this service in 1978, CP Hotels lost this source of business and it was not until the transfer of the hotels to the airline that these properties found a place in the hierarchy of Canadian Pacific where they could be utilized to their full potential.

During the late 1970s and into the 1980s, the Canadian government had moved gradually away from the concept of airline regulation as practised by the government of Mackenzie King in the 1940s. Indeed, by 1979 CP Air had been freed of all restrictions on the transcontinental route and was allowed to compete directly with Air Canada. However, with airline deregulation completed in the United States under the Carter presidency, there was pressure for Canadian authorities to introduce similar freedom of the skies north of the border. On May 10, 1984, the federal government introduced a new policy easing the restriction of competition between Canadian airlines. CP Air, following its co-operative agreement of 1983 with Eastern Provincial Airways, had begun negotiating with the Newfoundland Capital Corporation for the purchase of the airline and on August 31, 1984 purchased EPA and its subsidiary Air Maritime for $20 million. Unlike some well known U.S. airlines such as Braniff which went on an expansion spree following deregulation and subsequently went bankrupt, Canadian Pacific was more circumspect and in one purchase acquired an established airline and subsidiary which protected its traffic interests in the Maritimes.

Eastern Provincial Airways was formed as a non-scheduled airline at Gander, Newfoundland in 1949 and provided charter services throughout the island as well as operating forestry patrol and DEW support flights. Scheduled services were commenced in 1961 and, by the time of the acquisition, EPA had become eastern Canada's major air carrier. The airline's trunk routes connected Toronto, Montreal, Halifax, St. John's, Gander and Goose Bay and were operated by a fleet of Boeing 737-200s. Feeder services were provided by Air Maritime utilizing ageing British Aerospace 748s. These twin engine, turbo-prop aircraft operated between Halifax, Fredericton, Moncton, St. John, Charlottetown and the Magdalen Islands. Following the acquisition of EPA, the trunk services were integrated with CP Air's transcontinental flights and in July 1985 it was announced that the EPA Boeing 737 flights would be operated under the trade name CP Air thus making the airline a truly transcontinental system. It was also stated that Air Maritime would continue to operate feeder routes but subsequently CP Air decided to divest itself of these services and the local routes have been taken over by Air Atlantic, in which Canadian Pacific has a minority interest.

Another feature introduced by Colussy was a partial change in emphasis of CP Air's marketing strategy. From its earliest days, the airline had seen itself as Canada's second domestic airline and in many areas strove to compete directly with Air Canada for every passenger within Canada. On the international scene, the two airlines had their own general areas of operation where competition between them was minimized. Within Canada, however, both airlines now offer essentially the same trunk services but, obviously, with only one third the aircraft of Air Canada, CP Air could not hope to offer all the services that the government airline provided. Under Colussy's guidance, the company went after its own niche as the business traveller's airline.

For many years, business people who travelled on tickets which cost more than twice as much as discounted tickets, used primarily by vacationers, had complained that their expensive tickets gave them no benefits other than the ability to change their flights without penalty. Eventually, the airlines yielded to these complaints and in 1978 KLM was the first company to introduce extra facilities for full-fare passengers. From this stemmed the concept of separate business class cabins with improved amenities such as better food, free beverages and free headphones for in-flight entertainment although, at this time, no attempt was made to up-grade the seating and passengers remained in Economy seats with minimal space. Working under such conditions was impossible on a full flight but it was an improvement as airline personnel were directed to leave as much empty space as possible in the business sections of aircraft. To attract the business traveller between Toronto and Montreal, CP Air introduced "The Company Jet" service featuring low density seating and special services for the business traveller on September 15, 1980 but because of low passenger demand it was terminated before the six month market testing period was completed. Nevertheless, business class similar to that offered by KLM and other international carriers was introduced on CP's transcontinental and international flights on October 26, 1980 as Empress Class which continues to be provided by the company for the full fare economy passenger. CP Air was the first Canadian airline to offer this service and on January 28, 1983 introduced Royal Canadian Business Class on its Boeing 747 flights between Vancouver, Tokyo and Hong Kong. First Class accommodation was restricted to 12 fully reclining sleeperette seats in the upper cabin and the forward cabin was equipped to carry 28 passengers in former first class seats with considerably more hip room than that provided in economy seats. In airline terminology, "it features superior in-flight amenities including more spacious seats and a separate on-board cabin for a modest premium over the regular economy fare." During 1983, Royal Canadian Business Class was introduced to all the airline's international routes and has been well accepted by the business traveller.

Within Canada, however, the business traveller had no equivalent service to Royal Canadian Business Class until October 29, 1984 when CP Air introduced its Attaché business class on selected long haul domestic flights to test the concept in the market place. Using three Boeing 737s equipped with modified interiors and with specially designed seats, CP Air began services between Vancouver and Toronto and Montreal providing seating for eight first class and 54 business class passengers. In the business cabin, the seating is nominally three abreast but the centre seat is not sold and a convenient table can be lowered from the back of this seat. Full cabin service and upgraded meals make Attaché almost equivalent to Royal Canadian Business Class and there is room to work on the flight.

Although CPAL still emphasizes its commitment to the business traveller, there is little doubt that, with the arrival of Carty, Canadian Pacific has reverted to its previous concept of providing direct competition for Air Canada. The acquisition of Nordair and the recent marketing arrangements with commuter airlines throughout Canada indicate that Canadian Pacific Air Lines is again competing with the government airline for every passenger in the country.

Colussy was also responsible for the introduction of the first frequent flier program in Canada. Again, this is a concept that was introduced in the United States some years ago and rewards passengers' loyalty by providing free or reduced cost travel when sufficient mileage has been accumulated on the airline. CP Air introduced its Travel Bonus Program in July 1984 and passengers enrolled in the scheme receive points for each mile they fly with the airline. In addition, partner airlines credit mileage travelled on their systems and hotels and car rental companies also participate in the program. The success of the concept still has to be measured from the airline's point of view but there is no doubt that passengers who travel freqently have earned worthwhile bonuses. As Air Canada immediately followed the introduction of CP Air's Travel Bonus Program with a frequent flier plan of its own, no doubt some of the marketing impact of the concept was lost and both airlines have to provide the programs in order to retain their passengers' loyalty. It is nevertheless a fact that the CP Air Travel Bonus Program is more generous than Air Canada's plan as it allows comparable benefits to be claimed at lower mileages. Currently, 150,000 frequent fliers have enrolled in CP Air's Travel Bonus Program.

After only two years with CP Air, Colussy left the airline in late 1984 to pursue his own business interests in the United States. He was replaced by Donald J. Carty as President and Chief Executive Officer who took up his appointment in March 1985 after several years in senior management positions with American Airlines. Having been with a company which had successfully weathered deregulation in the United States, Carty was in an ideal position to ensure that CP Air achieved similar success in Canada. Soon after he arrived in Vancouver he stated that the airline must become more cost efficient, develop a stronger revenue base and increase its emphasis on attracting the business travellers. He indicated that although employee-management communications were fairly good, he wanted to build on this base. In addition, he said that he wanted CP Air to be larger with a bigger share of the market and that this could only be achieved with consistent profitability. Unfortunately, the airline had an operating loss of $8.9 million in 1985.

Soon after Carty joined CP Air, Attaché service was expanded to provide 24 flights each business day. Calgary, Edmonton and Winnipeg were provided with Attaché flights on April 28 - 29, 1985 and the Toronto - Halifax service commenced on May 13th. However, the Halifax and Winnipeg flights attracted insufficient business to warrant continuing Attaché service to these destinations and only Vancouver, Toronto, Calgary and Edmonton now enjoy these flights.

May 1985 brought two decisions from the Canadian government which will make Carty's drive for a bigger and more profitable airline more difficult to achieve. On May 6th, it was announced that San José, California had been agreed by the Canadian and United States governments as the United States' under-utilized airport for "no frills" flights between the two countries. Air California operates the San-José - Vancouver route and with San José only 50 miles south of San Francisco, this provides considerable competition for the Canadian carrier. Only four days later, Canadian Transport Minister Donald Mazankowski announced that Wardair was to be given the right to serve the United Kingdom as Canada's second scheduled carrier with flights to London, Prestwick and Manchester. Since CPAL was prevented from initiating service to Britain in 1961, it had been hoped that it eventually would receive permission to introduce these flights. The Canadian authorities, however, elected to award the routes to Wardair which has built up an excellent reputation for providing charter flights to Europe, the Caribbean and Hawaii.

Although facing stiffer competition on its San Francisco route and unsuccessful in its bid to obtain routes to Britain, CP Air was able to announce a major success on October 8, 1985 when Carty held a press conference with Jean Douville, President of Nordair, to state that the directors of CP Air and Nordair had agreed in principle to a merger proposal. Having successfully acquired Eastern Provincial Airways to protect its eastern flank, CP Air was anxious to expand its presence in Ontario and Quebec where it had had no local services since October 31, 1955 when it traded its routes in this region to Trans-Canada Air Lines in return for the Toronto - Mexico City service. In order to offer a truly competitive domestic service to that provided by Air Canada, the company had to bolster its route network in central Canada and Nordair was the most suitable available partner. On September 20th, Quebecair, the regional carrier owned by the Quebec provincial government had made an offer to purchase the remaining 65% of Nordair which it did not already own. However, the offer was rejected by Nordair's management and the majority of its shareholders. A protracted battle then ensued between CP Air and Quebecair and it was not until July 31, 1986, following the change of government in

Quebec, that this was settled. The provincial government sold its 35% interest in Nordair to Canadian Pacific Air Lines and Quebecair was sold to the owners of the CPAL commuter airline Nordair Metro. This allowed CPAL and Nordair to merge and to become an important integrated airline in central Canada. Total integration of the airlines took place on January 24, 1987.

Originally known as Boreal Airways, Nordair was formed on May 26, 1947 at St. Felicien, Quebec. In 1956, it acquired Mont Laurier Aviation and adopted the name Nordair. The following year it moved its main base to Dorval airport, Montreal and continued to expand serving communities in the Northwest Territories, Ontario and Quebec. In 1972, the airline was floated to the public and in 1979 Air Canada acquired 86.46 percent of the company's stock. However, the federal cabinet ordered Air Canada to return the airline to private enterprise though this was not achieved until 1984 when Innocan of Montreal acquired a controlling interest.

Nordair's fleet comprised ten Boeing 737-200s with three further aircraft on lease. Six of the company's 737s are Combis—equipped to carry passengers and cargo. These aircraft are fitted with deflectors for operations on gravel runways. Nordair also operated five Fairchild Hiller FH-227s, two of which are passenger/cargo aircraft and are used exclusively for supplying and maintaining the DEW which CPAL helped construct in the 1950s. The three remaining FH-227s operate scheduled services. Two Lockheed Electra L-188s operate ice-reconnaissance flights for Environment Canada.

Having acquired Nordair, Canadian

Pacific Air Lines now operates flights in the Yukon and the Northwest Territories as well as all Canada's provinces, with the exception of Saskatchewan where it is now represented by Norcanair. In some respects, the airline is similar to the conglomeration of routes that were forged together to form Canadian Pacific Air Lines in 1942. However, in the area of aircraft types there is little similarity. On July 1, 1942, Canadian Pacific Air Lines owned 77 aircraft which had been constructed by 13 different manufacturers. Over the years, the airline gradually standardized its fleet until, with the withdrawal of the last Boeing 727 in 1984, only three types were operated. The fleet comprised 19 Boeing 737s, four Boeing 747s and eight McDonnell Douglas DC-10s. Throughout the system, it was recognized that the Boeing 747s were the flagships of the fleet and, although they were ageing, they were very well accepted by the travelling public. It therefore came as something of a surprise on October 16, 1985 when Carty announced that CP Air was going to exchange its Boeing 747s for a similar number of DC-10-30s from Pakistan International Airlines. This exchange was being handled by Page Avjet Corporation of Orlando, Florida and Boeing 747 C-FCRE was handed over to its new owners on December 18, 1985. In return, CP air received PIA DC-10-30 PK-BBL which became the new *Empress of Canada* and was registered as C-FCRE. The entire exchange was completed in October 1986.

Although traditionalists mourn the passing of the 747 from the fleet, standardization on the DC-10-30 as the only long-haul aircraft has important financial considerations. The company has em-

barked on a plan to provide more flights to selected destinations and while the passenger traffic is not sufficient to warrant increased flights with the 409 seat 747s, additional flights with the 281 seat DC-10-30 are justified. Thus, the Boeing 747's continued service in the Canadian Pacific service could not be justified. In addition, the sale of the parts inventory and equipment for the 747s, together with the disposal of the 747 flight simulator is anticipated to provide approximately $20 million. Standardization will increase operating income by over $12 million annually and will improve aircraft utilization by an estimated ten percent — the equivalent of one additional DC-10.

Even greater standardization was to follow as it was announced on January 24, 1986 that the airline had negotiated with GPA Group Ltd. of Shannon, Ireland to exchange its three Boeing 737-300s for 737-200s. Prior to the second oil crisis of 1979, four Boeing 767s had been ordered but in 1983 the contract was changed to five 737-300s to be delivered in 1985 and 1986, with a further five being ordered for 1987 and 1988. The first 737-300 was accepted on April 12, 1985 and two further aircraft were delivered the following month. Exchanging these aircraft for the smaller 737-200 allows significant savings to be made through standardization with the rest of the 737 fleet and enables the airline to reduce its debt. The fourth and fifth 737-300s joined the fleet in April 1986 but these were disposed of to the GPA Group in December 1986. The order for the final five aircraft has been cancelled.

But the most surprising change of all to be introduced in 1985 was the De-

cember 17th announcement by Carty that the airline was reverting to its original name of Canadian Pacific Air Lines. Furthermore, the distinctive orange livery is being replaced by a Pacific Blue on the aircraft lower fuselages and tails, while the upper bodies will be Sky White and separated from the blue by a stripe of Corporate Red. The multimark has been redesigned and elongated to impart an airline character and, although retaining the triangle and semi circle, now has four pin stripes signifying speed and five rectangles symbolizing the five continents that the airline serves. On the upper body, forward of the wings, each aircraft will carry the name Canadian Pacific on one side and Canadien Pacifique on the other.

The name CP Air and the orange livery had been in use for 18 years and were introduced to emphasize the worldwide operations of the corporate parent, Canadian Pacific Limited. Strangely enough, it was in the overseas market that the abbreviated name had the least impact. While Canadian's have been familiar with the initials C.P.R. and C.P. for generations, such is not the case abroad and, to many, CP Air did not identify the airline as one of Canada's flag carriers. Worse, it caused confusion with Hong Kong based Cathay Pacific Airways which competes with CPAL on the Vancouver - Hong Kong route. The new name was introduced formally on January 12, 1986 when fully integrated operations with Eastern Provincial Airways began. DC-10-30 C-FCRE *Empress of Canada* was unveiled in the new livery and it was planned that other aircraft in the fleet would be repainted over the following three years.

▲ It is January 1986 and it's out with the orange and in with the red, white and blue. Boeing 737-217 Advanced C-GQCP *Empress of Richmond* is seen at Vancouver in the company of McDonnell Douglas DC-10-30 C-FCRE *Empress of Canada* soon after the new livery was unveiled.

In December 1986, came the news that Canadian Pacific Air Lines was to be purchased by Pacific Western Airlines Corporation of Calgary. This was all the more surprising as earlier in the year CPAL had taken steps to strengthen its domestic network and had begun an expansion of its international routes so that by year end it served 71 cities in 15 countries. However, with continued CPAL losses, Canadian Pacific Limited finally decided to dispose of its airline operations and the change of ownership will take place in 1987 when the necessary government approval has been obtained.

Pacific Western Airlines was formed at Fort St. James, British Columbia on July 1, 1945 as Central British Columbia Airways and provided charter services until 1953 when it obtained its first scheduled route licence. This authorized the company to operate between Vancouver and Kitimat. On May 15, 1953 the company adopted its current name and by expansion and acquisition grew to become Canada's third largest airline. Extensive services are operated with a fleet of 24 Boeing 737s throughout British Columbia, Alberta, Saskatchewan, Manitoba and the Northwest Territories. It operates airbus services between Calgary and Edmonton and also from Vancouver to Seattle. Charter services are operated to Mexico, the Caribbean and the United States. There is little doubt that the PWA/CPAL combination will offer Air Canada severe competition as the two companies dominate air services throughout Canada and, in order to protect itself in British Columbia, the government airline acquired AirBC two days before the CPAL sale was announced. As already described,

AirBC began operating a co-ordinated commuter service with CPAL from Vancouver in 1983 and in 1986 expanded its services in southern British Columbia. No doubt a realignment of services will take place but as Time Air of Lethbridge, which is 46% owned by PWA, operates competing services in this area, PWA/CPAL will remain with a commuter ally. On the east coast, Air Atlantic has taken over the feeder routes operated by Air Maritime and CPAL acquired a minority interest in Norcanair of Saskatoon. Since October 26th co-ordinated services connecting Edmonton, Calgary and Winnipeg with Saskatoon, Regina, Prince Albert and other points in Saskatchewan have been available. In addition, Norcanair offers jet service between Calgary, Saskatoon, Regina and Minneapolis using two Fokker F28s. Orginally formed as Saskatchewan Government Airways in 1947 to provide charter services, the company branched out into operating scheduled routes and the name Norcanair was adopted in March 1965.

In Quebec, Nordair, which is now owned by CPAL, has taken a 35% equity interest in Nordair Metro. This newly formed commuter airline, whose owners have purchased Quebecair, offers services to a number of Quebec centres and Ottawa from Dorval Airport, Montreal. The initial flights to Quebec City and Ottawa commenced on March 31st using three turbo-prop Convair 580s and the Dorval - Bagotville route began on April 14th. Other centres added during 1986 include Baie Comeau, Gaspé, Iles-de-la-Madeleine, Mont Joli, Rouyn-Noranda and Rimouski. The only area where PWA/CPAL has poor regional representation is in Ontario where CPAL has a commercial agreement with

PemAir covering the Toronto-Pembroke route. Work is underway to provide a comprehensive Ontario commuter alliance and it anticipated that such a service, utilizing modern turbo-prop aircraft, will be announced during 1987.

On the international scene, CPAL's plans to increase flight frequencies in developing markets became apparent with the introduction of the winter schedule on October 27, 1985. The Vancouver-Tokyo service was increased to six flights weekly with three of these offering same plane service from Toronto. negotiations with the Japanese author- Three non-stop flights weekly were offered between Vancouver and Hong Kong and now four such flights a week are available. On November 1, 1985 a Toronto-Auckland, New Zealand service was introduced. This was CPAL's first scheduled service to New Zealand since 1969 when the New Zealand government withdrew the airline's right to operate the route. A second weekly flight to Auckland commenced on September 14th when DC-10-30, C-FCRB, in the new livery operated this service. By arranging for the Vancouver-Sydney flight and the Toronto-Auckland service to meet in Honolulu, CPAL offers both Vancouver and Toronto boarding passengers rapid and convenient services to Auckland, Fiji and Sydney.

CPAL introduced the first non-stop flight between North America and the People's Republic of China on April 29th when it inaugurated its Vancouver-Shanghai service. This makes it viable to travel westbound from Europe to China rather than by the more normal eastbound service offered by other airlines. It also introduces a modern day equivalent of Canadian Pacific's

Far East service when the fastest means of reaching Shanghai from Europe involved taking a Canadian Pacific ship across the Atlantic, travelling to Vancouver on the Canadian Pacific Railway and then sailing across the Pacific on another Canadian Pacific ship. Current plans are to extend the Vancouver-Shanghai service to Beijing in 1987.

Bangkok will also be added to the CPAL route system during 1987, following the October 1986 announcement of a bilateral air agreement reached between Canada and Thailand. The airline's DC-10-30s overnight in Hong Kong four nights a week and the extension of the Vancouver-Hong Kong flight to Bangkok is logical and easy to implement. Furthermore, the bilateral agreement allows the airline to connect Amsterdam with Bangkok and CPAL may be the first Canadian flag carrier to offer an around the world service. Other Pacific Rim destinations anticipated to come on line before too much longer include Taipei and Seoul.

A Toronto-Rio de Janiero-Sao Paulo service will commence on May 2, 1987 and Vancouver-Brazil flights could be in operation within three years. Vancouver and Toronto flights to Mexico City are expected to be reintroduced within 18 months. On the North Atlantic, frequencies have been increased significantly and currently CPAL offers daily service from Vancouver-Amsterdam via Toronto as well as four flights a week on the Polar route. The company is also interested in obtaining additional landing rights in other European cities and is hopeful that current bilateral talks with the United States will result in further services to destinations south of the border.

CPAL 833

▲ Boeing 747-217B C-FCRA *Empress of Asia* over Mount Baker, Washington in 1974. Such was the impact of CP Air's orange livery that the Smithsonian Institution in Washington, D.C. incorporated an illustration of a CP Air 747 to highlight its display of this aircraft. Although the 747 no longer serves with CPAL, sales of the type remain strong and in 1986 Boeing sold 83 examples compared with only 42 in 1985.

The Aircraft

Canadian Pacific Air Lines owned 77 aircraft of 27 different types constructed by 13 manufacturers when it commenced operations. Today, it operates a fleet of 64 modern aircraft comprising 45 Boeing 737s, 12 McDonnell Douglas DC-10s, five Fairchild Hiller FH-227s and two Lockheed L-188C Electras. From one of the most diverse fleets in existence, Canadian Pacific Air Lines has standardized its aircraft to a degree which makes it the envy of many other operators.

The following pages contain photographs and histories of the 48 types of aircraft that the airline has operated. Aircraft types originally acquired from the constituent companies are illustrated on pages 45 to 68 and are arranged alphabetically. A chronological arrangement has been utilized for the aircraft acquired after July 1, 1942 and these types occupy pages 69 to 106. Aircraft of the commuter airlines are shown on pages 107-110.

To provide variety, wherever possible, previously unpublished photographs have been used. Unfortunately, some of the shots are not of the best quality but they have been included to illustrate, specific aircraft at work rather than using manufacturers' brochure illustrations. During the 1930s and 40s, cameras generally did not have the capabilities of today's single lens reflex equipment and allowances must be made for prints which have miraculously survived for over 40 years. Even Canadian Pacific Air Lines does not have a complete photographic record of the various aircraft types it has operated and as well as obtaining prints from the airline, other sources were necessary to complete the record. Bob Cameron of Whitehorse provided the prints of the American Pilgrim 100B, the Curtiss Condor, the Curtiss-Wright Kingbird and the Boeing 247D on pages 69 - 72. These aircraft were the first fleet purchases by Canadian Pacific Air Lines as they were acquired by Yukon Southern Air Transport, from British Yukon Navigation after the new airline commenced operations. Photographs of these aircraft, which served for extremely short periods with CPAL, are rare and Bob's generosity in allowing them to be included in this work is gratefully acknowledged.

Obtaining photographs of CPAL's Avro Anson Vs and its single Cessna C-37 Airmaster proved to be difficult. In fact, it was not possible to include a photograph of the Anson in CPAL's livery and the print on page 74 was kindly supplied by A.J. Shortt of the National Aviation Museum in Ottawa. It illustrates the museum's Anson V in RCAF livery. Just when all hope of finding a photograph of the Cessna C-37 Airmaster was fading, Ray Crone of Saskatoon came up with the shot of CF-BFE on page 50. This photograph has been blown up from a 2½ x 3 inch print. Phil Lucas of Okotoks, Alberta provided the excellent shot of Stinson Reliant CF-BEB seen on page 66. Nicholas Morant took the photograph of the Canadair C-4 seen on page 80. This shot is unusual in that airlines do not now normally take air to air photographs, instead relying on the aircraft manufacturers with fully equipped chase planes to provide the necessary prints. In 1949, it was a somewhat different world and the shot of CF-CPR was taken through the specially cleaned window of a DC-3! Nicholas also supplied the photograph on page 24 of the aircraft being serviced at Dorval prior to their Trans-Atlantic delivery flights. This was taken during his war-service with the National Film Board. Back with Canadian Pacific, he also took the excellent hangar shot of the Britannias on page 91. Thanks are extended to all who supplied photographs for inclusion in this work.

Organizations providing prints for the work include the National Archives, in Ottawa, the Provincial Archives of Alberta, Nordair, the Archives of the Canadian Rockies, British Aerospace and, of course, Canadian Pacific Air Lines. Thanks are extended to all these organizations for allowing their photographs to be included in this book. British Aerospace supplied the prints of the de Havilland Comets seen on pages 84 and 85. This company's generosity in providing these photographs of the airliner is gratefully acknowledged. Considering the type's initial record and CF-CUN's disaster at Karachi, few companies would have made such photographs available.

◀ Bristol Britannia CF-CZB *Empress of Vancouver* outside the newly constructed Britannia Hangar at Vancouver in May 1958.

44

Aircraft types acquired from the constitutent companies

The Barkley-Grow T8P-1 was the only aircraft produced by the Barkley-Grow Aircraft Corporation. An eight passenger, all-metal, twin engine, low wing monoplane, it showed a strong resemblance to both the Lockheed 12 and the Beech 18 except for its fixed undercarriage with spatted wheels and triple tail. The aircraft was designed by Archibald Barkley who had worked with the Wright brothers on their gliders prior to their first powered flight. In 1931, Barkley had constructed an aircraft of his own design incorporating his patented multi-spar, stress skinned wing with no ribs or bulkheads but of exceptional strength. Unfortunately the aircraft except for the wings, was destroyed on its maiden flight. Undaunted, Mr. Barkley and Harold B. Grow joined forces to produce the T8P-1, incorporating the patent wing and the initial example made its first flight in early 1937. After a series of demonstration flights in the United States, the prototype

came to Canada where it was registered as CF-BVE. Canadian Car & Foundry soon obtained the world-wide distributing rights for all but the United States where the builders retained these rights. Neither organization was very successful as marketers as only 11 T8P-1s were constructed and the Barkley-Grow Corporation was purchased by the American Manufacturing Corporation, which subsequently became part of the Consolidated-Vultee Corporation. Canadian Car demonstrated the aircraft to the Department of National Defence and the Department of Transport but apart from selling only one aircraft to the RCAF, no government orders were obtained, the RCAF preferring the Beech 18 which it acquired in large numbers. In a comparative test between the two aircraft in August 1938 the Department of Transport noted that, with the same load, the Beech 18 was superior to the T8P-1 in all respects except in the length of the landing run. As

the Beech 18 was also cheaper than the Barkley-Grow, it received the orders but the T8P-1 was a good aircraft with a robustness that enabled three of the 11 examples built to survive into the late 1960s. For a bush aircraft to exhibit such longevity, it has to be good.

Through the purchase of Yukon Southern Air Transport, Mackenzie Air Service and Prairie Airways, CPAL acquired a total of six Barkley-Grows. The prototype aircraft, CF-BVE, was sold in 1945 and BMG and BTX were written off in mishaps but CF-BLV, BMV, BMW and BQM continued in service until late 1949/early 1950 when they were replaced by more modern aircraft.

CF-BQM is being restored at the Aero Space Museum in Calgary.

▲ Barkley-Grow T8P-1s CF-BTX and CF-BMW, which were obtained from Mackenzie Air Service and Yukon Southern Air Transport respectively, are seen at Three Mile Island soon after the formation of CPAL.

Aircraft	Barkley-Grow T8P-1
Year of first flight	1937
Engines	Pratt & Whitney Wasp Junior (450 hp)
Wingspan	50 ft 8 in
Length	36 ft 2 in
Height	9 ft 8 in
Weight empty	5,880 lb
Weight loaded	8,750 lb
Cruising speed	185 mph
Range	1,000 miles
Crew	2
Passengers	6

CPAL 6712

This high performance, five seat, cabin, stagger-wing biplane was first produced in 1932 and, by the time the production line was closed in 1948, almost 800 had been produced including 270 constructed for the U.S. forces for liaison and communication duties. The aircraft was unusual in that it was extremely fast for a biplane and, in fact, a C-17-R won the New York to Los Angeles Bendix race in 1936 in 14 hours, 55 minutes. The type's maximum speed of 211 mph was achieved by fitting a Wright R-975-E 420 hp engine in a relatively streamlined fuselage. Retractable wheels added to the aerodynamic refinement of the C-17-R which sold for $14,500 in 1936. Two of the 18 C-17-Rs produced were delivered to Canadian customers and CPAL obtained one of these in the acquisition

of Starratt Airways & Transportation. One wonders why such a company would require a high speed sports aircraft of this type. Quite possibly, Mr. Starratt enjoyed flying!

In 1937, Beech Aircraft, which had previously fitted Wright engines to its Model 17s, experimented with the Pratt & Whitney Wasp-Junior 450 hp engine in this airframe and the resulting D-17-S obtained its certificate on July 16, 1937. A total of 66 aircraft of this type had been sold by the time the United States entered World War Two. A number of these had been obained by Canadian owners and, one, CF-BLU, entered CPAL service following the acquisition of Yukon Southern Air Transport. It was written off at Camp Canol, NWT on August 16, 1942 after hitting a sandbar on take-off during the construction

of the Canol Pipeline. CF-BIF was sold to an operator in Alaska in May 1944.

Aircraft	Beechcraft C-17-R	Beechcraft D-17-S
Year of introduction	1936	1937
Engine	Wright R-975-E (420 hp)	Pratt & Whitney Wasp Jr. (450 hp)
Wingspan	32 ft 0 in	32 ft 0 in
Length	24 ft 5 in	25 ft 11 in
Height	8 ft 2 in	8 ft 0 in
Weight empty	2,250 lb	2,540 lb
Gross weight	3,900 lb	4,200 lb
Cruising speed	202 mph	202 mph
Range	800 mils	800 miles
Crew	1	1
Passengers	3	3

▲ Starrat Airways & Transportation's Beechcraft C-17-R in winter guise equipped with streamlined skis. Subsequently many operators fitted aircraft with wheel skis where the wheel sat on the ski and provided some cushioning while the aircraft was taxiing, taking-off or landing.

The twin engined, all-metal, low-winged Model 18 made its first flight on January 15, 1937 and was certificated on March 4th. Powered by Wright R-760 Whirlwinds of 320 hp, the original Model 18 was an expensive aircraft and, at first, was of little interest to U.S. companies. However, Canadian operators recognized the potential of the aircraft and some of the first Model 18s went to Prairie Airways and Starratt Airways & Transportation. The latter company found the 18s ability to operate on wheels, skis and floats of considerable advantage. Nevertheless, sales remained slow and by the time war broke out in Europe, only 39 Model 18s had been sold even though no less than five versions powered by Wright, Pratt & Whitney and Jacobs engines had been manufactured.

The first military version of the Beech 18 was supplied to the Philippine Army Air Corps. Dwight D. Eisenhower, as Chief of Staff of the American mission to the Philippines, selected the Beech 18 for service with the Air Corps and subsequently large orders were placed by the USAAF and the U.S. Navy for various models of the aircraft. During and after the war it served as a pilot, navigational, gunnery and bombing trainer, an ambulance, a transport, a photo-reconnaissance aircraft and for directing radio controlled target aircraft. A total of 5,257 modified Beech 18s were produced for Allied forces and the type remained in service with the U.S. Army until 1976. After World War Two, over 2,200 Beech 18s were refurbished by Beech for the U.S. government. Commercial production re-commenced in 1945 with the D18s and by the time the last Beech Super H18 was delivered on November 26, 1969, over 9,000 examples had been produced. The Model 18 was in continuous production for 32½ years, the longest production run in aviation history.

CPAL operated five Beech 18s which were obtained from Prairie Airways and Canadian Airways when these companies were taken over. The two 18Ds obtained from Prairie Airways were sold to Transportes Aereos Centro Americanos of Venezuela in 1944 and the three Canadian Airways A-18As were disposed of by mid-1948.

Aircraft	Beechcraft 18D	Beechcraft A-18A
Year of first flight	1938	1940
Engines	Jacobs L-6 radials (300 hp)	Wright Whirlwind radials (350 hp)
Wingspan	47 ft 8 in	47 ft 8 in
Length	31 ft 11 in	34 ft 3 in
Height	9 ft 5 in	9 ft 5 in
Weight empty	4,336 lb	4,600 lb
Gross weight	7,200 lb	7,500 lb
Cruising speed	195 mph	205 mph
Range	800 miles	1,200 miles
Crew	1 - 2	1 - 2
Maximum passenger capacity	9	9

▲ Ex-Canadian Airways' Beechcraft A-18A BQQ awaits its next assignment. The Wright Whirlwinds of the A-18As were considered to be much superior to the Jacobs radials of the 18Ds. Prairie Airways found their aircraft to be extemely unreliable and the Jacobs engines were referred to derisively as "Shakey Jakes."

G.M. Bellanca designed a series of successful aircraft in the 1920s and 30s some of which earned an excellent reputation for working under adverse conditions. One of his CH-200s, powered by a Packard diesel engine established the non-refuelled endurance record of 84½ hours. Rather remarkably, this 1931 record was not broken until July 15, 1986.

The high winged, six seater CH-300 monoplane, equipped with a 300 hp Wright Whirlwind engine, first flew in late 1928 or early 1929 and around 36 of this type were built. The RCAF ordered six Pacemakers for aerial survey work and these were supplied from the United States. However, in late 1929, Bellanca Aircraft of Canada was formed to sell and service the company's aircraft. Thought was given to setting up a factory to manufacture

Bellancas in Canada should sufficient orders be received. These never materialized but Bellanca received an order for six further CH-300 Pacemakers and these were built in Montreal by Canadian Vickers utilizing welded steel fuselage skeletons supplied by the U.S. parent company. The first of these aircraft made its initial flight in May 1931 and the remaining aircraft of the RCAF order were completed later the same year.

In RCAF service, the Pacemaker was used primarily for aerial surveying but in 1937 four Pacemakers were sold to Canadian Airways. One of these, CF-BFA, was transferred to Quebec Airways in 1941 and was damaged beyond repair at Baie Comeau in December 1942. CPAL's only other Pacemaker was a U.S. built aircraft, CF-AMO, which was

purchased by Wings in 1940 and sold to Austin Airways of Toronto in 1944.

Aircraft	Bellanca CH-300 Pacemaker
Year of first flight	1928/1929
Engine	Wright J-6 radial (300 hp)
Wingspan	46 ft 4 in
Length	27 ft 9 in
Height	8 ft 4 in
Weight empty	2,363 lb *
Gross weight	4,300 lb *
Cruising speed	125 mph
Range	850 miles
Crew	1
Passengers	3

* On floats

▲ A typical scene in Northern Manitoba in the early 1940s as Wings Bellanca CH-300 Pacemaker CF-AMO brings in supplies to a remote settlement.

This large, single engined, cabin aircraft was designed for U.S. airline service but the introduction of regulations which severely restricted the use of single engined transport aircraft within the United States meant that the Bellanca Aircruiser could not find a niche in the market and the few examples built all were purchased by Canadian operators. Bellanca designed a large, high winged, cabin sesqui-plane in which the airfoil shaped stub wings and outer struts provided an additional lifting surface representing almost 30 percent of the total lifting area. This, coupled with a high horsepower engine enabled the Aircruiser to carry a load which was greater than the aircraft's own empty weight. Up to 15 passengers or two tons of cargo could be carried and the Aircruiser earned an excellent reputation as a Canadian bush aircraft.

The type received its certificate on March 16, 1935 and was available with a 670, 715, 730, 760 or 850 hp Wright Cyclone engine. These models were referred to as the 66-67, 66-70, 66-75, 66-76 and 66-85 respectively. With such power and lifting capacity, the Aircruiser exhibited an unusually good short field performance and the aircraft did excellent work in the Canadian bush. CPAL obtained a 66-70, CF-AWR, in the purchase of Canadian Airways and a 66-75, CF-BTW, and a 66-76, CF-BKV, from Mackenzie Air Service. The ex-Mackenzie Air Service aircraft went to Central Northern Airways of Winnipeg in 1944 and 1947, respectively. The Aircruiser 66-70 was damaged beyond economic repair in 1947 when it was forced down because of fuel starvation. CF-BTW is owned by Barney Lamm of Gimli, Manitoba and is still in operation. CF-AWR is being restored by the Western Canada Air Museum at Winnipeg where it is on display.

Aircraft	Bellanca 66-70 Aircruiser	Bellanca 66-76 Aircruiser
Year of introduction	1935	1935
Engine	Wright Cyclone radial (715 hp)	Wright Cyclone radial (760 hp)
Wingspan	65 ft 0 in	65 ft 0 in
Length	43 ft 4 in	43 ft 4 in
Height	11 ft 9 in	11 ft 9 in
Weight empty	5,983 lb	6,348 lb
Gross weight	10,853 lb	11,400 lb
Cruising speed	137 mph	137 mph
Range	700 miles	700 miles
Crew	1	1
Maximum passenger capacity	15	15

▲ Bellanca 66-70 Aircruiser CF-AWR showing its aerofoil-shaped stub wings and outer struts to good effect. Although serving with Mackenzie Air Service from March 1935 to May 1939, this aircraft was sold to Eldorado Gold Mines and then to Canadian Airways before becoming part of the CPAL fleet.

49

This small, high winged, cabin monoplane carried a pilot and three passengers and was aimed primarily at the private owner. Nevertheless, small commercial operators found the aircraft economical to operate for charter work.

The flight certificate was obtained on February 8, 1937 and almost 50 examples were constructed. Powered by a Warner Super Scarab engine of only 145 hp, the C-37 was one of the most efficient aircraft ever constructed. Two examples are known to have been delivered to Canada when new. One of these CF-BFE which was acquired by Prairie Airways and became part of the CPAL fleet in 1941. It was damaged beyond repair on March 17, 1943 when the propeller broke off in flight at Stalwart, Saskatchewan.

Aircraft	Cessna C-37
Year of first flight	1937
Engine	Warner Super Scarab (145 hp)
Wingspan	34 ft 2 in
Length	24 ft 8 in
Height	7 ft 3 in
Weight empty	1,304 lb
Gross weight	2,250 lb
Cruising speed	143 mph
Range	540 miles
Crew	1
Passengers	3

▲ Cessna C-37 Airmaster of Prairie Airways seen at Saskatoon in July 1938. Prairie Airways purchased the aircraft from Aircraft Company of Canada of Winnipeg on May 8, 1937.

CPAL 23823

The D.H.60 Moth two seat biplane made its first flight on February 22, 1925 and was the precursor of some 10,000 de Havilland Moths of various types in which countless thousands of pilots learned to fly. Originally powered by a 60 hp Cirrus 1 engine, the Moth soon became established with flying clubs throughout the world. From 1928, de Havilland equipped the Moth with the company's own Gipsy engine and this version was designated the D.H.60G Gipsy Moth. At the same time, to comply with requests for a more robust version of the Moth, the D.H.60M Moth with a fabric-covered, welded steel frame was also introduced. The prototype 60M, or Metal Moth, made its maiden flight on September 6, 1928 and was shipped to Canada in late 1928 for evaluation by the RCAF as a training aircraft. This resulted in an order for 50 D.H.60Ms in 1929. A further 90 were shipped to de Havilland's Canadian subsidiary for supply to the Ontario Provincial Air Service and various flying schools. A total of approximately 540 Metal Moths was produced including 35 assembled in Canada for the RCAF and civil purchasers.

The Tiger Moth was the ultimate development of de Havilland's line of biplane training aircraft. It was designed to meet the Air Ministry Specification 15/31 and differed from the original Moth in having an inverted engine, a fabric-covered wood and metal frame and a slight sweep back of the wings. Originally known as the D.H.60T Tiger Moth, eight prototypes were produced before the wing sweep back and lower wing dihedral were increased to produce the D.H.82 Tiger Moth. This version made its first flight on October 26, 1931. The success of this new design was immediate and by the time World War Two broke out some 1,150 Tiger Moths had already been produced.

The Canadian version stemmed from an attempt by the Toronto based subsidiary to sell the trainer to the RCAF in 1935. In 1936, the company was awarded a contract for 25 D.H.82As to be constructed in Canada. These were provided with various modifications to make the type more suitable for Canada's extreme climate. Improvements included a cabin heating system, a cockpit canopy and

strengthened undercarriage to allow operation on skis. The first Canadian built D.H.82A flew on December 21, 1937 following which the aircraft for the RCAF and three for civilian use were constructed. With the creation of the British Commonwealth Air Training Plan, the RCAF ordered large numbers of D.H.82Cs, fitted with wheel brakes and a tail wheel and this type made its maiden flight on March 12, 1940. de Havilland Canada had manufactured a total of 1,548 Tiger Moths when production ceased in 1942 and the company switched to construction of the D.H.98 Mosquito. British production was over 5,000 aircraft and over 1,400 D.H.82 Tiger Moths were constructed in Australia and New Zealand.

Starratt Airways & Transportation's D.H.60M CF-AGX became part of the CPAL fleet and continued to operate in northwestern Ontario until early 1945 when it was sold. D.H.82A CF-CGV was purchased by CPAL in June 1943 and served with the airline for one year.

▲ R.W. Starratt's Northern Transportation Company of Hudson, Ontario purchased de Havilland D.H.60M Moth CF-AGX in October 1932. It then became part of Starratt Airways & Transportation's fleet. CPAL sold the aircraft to H.A. Hennesy of Toronto in January 1945.

Aircraft	de Havilland D.H.60M Moth	de Havilland D.H.82A Tiger Moth
Year of first flight	1928	1934
Engines	de Havilland Gipsy 1 (100 hp)	de Havilland Gipsy Major (130 hp)
Wingspan	30 ft 0 in	29 ft 4 in
Length	23 ft 11 in	23 ft 11 in
Height	8 ft 9 in	8 ft 9 in
Weight empty	955 lb	1115 lb
Gross weight	1,750 lb	1,825 lb
Cruising speed	85 mph	93 mph
Range	320 miles	300 miles
Crew	1	1
Passenger	1	1

In the early 1930s small feeder airlines sprang up in all parts of the world and, to provide a suitable aircraft for these operators, de Havilland designed and built the four passenger, enclosed cabin D.H.83 Fox Moth based on the standard Tiger Moth wings, tail unit, undercarriage and engine mountings in order to keep the cost as low as possible. The prototype flew on January 29, 1932 and was then shipped to Canada where it was registered as CF-API and used to evaluate the type on skis and floats. Six other British built D.H.83s followed the prototype to Canada and two Fox Moths served with Canadian Airways. Quebec Airways operated one, and Ginger Coote Airway's first aircraft was the prototype CF-API which it owned from January

1937 to June 1938. One of the Canadian Airways Fox Moths, CF-APG, was still owned by the company when CPAL began operations but this was severely damaged in a storm at Cartierville, Quebec in September 1942 and withdrawn from use.

Ninety-eight D.H.83s were built in Britain and two were constructed in Sydney by de Havilland's Australian subsidiary. After World War Two, de Havilland Aircraft of Canada, Limited introduced a Canadian Fox Moth, the D.H.83C. This was equipped with a more powerful 145 hp de Havilland Gipsy Major engine, strengthened cabin floor for freight handling, and an enlarged left hand door among other improvements. Fifty three Canadian Fox Moths

were produced but none of these served with CPAL.

Aircraft	de Havilland D.H.83 Fox Moth
Year of first flight	1932
Engine	de Havilland Gipsy III (120 hp)
Wingspan	30 ft 11 in
Length	25 ft 9 in
Height	8 ft 10 in
Weight empty	1,071 lb
Gross weight	2,000 lb
Cruising speed	94 mph
Range	385 miles
Crew	1
Passengers	3

▲ Canadian Airways' D.H.83 Fox Moth CF-API draped with tarpaulins to enable it to be started. Each bush aircraft carried two Clayton and Lambert firepots which were filled with gasoline, lit and placed below the tarpaulins. It took about 50 minutes to get the engine warm enough to start in 60 below weather.

The Fox Moth was so successful in feeder line service that the British company, Hillman Airways, asked de Havilland to construct a twin engined aircraft which the airline intended to operate between London and Paris offering cut price fares. de Havilland designed an all-wood, six passenger biplane powered by two Gipsy Major 130 hp engines and the prototype D.H.84 Dragon flew for the first time on November 24, 1932. It commenced service with Hillman the following month and the airline began its Paris service in April 1933. Such was the popularity of the route, primarily because of the low prices, that the four DH-84 Dragons originally ordered by Hillman had to be supplemented by two further aircraft and all were converted to carry eight passengers.

Orders for the new aircraft were received from many small airlines and military customers. The Iraqi Air Force ordered eight military Dragons equipped with racks for sixteen 20 lb. bombs and fitted with three machine guns. Other military customers included the Danish Army Air Force and the Portuguese Air Force. The Irish and Turkish Air Forces purchased civilian Dragons which were modified for military service. Orders for civilian Dragons were obtained from companies in India, Czechoslovakia, Spain and three D.H.84s were shipped to Canada. CF-APJ was registered by Canadian Airways on May 13, 1933 and was used on Moncton, N.B. to Charlottetown, P.E.I. route for ten years, surviving the takeover by CPAL but being reduced to spares in October 1942 to enable

reconditioning of the airline's other D.H.84, CF-AVD. This was a Dragon II which had been registered by Quebec Airways in February 1935 and transferred to Canadian Airways on August 24, 1935. It was damaged beyond repair at Baie Comeau, Quebec on May 26, 1944. The other D.H.84, registered in Canada was also a Dragon II and also went to a Canadian Pacific company — Consolidated Mining & Smelting. Registered CF-AVI on October 2, 1935, the aircraft was returned to de Havilland Aircraft of Canada on November 10, 1937.

In total, 115 Dragons of both types were constructed in Britain and a further 87 were built by the Australian subsidiary which supplied the aircraft to the RAAF for radio/navigation training and communication duties.

▲ Canadian Airways' D.H.84 Dragon II CF-AVD arriving at Goldpines, Ontario

Aircraft	de Havilland D.H.84 Dragon 1
Year of first flight	1932
Engines	Two de Havilland Gipsy Majors (130 hp)
Wingspan	47 ft 4 in
Length	34 ft 6 in
Height	9 ft 4 in
Weight empty	2,300 lb
Maximum take-off weight	4,200 lb
Cruising speed	109 mph
Range	460 miles
Crew	1
Passengers	6

The D.H.89 Dragon Rapide was one of the most successful British commercial aircraft ever designed. It was originally conceived as an improved version of the D.H.84 Dragon offering higher speed and more comfort but in fact became a down-sized version of the 10 passenger, four engine D.H.86 which had been introduced as a longhaul airliner on the Empire route from London to Australia between Singapore and Brisbane. The Dragon Rapide, or Dragon Six as it was originally known, was designed to carry eight passengers at speeds of 130 mph on routes of less than 500 miles. It was conceived to operate on stages with limited traffic and where no subsidies were available. It was equipped with tapered wings and the two Gipsy Six engines and the fixed undercarriage was enclosed in streamlined nacelles. The prototype made its first flight on April 17, 1934 and a ready market was found for the new aircraft with both domestic and overseas airlines. Hillman Airways, which had been the first operator of the Dragon, also introduced the Rapide into commercial service.

In 1937, the D.H.89A with flaps outboard of the engines was introduced and many of the initial version were brought up to this standard. By the outbreak of World War Two, 205 Rapides had been produced. Prior to this, D.H.89M, was designed, equipped with a Vickers machine gun in the nose and a bomb bay for two 100 lb. and four 20 lb. bombs. A Lewis gun was fitted in a dorsal turret. A prototype was constructed to meet a requirement from the RAF for a Coast Command reconnaissance aircraft. The Anson (see page 70) was the successful contender.

With the outbreak of the war, many of the British registered Rapides were impressed into RAF and Royal Navy service. In addition, new construction as the D.H.89B MK.1 navigation and wireless/telegraphy trainer and the MK.2 communication aircraft was authorized. Christened the Dominie by the RAF, over 500 were constructed by 1947 when the 728th and last Rapide was completed.

CPAL acquired one D.H.89 and four D.H.89As in the purchase of the 75 percent interest in Quebec Airways. A further D.H.89A was obtained from both Canadian Airways and Ginger Coote Airways. The Quebec Airways aircraft were used on services along the St. Lawrence and the other two aircraft operated out of Vancouver. Of the seven aircraft, five were lost in mishaps and the remaining two were disposed of in mid-1947.

Aircraft	de Havilland D.H.89 Dragon Rapide
Year of first flight	1934
Engines	Two de Havilland Gipsy Six (200 hp)
Wingspan	48 ft 0 in
Length	34 ft 6 in
Height	10 ft 3 in
Weight empty	3,346 lb
Maximum take-off weight	5,500 lb
Cruising speed	132 miles
Range	578 miles
Crew	1
Passengers	8

Ginger Coote Airways' D.H.89A CF-BNG at Chilliwack Lake, B.C. in 1941.

In 1935, de Havilland introduced the five seat D.H.90 Dragonfly as a private owners' touring aircraft which was outwardly similar to the Rapide but different structurally as the fuselage was a monocoque, plywood shell similar to that of the D.H.88 Comet which won the MacPherson Robertson England to Australia air race in 1934. Struts and bracing for the wings were reduced from that seen in the Rapide and power was supplied by two Gipsy Major engines neatly cowled in nacelles which were extended to cover the undercarriage. The prototype made its first flight on August 12, 1935 and the second aircraft, fitted with variable position propellers, flew in February 1936, becoming the first production aircraft. Because of the mono-

coque shell, the cost of constructing the aircraft was much higher than the wood and fabric design of the Rapide and at £2,650 — then the equivalent of $13,250 — sales of the Dragonfly were limited to the very wealthy, government departments and established airlines. Two D.H.90s served in the CPAL fleet. CF-BPD, was constructed in 1937 and was obtained through the purchase of Ginger Coote Airways. In April 1943 it was groundlooped at Edmonton and written off. Prior to this, in December 1942, the newly incorporated airline purchased CF-BFF from the RCAF and this served for three years with CPAL before being sold to de Havilland Aircraft of Canada.

Aircraft	de Havilland D.H.90 Dragonfly
Year of first flight	1935
Engines	Two de Havilland Gipsy Majors (145 hp)
Wingspan	43 ft 0 in
Length	31 ft 8 in
Height	9 ft 2 in
Weight empty	2,487 lb
Maximum take-off weight	4,000 lb
Cruising speed	125 mph
Range	885 miles
Crew	1
Passengers	4

▲ Another aircraft of Ginger Coote Airways, D.H.90 Dragonfly CF-BPD which was purchased from Leavens Brothers Air Services of Toronto on September 1, 1941.

A.G. Sims, Public Archives Canada, C65258

The Fairchild FC-2W was a modification of the earlier FC-2 and proved to be one of the first real workhorses of civil aviation. It was a five seat, high wing, cabin monoplane and was powered by the 450 hp Pratt & Whitney Wasp. The type certificate was issued in December 1927 and in April 1928 it was an FC-2W that was first on the scene at Greenly Island, Labrador to offer assistance to the Junkers W33 *Bremen*, the first aircraft to cross the North Atlantic from east to west. The Junkers had crashed at the end of its epic flight.

Hard on the heels of the FC-2W came the FC-2W2 which was similar but larger than its predecessor. It was a seven place, high wing, cabin monoplane

which could carry a cargo of over 1,500 lb. It was a robust bush aircraft which received its type certificate in August 1928. After only a few FC-2W2s had been built, the design was further modified to produce the Fairchild 71. Some of the FC-2W2s, including the two owned by CPAL, were subsequently brought up to Fairchild 71 standards. CF-AHG of Dominion Skyways was converted to 71C standards by de Havilland in January 1941 while CF-BVU of Canadian Airways was also modified by de Havilland in December 1943. This aircraft was destroyed by fire at Fort Vermillion, Alberta in March 1944 and CF-AHG was sold in December 1946 as CPAL began to withdraw from bush operations.

Aircraft	Fairchild FC-2W2	
Year of first flight	1927	
Engine	Pratt & Whitney Wasp (420 hp)	
Wingspan	50 ft 0 in	
Length	33 ft 2 in	
Height	9 ft 6 in	
Weight empty	2,732 lb	3,072 lb on floats
Gross weight	5,500 lb	5,500 lb on floats
Cruising speed	108 mph	
Range	750 miles	
Crew	1	
Maximum passenger capacity	7	

▲ Dominion Skyways' Rouyn, Quebec base in 1935 with Fairchild FC-2W2 CF-AHG, Bellanca CH-300 Pacemaker CF-ANU and Fokker Super Universal CF-AJH owned by A.G. Sims in attendance.

The Fairchild 71 was a modified version of the FC-2W2 with improved aerodynamics which sustained Fairchild's reputation for designing and constructing reliable bush aircraft. It was a high-wing, cabin monoplane powered by a Pratt & Whitney 450 hp Wasp and made its first flight in 1928. The following year, Fairchild Aircraft Ltd. was formed in Canada to manufacture the Model 71 and between 1930 and 1938 the Canadian subsidiary produced eight 71Bs, 12 71Cs and one 71CM. Total American production of all variations of the Model 71 was 142 aircraft.

The first Canadian built version was the 71B and differed from the original 71 in that the fuselage fairing was simplified and the cabin interior was strengthened for transporting cargo. As this model was constructed for the RCAF, provision was made for taking oblique as well as vertical photographs. The first few Canadian built aircraft were built using U.S. assembled fuselage frames and the first Montreal constructed 71B flew in June 1930. All

eight Canadian 71Bs went to the RCAF but subsequently were sold to Canadian Airways although only one survived until CPAL commenced operations in 1942.

In order to improve the appeal of the Model 71 to bush operators, the 71C was designed in 1932. Among the improvements were an increase in the maximum operating weight to 6,000 lb. which required strengthening of the frame. Other improvements included further refinement to the cowling, the cabin heating system, etc. Subsequently, a larger left hand cargo door was provided to allow a 45 gallon drum to be rolled into the cabin. The single 71CM was constructed for Canadian Airways and was basically a 71C with a light aluminum skin in place of the customary fabric covering. Registered by Canadian Airways on August 15, 1933, the 71CM was written off in a windstorm at Senneterre, Quebec on August 19, 1934. No other metal skinned Model 71 was constructed but in 1933 Fairchild Aircraft began work on the Super 71 which was the first

aircraft to be designed exclusively for bush operations in Canada. The design was unusual in that the pilot was seated behind and above the enclosed cabin and the wing was of parasol design — i.e. it did not intersect the fuselage. Canadian Airways purchased the only Super 71 built — CF AUJ — and operated it from December 12, 1935 until it was written off in October 1940 when it hit a log on take-off.

CPAL obtained ten Fairchild 71s from the acquisition of Canadian Airways, Wings and Dominion Skyways. These aircraft provided communication to remote locations throughout the war but the arrival of surplus Norseman aircraft following the end of hostilities allowed the last of them to be withdrawn from service in mid-1947. Two ex-Canadian Pacific Air Lines' Fairchild 71s are being restored. CF-AKT is at the Western Canada Air Museum and CF-ATZ is being refurbished in Edmonton.

▲ Fairchild 71C CF-BKP of Canadian Airways has been hauled out of the water onto the ice and its floats are receiving attention.

Aircraft	Fairchild 71
Year of first flight	1928
Engine	Pratt & Whitney Wasp C (420 hp)
Wingspan	50 ft 0 in
Length	32 ft 10 in
Height	9 ft 4 in
Empty weight	2,940 lb
Gross weight	5,500 lb
Cruising speed	106 mph
Range	625 miles
Crew	1
Passengers	6

CPAL 1228

▲ Fairchild 82A CF-AXL was purchased by Starratt Airways & Transportation in March 1937 and was sold by CPAL in February 1947. In August 1965 it was repurchased from Alberta Fish Products of Edmonton. It was refurbished at Vancouver and this photograph illustrates the finished result, ready for presentation to the National Aviation Museum.

The Fairchild Super 71 did not attract any orders from bush operators because of its unusual layout with the pilot having to peer out between the wing and the fuselage. The all-metal design was also more expensive and Canada was in the midst of the Depression. Aircraft operators wanted basic machines at the lowest possible cost and Fairchild decided to do what it did best — producing metal framed, fabric covered aircraft of normal layout. In 1935, it designed the Fairchild 82 utilizing the 71C wings and an enlarged fuselage which could accommodate six passengers under normal conditions. Nine passengers could be carried if necessary. Large cabin doors were fitted to enable bulky freight to be loaded and the high wing monoplane could be fitted with a variety of engines. The 82A was equipped with a Pratt & Whitney Wasp of 550 hp. The 82B had a 600 hp Wasp as did the 82D which was similar to the 82B except for the enlarged fin and rudder. The single 34-42 Niska was fitted with a 420 hp Ranger engine which was subsequently replaced by a 600 hp Wasp and the aircraft was converted to 82D standards.

The prototype, CF-AXA, made its maiden flight on July 6, 1935 and the aircraft sold equally as well as its contemporary and main competitor, the Norseman. It was well liked by those who operated it and it was able to haul a good load over a useful range of about 500 miles. Twenty-four Fairchild 82s had been sold by the time production was halted in 1939 in order that the company could start construction of the Bristol Bolingbroke for the RCAF.

Seven Fairchild 82s came into the CPAL fleet from the purchase of Canadian Airways, Yukon Southern Air Transport, Wings, Starratt Airways & Transportation and Mackenzie Air Service. As war surplus Norseman became available, the 82s were disposed of and by mid-1947 all had been retired from CPAL service. In the mid-1960s, the airline repurchased Fairchild 82A CF-AXL and, after being refurbished in Vancouver, it was flown to Ottawa and presented to the National Aviation Museum.

Aircraft	Fairchild 82
Year of first flight	1935
Engine	Pratt & Whitney Wasp (550 hp)
Wingspan	51 ft 0 in
Length	36 ft 11 in
Height	10 ft 5 in
Weight empty	3,060 lb
Gross weight	6,325 lb
Cruising speed	128 mph
Range	657 miles
Crew	1
Passengers	6 - 9

Public Archives Canada PA 120006

The Fokker Universal was designed by Robert Noorduyn, who later found fame as the designer of the Norseman, and was the first Fokker design to be built in the United States. It appeared in late 1925 and 45 of these large, high winged, five to seven seat monoplanes were constructed for service in the United States and Canada. In 1928, the Super Universal appeared. This was a logical development of the original Universal. The 200 hp Wright Whirlwind was replaced by a 400 hp Pratt & Whitney Wasp, the cabin dimensions were increased and the pilots were provided with a fully enclosed cockpit.

A total of 80 Super Universals was constructed by the Atlantic Aircraft Corporation at Teterboro, New Jersey and 47 were built under licence in Japan. Canadian Vickers of Montreal also produced 14 licence built Super Universals in Montreal and CF-AJB, which was the only Super Universal to be owned by CPAL, was one of these. Obtained in the acquisition of Starratt Airways & Transportation, the aircraft was withdrawn from service in late 1942 and dismantled. It was the last operational Fokker Super Universal in Canada.

Aircraft	Fokker Super Universal
Year of first flight	1928
Engine	Pratt & Whitney Wasp (420 hp)
Wingspan	50 ft 8 in
Length	36 ft 7 in
Height	8 ft 11 in
Weight empty	3,200 lb
Gross weight	5,550 lb
Cruising speed	118 mph
Range	675 miles
Crew	1
Maximum passengers capacity	7

▲ Starratt Airways & Transportation's Fokker Super Universal CF-AJB was built in 1929 by Canadian Vickers but because of the economic situation remained unsold until purchased by R.W. Starratt's Northern Transportation Company in February 1934. It was withdrawn from service in November 1942.

Public Archives Canada C57862

Hugo Junkers was responsible for the design and construction of the world's first all-metal aircraft which was produced for the German military forces in 1915. Following World War One, Junkers turned to producing all-metal civil aircraft and in June 1919 his F.13, a low wing, single engined monoplane with accommodation for two crew and four passengers, made its first flight. Because the market was full of war surplus aircraft, the F.13 did not sell well initially. However, by 1921 Junkers had established his own airline which employed 60 of his F.13s on over 40 routes within Germany and on international services into neighbouring countries.

Following on from the F.13, Junkers designed the larger but similar W.33 capable of carrying up to

six passengers. This aircraft, powered by a liquid-cooled, six cylinder, in-line Junkers 310 hp engine, made its first flight in 1926 and 199 had been built when production ceased in 1934. The W.34 was an almost identical aircraft except that it was powered by a nine cylinder, radial 420 hp Gnome-Rhône engine. Approximately one hundred commercial W.34s were constructed although almost 1700 of the military equivalent, the K3, were also produced.

Both the W33 and W34 benefited immensely from the publicity obtained from the W.33 *Bremen* which on April 12-13, 1928 was the first aircraft to make the east-west crossing of the Atlantic. From Baldonnel, near Dublin, to Greenly Island, Labrador, this aircraft flew more than 2,000 miles in 37 hours.

Like the first west-east non-stop crossing by Alcock and Brown in 1919, the flight ended in a crash landing but Koehl, von Huenfeld and Fitzmaurice had proved that such flights were possible. As a result, W-33 and W-34 sales were made in many parts of the world and Canadian Airways had four W-34s when CPAL commenced operations. One of these had been built as a W-33 in 1931 but in 1936 was converted to W-34 standards by replacing the liquid cooled engine with a 420 hp Pratt & Whitney radial engine. All four Junkers remained in service until 1945 when one was cannibalized for spares to keep the others aircraft in service. The final aircraft was withdrawn in 1947 when it was replaced by a war-surplus Norseman.

▲ Canadian Airways' Fort McMurray, Alberta base in 1933 showing Junkers W-34f CF-AMZ, Fairchild 71C CF-ATZ and Fairchild FC-2W2 CF-AAO.

Aircraft	Junkers W33	Junkers W34
Year of first flight	1926	1926
Engines	Junker L.5 (310 hp)	Gnome-Rhône Jupiter or Pratt & Whitney Wasp (420 hp)
Wingspan	58 ft 3 in	58 ft 3 in
Length	34 ft 6 in	33 ft 8 in
Height	11 ft 8 in	11 ft 8 in
Empty weight	2,684 lb	3,630 lb
Gross weight	5,500 lb	7,050 lb
Cruising speed	93 miles	108 miles
Range	620 miles	530 miles
Crew	1	1
Passengers	6	6

It may surprise some to learn that CPAL flew a Junkers JU 52 and they may be even more surprised to learn that this was a single engined aircraft. More people are familiar with the three engined JU 52/3m which was the Luftwaffe's major transport in World War Two and of which more than 4,000 were constructed. However, the three engined version was actually a development of the JU 52 and the switch to a trimotor configuration was made after five single engine aircraft had been constructed. CF-ARM was, in fact, the last JU 52 to be built.

It was designed by Hugo Junkers as a freight aircraft with an unobstructed cargo space and large door allowing bulky items to be loaded with relative ease. The low wing, cantilever monoplane prototype made its maiden flight on October 13, 1930 and Canadian Airways registered CF-ARM on October 26, 1931. It remained in service with its original owners and CPAL until withdrawn from service in 1943. It was the largest aircraft in Canada until 1938 when TCA received its first Lockheed 14 and never lost its distinction of being the largest single engine aircraft to operate in Canada. It was referred to as the "Flying Box-car" and was used all over Canada, hauling bulky items to remote locations. Such was the capacity of the aircraft's cargo space that horses and oxen, suitably drugged and strapped to pallets, were carried without difficulty. Cargo capacity of the 21 ft. by 5 ft. 6 in. hold was two tons and this load could be carried almost 1,000 miles without making a stop. During the 1930s, the corrugated duraluminum skinned aircraft was a familiar sight at nearly all large-scale construction projects in remote areas of Canada.

Originally powered with a BMW VIIau engine of 755 hp, the aircraft was designated as a JU 52ce. Soon after arrival in Canada, the aircraft was tested to determine its load carrying capacity and on one of these tests it carried 7,590 lb. aloft. However, the BMW engine proved to be extremely unreliable and in 1936 CF-ARM was equipped with an 825 hp Rolls Royce Buzzard, thus becoming a JU 52 cao. A replica of CF-ARM is on display at the Western Canada Air Museum at Winnipeg.

▲ Junkers 52 CF-ARM seen at Casummit Lake, Ontario in August 1936 prior to the BMW VIIau engine being replaced by the Rolls Royce Buzzard.

Aircraft	JU 52
Year of first flight	1930
Engine	BMW Type VII (755 hp)
Wingspan	96 ft 9 in
Length	60 ft 0 in
Height	20 ft 8 in
Weight empty	8,360 lb
Gross weight	15,840 lb
Cruising speed	100 mph
Range	932 miles
Crew	1

In 1926, Allan and Malcolm Loughead formed the Lockheed Aircraft Company, changing the spelling of the family name slightly to ensure no problems with pronunciation. At this time, Ford and Fokker were manufacturing relatively large aircraft capable of carrying 12 passengers but at slow speeds. At Lockheed it was believed that there was a need for a small but fast aircraft which could carry four passengers over distances comparable to those of the Ford & Fokker aircraft. To test this belief, Allan Loughead and John K. Northrop designed and built the revolutionary Lockheed Vega which made its first flight on July 4, 1927. By paying very careful consideration to aerodynamics, the high-wing, all wood, monoplane which, though powered only by a Wright Whirlwind 220 hp engine, had a top speed of an amazing 138 mph. The cigar shaped, monocoque fuselage was constructed of

plywood and the one piece wing had no struts or wires.

The first Vega, built for George Hearst and christened *Golden Eagle*, was entered in the Oakland to Hawaii race of August 1927. This aircraft disappeared at sea without trace. Despite this disastrous start, a second aircraft was constructed to serve as a demonstrator and many orders were received for the new aircraft which was considered well suited to expeditionary, long distance record breaking and airline service. International Airlines introduced the type to commercial service on September 17, 1928.

The Vega 1 was followed by the Vega 5 which used the same fuselage design and, with a Pratt & Whitney 400 hp Wasp engine, was capable of 170 mph. The Vega 5 broke many long distance and

speed records leading the company to adopt the slogan "It takes a Lockheed to beat a Lockheed". Perhaps the most famous Vega 5 of all was Wiley Post's *Winnie Mae* in which he and Harold Gatty flew around the world in 8 days, 15 hours and 51 minutes. This flight started from New York on June 23, 1931 and was the first round the world flight by a commercial aircraft. In July 1933, Post completed a solo round the world flight in 7 days, 18 hours, 49 minutes — a record which endured for 14 years.

One hundred and thirty-one Vegas of all types were constructed. Canadian Airways' Vega 1 CF-AAL was the 30th of the series to be built. It was the only Vega aircraft owned by CPAL and was disposed of in June 1944.

▲ Lockheed Vega 1 CF-AAL was constructed as a Vega 1 and equipped with a Wright Whirlwind J5 200 hp engine. It was purchased by Commercial Airways of Edmonton in April 1929 and the original engine was replaced with a Wright Whirlwind J6 of 300 hp. It thus became a Vega 2 prior to its purchase by Canadian Airways in May 1931.

Aircraft	Lockheed Vega 1	Lockheed Vega 2
Year of first flight	1927	1929
Engine	Wright Whirlwind 220 hp	Wright Whirlwind 300 hp
Wingspan	41 ft 0 in	41 ft 0 in
Length	27 ft 8 in	27 ft 6 in
Height	8 ft 6 in	8 ft 4 in
Weight empty	1,875 lb	2,140 lb
Maximum take-off weight	3,470 lb	3,853 lb
Cruising speed	118 mph	133 mph
Range	900 miles	800 miles
Crew	1	1
Passengers	4	4

During the 1930s, Boeing, Douglas and Lockheed almost totally dominated the manufacture of transport aircraft through the introduction of modern, twin engined, metal aircraft. But whereas Boeing and Douglas concentrated on larger aircraft, Lockheed specialized in smaller, fast, economical transports and the first of these was the Lockheed 10 Electra which carried a crew of two and ten passengers over stages of up to 500 miles at 185 mph. The first Electra flew at Burbank, California on February 23, 1934 and subsequently a further 148 were built. In 1936, Canadian Airways bought two Electras, CF-AZY and CF-BAF, for service on the Vancouver-Seattle route. These aircraft were sold to Trans-Canada Air Lines in 1937.

Lockheed followed the Model 10 Electra with a smaller version of the same aircraft known as the Model 12 Electra. Aimed at providing a modern aircraft for feeder routes, the Model 12 carried six

passengers at speeds of over 200 mph. It made its first flight on June 27, 1936 and over 100 of the type were constructed. None of the CPAL constituent companies purchased the aircraft.

Lockheed's next design was the Model 14 Super Electra which provided for a crew of two and 14 passengers but was not simply a scaled up version of the Model 10. It incorporated a new wing design and was strengthened to enable it to operate either as a passenger or cargo transport. The first flight was made on July 29, 1937 with deliveries commencing the following September to Northwest Airlines where the type was introduced into commercial service. Among the Super Electra's more notable accomplishments was Howard Hughes' round the world flight in July 1938 when 15,432 miles were covered in three days, 19 hours and 17 minutes. On a more sombre mission, Neville Chamberlain, the British Prime Minister travelled

in a Super Electra to his meeting with Adolph Hitler at Munich in September, 1938. His famous "Peace for our time" speech was made just after he returned to Croydon in G-AFGN. Total production of the Super Electra was only 112 aircraft but subsequently the type was developed into the Lockheed Hudson maritime patrol bomber of which 2,940 were produced. In addition, 240 military transport versions and derivatives were built by Tachikawa and Kawasaki.

Trans-Canada Air Lines had a fleet of 16 Super Electras but two of these aircraft, CF-TCR and CF-TCS, were transferred to Yukon Southern Air Transport in July/August 1941. They thus were part of the CPAL fleet when the airline began operations in July 1942. On November 17, 1942 they were re-registered as CF-CPC and CF-CPD. In addition, six war surplus Hudson III aircraft were obtained.

▲ Lockheed 14-H2 Super Electra CF-TCS was one of two aircraft allocated to Yukon Southern Air Transport from Trans-Canada Air Lines to ensure that the airline's trunk lines could continue to operate when two Lockheed Lodestar 18-40s were returned to the United States. One of these Lodestars CF-BTZ is seen behind the Super Electra that replaced it.

Aircraft	Lockheed 14 Super Electra	Lockheed Hudson III (as military freighter)
Year of first flight	1937	
Engines	Two P & W Hornet (750 hp)	Two Wright Cyclone radials (1,200 hp)
Wingspan	65 ft 6 in	65 ft 6 in
Length	44 ft 3 in	44 ft 4 in
Height	11 ft 6 in	11 ft 10 in
Weight empty	9,685 lb	12,929 lb
Maximum take-off weight	15,000 lb	21,000 lb
Cruising speed	241 mph	223 mph
Range	1,000 miles	1,760 miles
Crew	2	4
Passengers	12	14

▲ Noordyn Norseman IV CF-BAW was the 9th Norseman built and was purchased from E & M Transport of Sherridon, Manitoba by Arrow Airways in May 1941.

The Norseman was the first Canadian aircraft purpose-built for bush flying. Its designer, Robert B.C. Noorduyn, obtained his early training with the British firms of Sopwith Aviation and Sir W.G. Armstrong Whitworth before joining the Fokker company in 1920. He moved to the United States to work as Anthony Fokker's assistant and was responsible for the design and construction of the Fokker Universal. Subsequently, Noorduyn worked for the Bellanca and Pitcairn companies before moving to Montreal where he formed Noorduyn Aircraft Limited in 1934. Noorduyn Aviation Ltd. was incorporated the following year to construct the conventional high winged monoplane capable of operating on wheels, skis and floats.

Construction of the prototype commenced in early 1935. Powered by a 420 hp Wright Whirlwind engine, the fabric covered wood and metal framed CF-AYO made its first flight on November 14, 1935 at Pointe aux Trembles, Montreal. Although underpowered, the Norseman 1 was a considerable improvement over previous bush aircraft and the prototype was delivered to Dominion Skyways in mid-January 1936. It survived to operate with CPAL and was written off at Round Island Lake, Ontario long after it had been sold to other operators. The first production aircraft, CF-AZA, a Norseman II,

made its maiden flight in May 2, 1936 but only two more of this type were constructed. These were slightly heavier than the prototype and the track of the floats was increased to improve the aircraft's stablility on water. It was still underpowered although two Mk IIs were sold.

The Norseman III was essentially a development phase leading to the Mk IV which became the main production type. Fitted with a Pratt & Whitney Wasp SC engine rated at 420 hp, the prototype Mk III CF-BAM first flew on September 4, 1936 but this was soon followed by the first Mk IV, CF-BAU. This latter aircraft was powered by a 600 hp Pratt & Whitney Wasp S3H1 engine. Canadian bush operators recognized the value of the new aircraft and CF-BAU was sold to Canadian Airways in December 1936.

In 1938, the RCMP purchased a Norseman IV and eight were ordered by the RCAF for service as bomber and navigational trainers. A further 47 Norseman were ordered by the RCAF in 1940 and in 1941 the USAAF requested six Norseman to assist in establishing and maintaining the Greenland section of the North Atlantic aircraft staging route. These aircraft were supplied from the RCAF order, modified to meet USAAF requirements and supplied as YC-64s towards the end of 1941. Following the United States' entry into World War Two, the company received several orders for a modified Norseman equipped with two belly fuel tanks. This version was known as the Mk VI which was designated the C-64A by the USAAF and total production of the Norseman during the war was over 800 aircraft, of which 767 were C-64As. They served

throughout North America, including British Columbia and the Yukon during the construction of the Alaska Highway. The Norseman also operated in Europe, Asia and the South Pacific. In the European war they served with distinction, evacuating casualties from battle areas to base hospitals.

Towards the end of the war, the Mk V was produced, this being a civil version of the Mk VI. Noorduyn had reserved the designation V to indicate Victory in the war. Unfortunately, the Mk V did not sell well because of the large number of surplus Mk VI's available once hostilities ceased. In April 1946, the Noorduyn company was sold to Canadian Car and Foundry. A Mk VII will all-metal wings and a 36 inch fuselage stretch was designed and built, making its first flight in mid-1951. However, because of its other commitments in support of the Korean

War, the company did not proceed with the new model and the single example of the Mk VII was destroyed in a hangar fire in 1958. On May 22, 1953 a group headed by Robert Noorduyn recovered the Norseman project and continued production of the aircraft until the last Norseman V made its maiden flight on December 17, 1959. There is some doubt over the actual number of Norseman aircraft produced as records have been destroyed but it is estimated that approximately 905 aircraft of this type were manufactured.

As can be seen from Tables 1 and 2, no less than 27 Norseman aircraft operated with CPAL including six which were acquired from the constituent companies and 13 which were purchased directly from Noorduyn or Canadian Car. The final purchases were ex-RCAF aircraft made available following the

end of World War Two. Until the acquisition of Eastern Provincial Airways, the Norseman was the aircraft which CPAL had operated in the largest numbers. With the merger with EPA, the Boeing 737 fleet finally outnumbered that of the Norseman. But while the 737 fleet continues to grow, the Norseman had a relatively short service life with CPAL as the company withdrew from bush flying and the last Norseman was disposed of in the mid-1950s.

One interesting item of trivia which cannot be gleaned from Tables 1 and 2 is the fact that **all** of the first 15 Norseman aircraft built served with either CPAL or one of its constituent companies.

▲ Somehow the Norseman never seems to grow old and this Norseman V built in 1945 and purchased by CPAL does not look out of place beside Edmonton Municipal Airport's former terminal.

Aircraft	Noorduyn Norseman MK V
Year of first flight (Mk 1)	1935
Engine	Pratt & Whitney Wasp (600 hp)
Wingspan	51 ft 8 in
Length	32 ft 4 in
Height	10 ft 3 in
Weight empty	4,250 lb
Weight loaded	7,400 lb
Cruising speed	141 mph
Range	464 miles
Crew	1
Passengers	8

Phil Lucas

The Stinson Reliant, a high wing, four seater, cabin monoplane, received its flight certificate in June 1933. At a price of just under $4,000, the Reliant was an immediate success and the design was refined progressively until 1940 when the Stinson Company was absorbed by Vultee Aircraft. The Stinson Reliant then became the Vultee V-77 and subsequently 500 examples were produced as navigational trainers for the Royal Navy.

The original Reliant SR was powered by a 215 hp Lycoming R-680 radial engine and 88 examples were constructed. During 1934, the SR-5 series was introduced and the SR-5A received its certificate on May 5, 1934. This model was designed to cater to the upper end of the private operator/small airline market and many SR-5As were equipped with extras such as a variable pitch propeller, superior navigational aids and night flying instruments. Power was supplied by a 245 hp Lycoming R-680-6 engine and the type could be operated on wheels, floats or skis. Over 70 SR-5As were produced.

In 1936 the SR-8 series was introduced with a double tapered wing which gave the aircraft a 'gull-winged' appearance. The four seat 8A was powered by a 225 hp Lycoming engine. The 8B and 8C, with slightly wider fuselages could accommodate an extra passenger. They were equipped respectively with the 245 and 260 hp Lycoming radial engines. The two CPAL SR-8CMs were dual-purpose aircraft suitable for passenger and freight operations.

The SR-9 was introduced for 1937 and received its type certificate on December 30, 1936. The 9A, 9B and 9C were similar to the SR-8 series except that they were equipped with a large, curved windshield. The SR-9D and SR-9E were equipped with the Wright R-760 radial engine of 285 or 350 hp respectively. These types received their flight certificates on February 2, 1937. CPAL's SR-9DM was a dual-purpose aircraft with similar features as the SR-8CMs received from Canadian Airways.

CPAL's single SR-5A was obtained in the acquisition of Starratt Airways & Transportation and was sold in October 1942. Two SR-8CMs were acquired when Canadian Airways was taken over and remained in service until they were sold in 1943 and 1944. The single SR-9CM was also acquired from Canadian Airways. This aircraft was severely damaged at Edmonton in August 1943 and withdrawn from use at that time. As of 1986, there were 14 active Reliants in Canada.

▲ Stinson SR-9DM Reliant CF-BEB seen outside the CPAL hangar at Edmonton's Municipal Airport ready to take pilots to Great Falls, Montana to pick up Lockheed Lodestars.

Aircraft	Stinson Reliant SR-5A	Stinson Reliant SR-8CM	Stinson Reliant SR-9DM
Year of Introduction	1934	1936	1937
Engine	Lycoming R-680-6 radial (245 hp)	Lycoming R-680-B5 radial (260 hp)	Wright Whirlwind R-760-E1 radial (285 hp)
Wingspan	41 ft 0 in	41 ft 7 in	41 ft 11 in
Length	27 ft 3 in	27 ft 0 in	28 ft 1 in
Height	8 ft 5 in	8 ft 6 in	8 ft 6 in
Weight empty	2,315 lb	2,370 lb	2,600 lb
Gross weight	3,390 lb	3,750 lb	4,050 lb
Cruising speed	120 mph	140 mph	148 mph
Range	620 miles	630 miles	630 miles
Crew	1	1	1
Passengers	3	4	4

CPAL 5060

The Travel Air 6000, a six seat, cabin monoplane, made its first flight in 1928. It was powered by a Wright Whirlwind engine of 220 hp. It received its airworthiness certificate in January 1929 and was advertised by the manufacturer as the "Limousine of the air". Airlines, however, demanded more performance than the 220 hp version could provide and in February 1929 the A-6000-A, with a 450 hp Pratt & Whitney Wasp engine received its certificate. A total of 25 A-6000-As was constructed and, of these, nine were in airline service with seating for six passengers.

To provide a similar transport suitable for bush operations to remote areas, Travel Air developed the SA-6000-A which was more or less a standard A-6000-A equipped with Edo floats. Capable of carrying an 800 lb pay load, this version had a large door in the rear of the cabin to enable cargo to be loaded. Cabin heating was supplied from the exhaust manifold and the cabin was insulated to ensure that winter operation in Canada and Alaska was reasonably comfortable. Only one SA-6000-A came into the CPAL fleet. This was CF-AEJ which had been operated by Starratt Airways & Transportation.

Aircraft	Travel Air SA-6000-A
Year of first flight	1929
Engine	Pratt & Whitney Wasp (450 hp)
Wingspan	54 ft 5 in
Length	33 ft 9 in (including floats)
Height	10 ft 6 in (in water)
Weight empty	3,676 lb
Gross weight	5,500 lb
Cruising speed	108 mph
Range	540 miles
Crew	1
Passengers	5

▲ Travel Air SA-6000-A CF-AEJ was constructed as a float plane in 1929 and acquired by R.W. Starratt's Northern Transportation Company of Hudson, Ontario in 1933. Note the springing on the skis which made take-offs and landings less uncomfortable.

Public Archives Canada PA14874

In 1934, Waco Aircraft introduced the UKC and YKC series which were similar four seater, cabin type, biplanes, the main difference being in the powerplants. The UKC was equipped with a 210 hp, seven cylinder Continental radial engine while the YKC had a 225 hp seven cylinder Jacobs radial engine. With the additional power providing slightly better performance, the YKC became the company's best selling aircraft for 1934. In 1935, the YKC was refined by the removal of features which contributed nothing to the aircraft's performance and this model became known as the YKC-S. Further refinements in 1936 led to a model designated the YKS-6. With a price of only $4,995, this type sold extremely well. The later examples of the YKS-6 were equipped to accommodate four passengers and this feature particularly appealed to bush operators as did the aircraft's adaptability to wheels, skis or floats.

Also available from Waco was the C series of Custom Cabin biplanes. In 1936, this group included the YQC-6, ZQC-6 and AQC-6 which were powered respectively with 225, 285 and 330 hp Jacobs seven cylinder radial engines. All aircraft in this series accommodated the pilot and four passengers. CPAL's fleet included three YKC-Ss, one YKS-6 and four ZQC-6s acquired through the purchase of the constituent companies. In addition, ZQC-6 CF-BDL was purchased from Fleet Aircraft in July 1943, probably to replace the YKS-6 which had been severely damaged earlier the same month when it ran out of fuel at Cooking Lake, Alberta.

▲ Waco YKS-6 CF-AYT was purchased by Wings in July 1936 and was re-engined with a Jacobs L-5MB in 1937 to become a ZKS-6. In July 1943, on a flight from Cold Lake to Cooking Lake, Alberta the aircraft ran out of fuel and was severely damaged. It was sold in August 1944.

Aircraft	Waco YKC-S	Waco YKS-6	Waco ZQC-6
Year of introduction	1935	1936	1936
Engine	Jacobs L-4 radial (225 hp)	Jacobs L-4 radial (225 hp)	Jacobs L-5 radial (285 hp)
Wingspan	33 ft 3 in	33 ft 3 in	33 ft 0 in
Length	25 ft 4 in	25 ft 4 in	26 ft 8 in
Height	8 ft 6 in	8 ft 6 in	8 ft 8 in
Weight empty	1,800 lb	1,809 lb	2,023 lb
Gross weight	3,000 lb	3,250 lb	3,500 lb
Cruising speed	124 mph	130 mph	150 mph
Range	450 miles	480 miles	600 miles
Crew	1	1	1
Passengers	3	4	4

Aircraft types obtained after July 1, 1942

L. Ryder, Collection of R. Cameron

In 1930, the Fairchild Airplane and Engine Corporation introduced the Fairchild 100 but in April 1931 the assets of the company were acquired by the American Airplane and Engine Corporation and the new aircraft was redesignated the Pilgrim 100A. Aviation Corporation, the parent company of both American Airways and the American Airplane and Engine Corporation, arranged for the production of 16 Pilgrim 100As for American Airways and the high winged, metal framed, fabric covered, cabin monoplane with accommodation for nine passengers received its certificate of airworthiness on August 21, 1931. Slightly larger than the Fairchild 100, the Pilgrim 100A was powered by a 575 hp Pratt & Whitney Hornet radial nine cylinder engine. American Airways introduced the aircraft on several sectors of its transcontinental service in 1931. The pilot's accommodation, located above the main cabin, offered excellent visibility. The passenger

cabin was furnished with six individual seats facing forward plus a rearward facing bench for three passengers on the front bulkhead. A toilet was provided at the rear of the compartment and passengers' baggage was carried in three underfloor compartments. Additional stowage, for mail and express, was located below the pilot's seat.

The order from American Airways for sixteen 100As was followed by the purchase of six 100Bs which were very similar to the initial model except that they were equipped with a 575 hp Wright Cyclone engine. Indeed, three 100As were converted to 100Bs by American Airways in 1934 when six aircraft exchanged their engines. It is not known whether this change was deliberate but the Pilgrim 100 obtained by Yukon Southern Air Transport in 1942 was one of the 100As which became 100Bs.

By 1932, the 22 American Airways Pilgrim 100s

were in widespread use across the system but their service with the airline was brief as faster, more modern, twin engined aircraft soon replaced them and by June 1935 all had been withdrawn and were offered for sale at Cleveland. With its large hold, rugged construction and excellent airfield performance, other operators purchased the entire fleet and at least nine Pilgrim 100s operated in Alaska. As late as 1965 one 100A was still active in the U.S.

The single Pilgrim 100B in the CPAL fleet was purchased by Yukon Southern Air Transport on August 7, 1942 after CPAL had commenced operations. It was acquired from British Yukon Navigation of Vancouver. In January 1944, it was sold to the Honduran portion of Transportes Aeroes Centro Americanos.

▲ American Pilgrim 100B CF-BUA seen at Atlin, B.C. Note the wheel skis and the mechanic's tool box.

Aircraft	American Pilgrim 100B
Year of first flight (Fairchild 100)	1930
Engine	Wright Cyclone (575 hp)
Wingspan	57 ft 0 in
Length	38 ft 0 in
Height	12 ft 3 in
Weight empty	4,362 lb
Weight loaded	7,750 lb
Cruising speed	117 mph
Range	500 miles
Crew	2
Passengers	9

The Curtiss T-32 Condor was the first aircraft to offer sleeping accommodation for passengers and was introduced to make transcontinental air travel more appealing to passengers who normally travelled by luxury trains operated by the United States railways. Curtiss designed the aircraft as a successor to its Model 18 which had attracted sales for only six aircraft. The new aircraft was also a biplane and proved to be the final civil transport biplane to be constructed in the United States. However, the two 650 hp Wright Cyclone engines enabled the aircraft to carry up to 18 passengers and a steward in daytime configuration. Twelve sleeping berths were available for night flights. Considerable thought was given to aerodynamic design and the Condor had a cruising speed of 145 mph — a significant increase over the type's

competition when it made its first flight in July 1930.

Eastern Air Transport and American Airways both ordered the Condor and Eastern introduced service with the type on December 10, 1930. Forty five Condors were constructed but the type's success was short-lived as the Boeing 247 offered severe competition and the arrival of the Douglas commercial aircraft spelled the end of commercial biplane operation with the major U.S. airlines even though a number of the Condors were modified to T-32-C standards with the fitting of 720 hp Wright Cyclones. This increased the Condor's cruising speed to 160 mph but the day of the biplane had passed and the aircraft were dispersed to secondary airlines. CPAL's only Condor was one of nine aircraft of this type originally supplied to American Airlines and

acquired by Yukon Southern Air Transport in August 1942 from British Yukon Navigation. In 1944, it was sold to C.H. Babb Inc. of Glendale, California.

▲ A 1942 shot of Curtiss Condor CF-BQN at the "steamboat" hangar at Whitehorse. The Condor was flown to Edmonton and remained in the hangar seen on page 66 before being sold.

Aircraft	Curtiss Condor T-32-C
Year of first flight (T-32)	1930
Engines	Two Wright Cyclone radials (720 hp)
Wingspan	82 ft 0 in
Length	48 ft 10 in
Height	16 ft 10 in
Weight empty	11,470 lb
Gross weight	17,500 lb
Cruising speed	160 mph
Range	650 miles
Crew	2
Maximum passenger capacity	18

Collection of R. Cameron

This twin engined, eight seat, cabin monoplane was designed and built by Curtiss-Robertson to operate safely on only one engine and to achieve this the engines were mounted well forward and as close to the aircraft's centre line as possible. During 1930 demonstration flights were conducted with a D-1 Kingbird with a full load which accomplished climb outs from 50 feet on only one engine. It was, however, decided that more power was desirable and the D-2 was produced equipped with Wright J6 300 hp engines and the type received its flight certificate on August 16, 1930. Orders were received from Eastern Air Transport and Pan American-Grace Lines, the Eastern aircraft operating on the company's trunk routes until 1935. Approximately 15 Kingbird D-2 aircraft were constructed.

In late 1930, Curtiss Robertson became the Curtiss Wright Airplane Company and it was this organization which constructed the single Kingbird D-3 in 1931. This was an improved model with greater performance which was achieved by reducing the number of passengers to five and fitting the aircraft with two Wright R-975-E 330 hp engines. However, the airlines wanted larger aircraft not smaller ones and the D-3, which had obtained its flight certificate on August 6, 1931, remained the property of the Curtiss-Wright Airplane Company until 1935. In 1941, British Yukon Navigation bought the D-3 from White Pass Airways of Skagway, Alaska. It was purchased by Yukon Southern Air Transport in August 1942, after CPAL had commenced operations but in November 1942 it was withdrawn from service.

Charles H. Babb Inc. of Glendale, California bought the D-3 in September 1943.

Aircraft	Curtiss-Wright Kingbird D-3
Year of first flight (D-3)	1931
Engines	Two Wright R-975-E radials (330 hp)
Wingspan	54 ft 6 in
Length	34 ft 9 in
Height	10 ft 0 in
Weight empty	4,215 lb
Gross weight	6,600 lb
Cruising speed	122 mph
Range	550 miles
Crew	1
Passengers	5

▲ Curtiss-Wright Kingbird D-3 also seen at the Whitehorse steamboat hangar. This 1941 shot was taken before British Yukon Navigation purchased the aircraft from White Pass Airways of Alaska.

L. Ryder, Collection of R. Cameron

The Boeing 247 was the first all-metal, cantilever-winged, monocoque commercial transport with a retractable undercarriage to be manufactured in quantity and, as such, was the world's first modern airliner. In the early 1930s, there was a need to replace the existing Ford Trimotors and Fokkers then in airline use with more advanced aircraft and Boeing designed the 247 utilizing its experience obtained from the Monomail mail plane and the Boeing B-9 bomber. With the stressed skin of the 247 adding to its structural strength, Boeing was in the forefront of technological advances and when it was only in the mock-up stage in 1932, United Aircraft & Transport ordered 59 aircraft of this type. These were powered by two Pratt & Whitney 525 hp Wasp engines which, unlike many previous aircraft, were enclosed in drag reducing cowlings. The main wheels retracted into the engine nacelles and the aircraft was fitted with three blade, fixed pitch propellers. Rather surprisingly, the windshield sloped forwards from base to top. The first flight was at Seattle on February 8, 1933 and it entered service on March 30, 1933 with Boeing Air Transport, which was part of the United Aircraft & Transport group.

The 247 had accommodation for ten passengers, two pilots and a flight attendant — then called a stewardess. It was the latter's job to look after the passengers, to serve meals which were kept hot in vacuum flasks and to assist the flight deck crew as required. This included loading baggage on occasions. With a cruising speed of 150 mph, the 247 was 50 mph faster than any other airliner then in service, but it did have two serious drawbacks. At high altitude airports, the 247's take-off performance was poor but this problem was overcome with the introduction of the 247D which was equipped with variable pitch propellers and 550 hp Wasp engines. The new model had a normally sloping windshield and with these improvements the 247's take-off run was reduced by 20 percent, the climb rate was increased by over 20 percent and cruising speed was improved to over 150 mph. United ordered 13 of the new type and earlier 247s were brought up to 247D standards. However, the other drawback was the result of the main spar passing through the cabin. This effectively cut the passenger area in two and proved to be impossible to overcome. Nevertheless, the Boeing 247 was the first modern airliner and, as such, played an important part in developing the airline industry in the United States. United Airlines was formed from the constituent companies of United Aircraft & Transport on May 1, 1934 and the new company took over the fleet of 247s. Although the 247 was soon superseded by the DC-2 and DC-3, United maintained its fleet of Boeings until they were transferred to the USAAF in 1942. Considering the fact that only 75 Boeing 247s were built, the impact of the aircraft was profound as it was the stimulus which brought about the DC-1 and its successors.

Following the commencement of operations by CPAL on July 1, 1942 five Boeing 247Ds were acquired by the airline. These were CF-BVF, BVT, BVV, BVW, BVZ and BVX. In fact, the five latter aircraft were on loan from the RCAF from earlier in 1942 to enable Yukon Southern Air Transport and Quebec Airways to maintain services when there was an acute shortage of aircraft. CF-BVT and BVV were loaned to YSAT in early 1942 and not registered by CPAL until October 1943. In addition, YSAT acquired CF-BVF in August 1942 from British Yukon Navigation of Vancouver. CF-BVW, BVZ and BVX were loaned to Quebec Airways by the RCAF in the first half of 1942 and were also registered by CPAL in October 1943. All the 247s had been disposed of by mid-1945.

▲ White Pass Airways' Boeing 247D NC13325 seen at Whitehorse in 1941. It subsequently was registered as CF-BVF by British Yukon Navigation on October 30, 1941 and on August 7, 1942 was taken over by Yukon Southern Air Transport. In July 1945, CPAL sold the aircraft to C.H. Babb Inc. of Glendale, California.

Aircraft	Boeing 247D
Year of first flight (247)	1933
Engines	Two Pratt & Whitney Wasp radials (550 hp)
Wingspan	74 ft 0 in
Length	51 ft 4 in
Height	12 ft 2 in
Weight empty	9,144 lb
Maximum take-off weight	13,650 lb
Cruising speed	189 mph
Range	745 miles
Crew	2
Passengers	10

The final development of Lockheed's fast twin concept was the Model 18 Lodestar which was a stretched and more powerful Model 14. In fact, the prototype was a Northwest Airlines Lockheed 14 converted into a Lodestar with accommodation for two pilots, a flight attendant and 14 passengers. The modified airplane made its first flight on September 21, 1939. Two further Lockheed 14s were converted before the first new Lodestar was produced on February 2, 1940. The Lodestar could operate over stages of up to 1800 miles at speeds of 229 mph and represented the ultimate in the concept of the small, high speed, limited payload airliner. Production of the seven Lodestar versions

totalled 625 aircraft and the last one was completed in 1943. CPAL operated 12 Lodestars of three subclasses, 08, 14 and 56. The first two subclasses were fitted with Pratt & Whitney Twin Wasps of 900 and 1,050 hp, respectively, while the 56 was fitted with Wright Cyclones producing 1,000 hp. Two of the new Lodestars were allocated to CPAL by the U.S. Joint Chiefs of Staff because of the importance of the airline's contribution to the war effort and seven were allocated by the USAAF for the same reason. The airline needed the increased capacity to meet its commitments in northwestern Canada relating to the Alaska Highway and Canol Pipeline construction.

Aircraft	Lockheed 18-56 Lodestar
Year of first flight	1939
Engines	Two Wright Cyclone (1,000 hp)
Wingspan	65 ft 6 in
Length	49 ft 10 in
Height	11 ft 11 in
Weight empty	12,195 lb
Maximum take-off weight	17,500 lb
Cruising speed	229 mph
Range	2,030 miles
Flight deck crew	2
Passengers	14

▲ Lockheed Lodestar 18-56 CF-CPF, seen at Edmonton Municipal Airport, was allocated to CPAL by the USAAF in 1943 because of the importance of the airlines' contribution to the North West Staging Route. In May 1951, she was sold to C.H. Babb Inc. of Glendale, California.

73

In May 1933, G.E. Woods-Humphery, managing director of Imperial Airways, approached Avro with a request for a fast, long range, twin engined aircraft similar to those being developed in the United States by Lockheed, Douglas and Boeing. Avro liked the concept and by August of the same year had designed the model 652 with a fabric covered steel fuselage, a wooden mainplane and accommodation for a crew of two and four passengers. Imperial Airways ordered two aircraft but at more or less the same time, the British Air Ministry invited Avro to submit a design for a twin engined coastal patrol aircraft. Avro merely adapted the 652 design to meet the Air Ministry's requirement, submitting their proposal on May 19, 1934. This resulted in an order for a single prototype to be delivered in March 1935. Rather interestingly, the Air Ministry also ordered a militarized prototype D.H.89 at the same time.

The first Anson for Imperial Airways made its initial flight on January 7, 1935 and both aircraft were delivered to the airline on March 11, 1935. On March 24th, the military 652 made its maiden flight and it eventually proved superior to the D.H.89M in trials held in May 1935 although minor modifications including an increase in the tailplane span had to be made. The Air Ministry then issued a specification written around the 652 and on May 25, 1935 ordered 174 aircraft of this type. The production prototype first flew on December 31, 1935 and subsequently the type received the RAF name Anson Mk.I Accepted into squadron service on March 6, 1936, the Anson became the RAF's first operational monoplane and its first type with retractable undercarriage. Ansons were placed in front line service with the RAF's Coastal Command and continued in this role until displaced by Lockheed Hudsons in the early years of World War Two. The bulk of the 11,020 Ansons constructed served as trainers and on communication duties.

The Anson V was a Canadian built derivative of the original Anson. It had a moulded plywood fuselage and was powered by two 450 hp Pratt & Whitney Wasp Jrs. The prototype was constructed by Federal Aircraft in Montreal and made its first flight on January 4, 1943. Originally, it had been planned to construct 2,300 Ansons for use as navigation/bombing trainers but when production ceased late in 1945, only 1,049 Canadian Ansons had been completed. With its wooden fuselage, the Anson V aircraft was comfortable to operate even in cold weather and the type became a very popular trainer being used extensively to train bomber navigators. Following the war, large numbers were made available to private operators who used them as freight aircraft and for photographic survey work. CPAL acquired a total of nine Anson Vs after the war ended and these were used for photographic survey and freight work. Examples of the Anson V can be seen at the Canadian Warplane Heritage Collection in Hamilton, Ontario and at the National Aviation Museum in Ottawa.

▲ The Avro Anson, unlike most military transport aircraft, proved to be suitable for use by commercial operators and CPAL used nine Anson Vs for photographic and transport services.

Aircraft	Avro Anson V (in military service)
Year of first flight (Anson V)	1943
Engines	Two Pratt & Whitney Wasp Jr. radials (450 hp)
Wingspan	56 ft 6 in
Length	42 ft 3 in
Height	42 ft 3 in
Weight empty	6,693 lb
Gross weight	9,275 lb
Cruising speed	145 mph
Range	680 miles
Crew	5

▲ Douglas DC-3 CF-CRW flies over Vancouver's unmistakable but now considerably changed shoreline in 1947 not long after the aircraft was purchased from C.H. Babb Inc. of Glendale, California.

Provincial Archives of Alberta PA535/5

▲ In the late 1940s and early 1950s the 17 DC-3s acquired by CPAL operated most of the company's trunk services. In this photograph CF-CVC and another unidentified DC-3, in company with Convair 240 CF-CUV, are seen at Edmonton Municipal Airport in the mid-1950s.

The DC-3 was developed as a result of the Boeing 247's success. As outlined previously, United Air Transport had ordered 59 Boeing 247s in early 1932 and Boeing refused to supply the type to other airlines until this order was completed. Transcontinental & Western Air, the forerunner of TWA, tried to order the 247 from Boeing but was informed that this would involve a two year wait before the first aircraft could be supplied. Transcontinental, not being prepared to accept such a lengthy wait, issued its own requirement for an all-metal, three engine monoplane with 550 hp engines, a crew of two and the capability of carrying at least 12 passengers at speeds of not less than 150 mph. Furthermore, the aircraft had to be able to take off fully laden with one engine shut down. In August 1932, five companies were invited to provide designs and Douglas, which at that time was a small company having previously built only military aircraft, constructed a twin engined, all

metal, low winged cantilever, monoplane, powered by two 690 hp Wright engines and capable of carrying 12 passengers. This was the DC-1 — the initials representing Douglas Commercial — and it made its first flight on July 1, 1933. Transcontinental liked the aircraft, especially the unobstructed cabin floor unlike that in the Boeing 247 where the main spar effectively cut the passenger accommodation in two. Douglas was persuaded to lengthen the fuselage to provide seating for 14 passengers and Transcontinental ordered 20 of these new aircraft which were designated DC-2s. The first flight was on May 11, 1934 and the type entered service exactly a week later making the various Fokkers, Trimotors and Boeings obsolescent. American, Eastern, KLM and Swissair also ordered the 190 mph airliner and approximately 200 were constructed — an extremely large production run for an aircraft in the 1930s.

The DC-3 evolved from the DC-2 because Ameri-

can Airlines required an aircraft to replace its Curtiss Condor biplanes which were then flying sleeper services across the United States. The airline wanted an aircraft with the economics and performance of the DC-2 but the space of the Condor and, after much difficulty, prevailed upon Douglas to stretch the DC-2 to provide sufficient space for 14 berths. American required that the aircraft be capable of flying between New York and Chicago non stop and Douglas obliged with a larger aircraft with an increased wing span, a fuselage of greater length, rounded sides and powered by 920 hp Wright Cyclone engines. The airline ordered 20 of the new aircraft in July 1935, eight to be in sleeper configuration and the remainder to be standard 21 seat airliners. The two types, which were identical except for their interior fittings, were designated as the Douglas Sleeper Transport (DST) and the DC-3 respectively. The DST, made its first flight at Santa Monica, California on December 17, 1935,

and the type was granted a certificate of airworthiness on April 29, 1936. Incredibly, the first DST was delivered to American Airlines the same day. At first only the DST version was available and American introduced the type into service on June 25, 1936 between New York and Chicago. Initially, these aircraft were temporarily fitted with seats as the first DC-3 was not delivered to American Airlines until August 18, 1936. As more DC-3s arrived, the DST's were refitted and diverted to the transcontinental service which started on September 18, 1936. Eventually, only 40 DSTs were supplied, these being purchased by Eastern, United, TWA, Western Air Express and American Airlines. Meanwhile, the DC-3 was earning itself an excellent reputation and was proving to be the first truly economic airliner. For only a 10 percent increase in operating costs, Douglas had provided an aircraft with 50 percent more capacity. Such was the impact of the DC-3 that by the time the United States entered

World War Two, 90 percent of all airline travel in the U.S. was on this aircraft and over 400 DC-3s had been supplied to airlines while a further 73 had been built for the U.S. forces where they were designated C-47s. During the war, vast numbers of C-47s were constructed for the United States and allied air forces. The last DC-3 was a civil version delivered to Swissair in May 1946 and this represented the last of 10,655 U.S. built aircraft of this type. To this must be added 571 licence built L2Ds constructed in Japan and a further 2,700 + Russian built Lusinov Li-2s.

CPAL acquired a fleet of 17 war surplus C-47s during 1946 and 1947. These were refurbished to airline DC-3 standards and were operated on domestic services where they were the first true airliners to serve many of Canada's remote communities, allowing CPAL to withdraw a number of its bush aircraft. With the withdrawal of the airline from services to remote localities and the acquisition

of the Convair 240s and DC-6s, it was possible to start selling off the DC-3s in the mid to late 1950s although, as noted elsewhere, CF-CRX remained with the airline until October 1974.

▲ Only one DC-3, CF-CRX, remained with the airline in 1968 and obtained the orange livery of CP Air. In this specially posed photograph, CF-CRX is seen with Boeing 727-117 CF-CUR and Douglas DC-8-43 CF-CPH *Empress of Lima*. In the background is one of Vancouver's notorious ground fogs.

Aircraft	Douglas DC-3
Year of first flight	1935
Engines	Two Pratt & Whitney Twin Wasp radials (1,200 hp)
Wingspan	95 ft 0 in
Length	64 ft 6 in
Height	16 ft 11 in
Weight empty	17,200 lb
Maximum take-off weight	25,200 lb
Cruising speed	165 mph
Range	1,510 miles
Crew	2
Maximum passenger capacity	36 (28 in CPAL service)

▲ Awaiting departure from one of CPAL's west coast terminals in the early 1950s, Canso A CF-CRV is seen ready for its passengers to board through what was once one of the machine gun ports when this aircraft served with the RCAF as No. 9755.

During 1933, the Consolidated Aircraft Corporation of Buffalo designed a streamlined, all-metal, high winged monoplane, flying boat, powered by two Pratt & Whitney Twin Wasp 800 hp engines, for use as a long range maritime patrol aircraft. The U.S. Navy contracted for one XP3Y-1 on October 28, 1933 and the new aircraft made its first flight on March 28, 1935. The XP3Y-1 competed with the Douglas XP3D-1 for a Navy contract and, in the event, Consolidated won an order for 60 P3Y-1s as their unit price of $90,000 was some $20,000 less than that of Douglas.

Consolidated decided to build the P3Y-1s in a new factory at San Diego. In the meantime, the prototype was re-equipped with 900 hp Wasps which improved maximum speed from 169 mph to 184 mph. As a result, the U.S. Navy decided to order a further 50 of the Wasp equipped version. This contract was signed on July 25, 1936 and these

aircraft became PBY-2s, the P3Y designation being changed to PBY in August 1936 to signify "Patrol Boat Consolidated". A further 66 PBY-3s with 1000 hp engines were ordered on November 27, 1936 and 33 PBY-4s with 1050 hp Wasps were ordered on December 18, 1937. These latter aircraft had a top speed of 297 mph at 12,000 ft. In addition, a single PBY-4 was built for the Royal Air Force and was delivered in July 1939, thus making the first trans-Atlantic delivery flight of a military aircraft. The last PBY-4 to be produced was converted to an amphibian by equipping it with retractable tricycle landing gear. Designated the XPBY-5A, this aircraft made its first flight on November 22, 1939 and had it not been for World War Two, it is likely that PBY production would have ended with this the 210th aircraft of this type. Other modern flying boats were in the prototype stage but when hostilities commenced it was vital to acquire large numbers of a fully developed patrol aircraft as soon as possible

rather than wait for more advanced but still untried designs to become available. Accordingly, the U.S. Navy ordered 200 PBY-5s to patrol the Neutrality Zone while Britain, France, Australia and Canada arranged to acquire a further 174 similar aircraft. Because the French quota of aircraft was still under construction when France capitulated, this order was taken over by Britain where the type was designated the Catalina. In October 1941, the U.S. Navy also adopted the name but in Canadian service the PBY was always known as the Canso. The RCAF ordered 50 PBY amphibians but, before the first was delivered, nine purely flying boat versions were obtained from the RAF to combat German submarines in the western Atlantic. Deliveries of the Canadian amphibians started in June 1941 and some of these aircraft were transferred to the RAF to replace the flying boats received from Britain. Additional orders were obtained from the U.S., Netherlands, Australian and New Zealand navies

as well as the USAAF and when production ended after hostilities ceased, 2,029 PBY flying boats and 1,402 amphibians had been produced in the United States and Canada. This total of 3,431 makes the PBY family the most produced flying boat in history. To this figure must be added approximately 150 Russian built versions constructed under licence prior to the advancing German armies overrunning Taganrog in 1941.

In 1940, Boeing Aircraft of Canada, based in Vancouver, and Canadian Vickers of Montreal were licensed to build the PBY. In spite of its 2,800 lb. weight disadvantage, the RCAF considered the amphibian version of the PBY to have sufficiently more operational flexibility to make the penalty acceptable. As a result, the only flying boat versions of the PBY in the RCAF were the original Catalinas from the RAF and these were known as Cansos. The amphibian version was designated the Canso

A. The first of an order for 55 Canso As produced by Boeing for the RCAF was completed in late 1942 and the initial Canadian Vickers, Canso A made its maiden flight on December 2, 1942. Vickers manufactured 139 Canso As for the RCAF. Total Canadian production of all PBY variants was 362 from Boeing while Canadian Vickers and its successor Canadair Ltd. produced 360 aircraft of this type.

RCAF Canso As served with ten squadrons and one OTU. No. 162 Squadron was based in Iceland and northern Scotland and between April 17 and June 30, 1944 was involved in the sinking of six U-boats. Following the war, a number of aircraft were declared surplus but Canso As continued in RCAF service until 1962, primarily engaged in search and rescue, and survey work. CPAL acquired four Canso As from Crown Assets in 1946 and these were converted to passenger configuration and used on the lightly travelled routes to remote

locations along the westcoast of British Columbia before airports were built. Centres served from Vancouver included Prince Rupert and Sandspit. The most notable of these PBYs was CF-CRR which, as 9767P of 162 Squadron RCAF sank the U-342 on April 17, 1944. Not many airlines have operated a fully blooded combat aircraft.

▲ Fresh from overhaul at Vancouver, Canso A CF-CRV illustrates the blister over the entry port and the recess for the wheel can be seen clearly. Note the more elaborate livery than that shown on the same aircraft in the previous page.

Aircraft	PBY-5A Canso A (in military service)
Year of first flight (Canso A)	1942
Engines	Two Pratt & Whitney Twin Wasp radials (1,200 hp)
Wingspan	104 ft 0 in
Length	63 ft 11 in
Height	20 ft 2 in
Weight empty	20,910 lb
Weight loaded	33,975 lb
Cruising speed	117 mph
Range	1,570 miles
Crew	8/9 (2 in passenger service)

▲ For its trans-Pacific services, CPAL purchased four Canadair Fours. This photograph shows the second example, CF-CPR, flying over the Gulf Islands off Vancouver in 1949. The typical Douglas shape and the liquid cooled Rolls-Royce Merlin engines can be seen clearly.

Trans-Canada Air Lines commenced trans Atlantic service using Lancastrian CF TMS on July 23, 1943 but it was recognized right from the beginning of this operation that the converted bomber was just a stop-gap measure until more suitable aircraft became available. Around the same time, the Canadian government decided to foster the domestic aircraft industry by acquiring the rights to manufacture the DC-4 in Canada but left the choice of engines for the aircraft to Trans Canada Air Lines. After considering all the more suitable engines available, Trans Canada Air Lines chose the Rolls Royce Merlin 620. While it is true that the liquid cooled Merlin had served well in such famous aircraft as the Hurricane, Spitfire, Mustang, Mosquito and Lancaster, its choice for a commercial aircraft is still somewhat mystifying. Engines for military aircraft are robust and are designed to give reliable performance under arduous combat conditions.

Relatively little attention is paid to weight and fuel consumption — two serious liabilities in the competitive world of air carriers.

Perhaps because of its proved dependability, the Merlin was chosen and the design to incorporate it into a DC-4 airframe commenced in 1944. The prototype CF-TEN-X was a C-54GM equipped with Merlin engines and made its first flight on July 15, 1946 at Cartierville, Quebec. At its official debut, five days later, the wife of C.D. Howe, the Minister of Reconstruction and Supply, named the aircraft *North Star*. The RCAF and TCA subsequently referred to all the Merlin powered DC-4s with this name but BOAC adopted the name of Argonaut for the type and CPAL called theirs Canadair Fours. The airline versions had pressurized cabins but the RCAF aircraft did not have this feature. Because developing the pressurization system delayed TCA's order for 20 aircraft, six of the 24 unpressurized version ordered

by the RCAF were finished to airline standards and used by TCA until its own pressurized DC-4M 2/4's were delivered. The first 24 North Stars were acquired by the RCAF. TCA then received the 20 DC-4M2 pressurized versions and commenced operations with the type on the Atlantic service on April 15, 1947. BOAC received its first two C-4s in March 1949 and CPAL was supplied with the 47th to 50th production line aircraft between April and June 1949. These were designated as C-4-1s and were identical to the BOAC machines though finished to CPAL specifications. As such they operated at a maximum weight of 82,300 lb. compared with the 79,600 lb. of the TCA machines. Following the completion of CPAL's last Canadair Four, production switched to the remaining 20 BOAC aircraft and the final Argonaut was delivered in November 1949. This, the 71st example, was completed in 1950. It was powered with Pratt & Whitney 2,100 hp R-2800

engines and was supplied to the RCAF where it was known as the C-5.

TCA used the North Star on its European and Caribbean routes as well as on the transcontinental service. BOAC equipped its fleet to handle 40 first class or 54 tourist passengers and the Argonaut became a stalwart on the African and Far East routes from its introduction in August 1949 until the remaining fleet was retired on April 8, 1960. TCA withdrew the type from service in 1961, long after CPAL had sold its three surviving examples to the government airline. Unable to make the type economic on the then under-utilized southern and northern Pacific services to Auckland, Sydney, Tokyo and Hong Kong, CPAL had replaced its Canadair Fours with the more economical DC-4.

Ask anyone who flew in the North Star what impression the aircraft made and one will almost invariably be told how noisy it was. Comfort was another factor low in the consideration of designers working on equipment for military use and the noise of the Merlin engine was prodigious. Even cabin soundproofing could not reduce the bellow of the four 12 cylinder engines to comfortable levels and it was only after a cross-over exhaust system had been developed to deflect some of the sound away from the passenger cabin that the North Star became somewhat more bearable. At the same time, the cross over exhausts removed the problem of passengers being able to see the blue flames from the short inboard exhaust stacks, another hallmark of the Merlin engine.

Following their disposal by TCA and BOAC, many North Stars/Argonauts operated with smaller airlines including Aden Airways and East African Airways. The Royal Rhodesian Air Force purchased four while most of the TCA fleet went into freighter service in North, Central and South America. The last surviving North Stars were retired in 1976.

Aircraft	Canadair Four (North Star)
Year of first flight (North Star)	1946
Engines	Four Rolls-Royce Merlin 626 (1,760 hp)
Wingspan	117 ft 6 in
Length	93 ft 7 in
Height	27 ft 6 in
Weight empty	46,832 lb
Maximum take-off weight	82,300 lb
Cruising speed	280 mph
Range	2,885 miles
Crew	4/5
Passengers	40

▲ It is July 15, 1949 and Canadair Four CF-CPI *Empress of Sydney* is seen at Mascot Airport, Sydney preparing to depart on the return leg of the pre-inaugural Australian flight.

CPAL 26210

Even before the DC-3 made its first flight, Douglas and United Airlines were discussing the possibility of constructing a four engine aircraft with double the capacity of the DC-3. In 1936 Eastern, American, Pan American, TWA and United Airlines each put up $100,000 for Douglas to design and construct a prototype. Pan American and TWA subsequently withdrew from the venture in favour of the Boeing 307 Stratoliner but Douglas nevertheless continued with the project. The result was an all-metal, unpressurized aircraft with a capacity of up to 52 passengers which made its first flight on June 7, 1938. Power was provided by four Pratt & Whitney 1,450 hp Twin Hornets and the aircraft had a dihedral tailplane with triple fins. Unlike the DC-3, it was equipped with tricycle undercarriage but unfortunately the DC-4 was too large, too complex and a maintenance nightmare. United flew demonstration and proving flights but the aircraft never entered regular, scheduled service and it was returned to Douglas. When the decision was made to construct the scaled down DC-4 the original aircraft became the DC-4E to denote that it had been built for experimental purposes. Douglas subsequently sold

it to the Mitsui Trading Company of Japan and it became the basis for the Japanese Navy's Nakajima G5N1 Shinzan four engine bomber. This too was equally unsuccessful and only six prototypes were built.

During 1939, Douglas commenced designing the smaller less complex four engined airliner which eventually became the DC-4. On January 26, 1940 Eastern, American, United and Pan American signed contracts for 61 aircraft of this type. Progress, however, was slow because of sales of military aircraft and the original delivery date of early 1941 was missed with the first flight not taking place until February 14, 1942. By this time, the United States was embroiled in World War Two and the DC-4 became the C-54 Skymaster and 1,163 aircraft of this type were built for the USAAF and the USN. Some C-54s were released to airlines for contract work for the military but none became available for civilian use until after hostilities ceased. United ordered 15 DC-4s on September 11, 1944 but this order was cancelled in October 1945 as the U.S. forces began to sell large numbers of surplus C-54s. Indeed it was an ex-C-54 of American Export Airlines

which made the first civilian postwar landplane flight across the Atlantic from New York to England via Gander and Shannon on October 23/24, 1945. Even though it was unpressurized, the DC-4/C-54 was a big improvement over the DC-3 as it could carry as many as 86 passengers in high density seating configuration at speeds of more than 100 mph faster than a DC-3. As the U.S. government sold off surplus aircraft, the world's airlines rapidly brought these military transports up to airline standards and during the late 1940s the DC-4 occupied a position of importance in civil aviation similar to that enjoyed by the DC-3 at the beginning of the decade. New DC-4s were also built but the last aircraft of this type was delivered in August 1947 when a total of 79 true DC-4s had been built. With the return to peace, aircraft manufacturers could devote people, time and money to introducing new aircraft and the appearance of postwar aircraft such as the DC-6 and the Constellation rapidly swept the relatively utilitarian DC-4 from the ranks of the world's major airlines.

Because of the Canadair Four's high fuel consumption, CPAL decided to replace this aircraft

▲ Douglas DC-4 CF-CUL was one of five aircraft purchased from Pan American to replace the Canadair Fours on the trans-Pacific services.

with the DC-4 and five examples were obtained from Pan American in 1950 and 1951. With the acquisition of new DC-6s from 1953 onwards it was possible to replace the DC-4s with pressurized and faster aircraft.

Aircraft	Douglas DC-4
Year of first flight	1942
Engines	Four Pratt & Whitney Twin Wasp radials (1,450 hp)
Wingspan	117 ft 6 in
Length	93 ft 11 in
Height	27 ft 7 in
Weight empty	46,000 lb
Maximum take-off weight	73,000 lb
Cruising speed	246 mph
Range	3,100 miles
Crew	4
Passengers	44

One of the most common descriptions of new designs of aircraft in the 20 years following World War Two was "DC-3 replacement". One of the first designs to be described as such was the Convair 240 which resulted from an early 1945 request from American Airlines to the U.S. aircraft constructors to design a larger, faster, twin engined successor to the DC-3 for operations on routes of up to 1,000 miles. Convair designed the 30 passenger Model 110 to meet this specification, powered by Pratt & Whitney 2,100 hp Double Wasps and this aircraft made its first flight on July 8, 1946. American then decided on a slightly larger and more powerful aircraft and the 110 did not go into production. The design was replaced by that of the Model 240 which could accommodate 40 passengers and was equipped with 2,400 hp Double Wasps. American ordered 100 Convair 240s off the drawing board although this was subsequently reduced to 75 and

the first flight of the new type was made on March 16, 1947. It was 3 ft. 8 in. longer than the 110 and featured "aspirated cooling", a form of thrust augmentation where cooling air and exhaust gases pass through a venturi and give added propulsion to the aircraft. Production commenced in late 1947 and American made the first commercial flight with the type on June 1, 1947. Other airlines acquiring the 240 included Western, Continental, Northeast, Pan American, Trans-Australia Airlines, KLM and Swissair and subsequently the type was sold to many other airlines. Civilian orders for the 240 totalled 176 aircraft while military orders from the USAF accounted for a further 395 examples. These were primarily T-29 navigational trainers together with some C-131A Samaritan aeromedical versions and VC-131A staff transports. Production continued until 1958.

CPAL purchased five Convair 240s in late 1952/early 1953. These were ex-Continental Air Lines aircraft and were used primarily on the British Columbia routes until being sold for further service in Japan in 1963 and 1964.

▲ Five Convair 240s were purchased from Continental Air Lines in 1952 and 1953 to supplement the company's DC-3s on the trunk routes. In this mid-1950 photograph CF-CVW is seen at Edmonton. Thirteen Convair 240s are still in airline service with five operators.

Aircraft	Convair 240
Year of first flight	1946
Engines	Two Pratt & Whitney Double Wasp radials (2,400 hp)
Wingspan	91 ft 9 in
Length	74 ft 8 in
Height	26 ft 11 in
Weight empty	30,345 lb
Maximum take-off weight	43,575 lb
Cruising speed	284 mph
Range	1,025 miles
Crew	2
Maximum passenger capacity	40

British Aerospace 6466A

▲ On August 1, 1952 de Havilland D.H. 106 Comet 1A CF-CUM is seen in the final stages of preparation for Canadian Pacific Air Lines. Note that the aircraft's tail could not be accommodated within the hangar. Since 1952, toleration of smokers has diminished considerably!

The de Havilland 106 Comet was the world's first jet airliner. The concept for this pioneering aircraft stemmed from the Second Brabazon Committee of May 1943 which deliberated on what types of aircraft should be constructed in Britain following World War Two. During 1944, drawings were prepared showing what was to become the Comet as a tailless design but by 1945 the proposed aircraft had a conventional configuration and a capacity of 24-32 passengers. It was to have the range to operate over the North Atlantic at the then unheard of cruising speed of 505 mph.

On January 21, 1947 BOAC (now British Airways) placed an order for eight Comet 1s which was subsequently increased to nine aircraft. The prototype G-ALVG first flew on July 27, 1949 and, while this operated most satisfactorily, it was apparent from the beginning that the plane did not have the range to operate across the North Atlantic. Nevertheless it was suitable for BOAC's Empire routes to Africa and the Far East. The first production aircraft flew on January 9, 1951 and BOAC's first service flight with the Comet left London for Rome, Beirut, Khartoum, Entebee, Livingstone and Johannesburg on May 2, 1952. Subsequently, the nine 36 seat Comet 1s inaugurated jet service on BOAC's Far East and Africa where they proved to be extremely popular with passengers as the 80 percent load factors testify.

The success of the nine Comet 1s led to orders for ten 1As which had an additional fuel capacity of 1,000 imperial gallons and passenger capacity was increased to 44. This model was ordered by Air France, UAT, the Royal Canadian Air Force and CPAL. Grant McConachie, the airline's president wanted to use the two Comet 1As on the south

Pacific route between Sydney, Fiji, Canton Island and Honolulu. Much as he would have liked to have the two jets handle the entire trans-Pacific flights, even with the increased fuel capacity, the 1As did not have the range to fly from Honolulu to Vancouver. Because of this lack of range, the CPAL Comet 1A CF-CUN left England for Sydney via the Far East on March 1, 1953 but at Karachi, Pakistan on take off for Singapore, the aircraft crashed and all aboard were killed. The accident was attributed to pilot error, as was that of a Comet 1 at Rome on October 26, 1952. It was found that, if the nose were lifted too soon, the engines' effectiveness was reduced and the aircraft could not reach flying speed. To overcome this problem, the Comets were fitted with drooped leading edges but with the Karachi crash CPAL's interest in the Comet waned and the company's other 1A, CF-CUM was sold to the Royal Aircraft Establishment where it became

British Aerospace 6858C

G-ANAV. It never flew for CPAL.

On January 10, 1954 BOAC's Comet 1 G-ALYP disappeared soon after leaving Rome and on April 8th G-ALYY went into the Mediterranean off Crete. This caused the Certificate of Air worthiness to be withdrawn and the Comet never regained the world leadership that it had enjoyed. Eventually, it was determined that these accidents were the result of metal fatigue brought about by flexure caused by pressurization but the time taken to reach this conclusion wiped out much of the Comet's early lead and CPAL's order for later model Comets were allowed to lapse. The RCAF's two 1As were rebuilt as 1XBs to overcome fatigue problems and re-entered service in September 1957.

Although no later model Comets were registered in Canada, the type has an interesting subsequent history. A Comet 3 with an 18 ft. 6 in. (5.6m) fuselage stretch to carry up to 78 economy passengers across the North Atlantic never reached production although ordered by Pan American, Air India and BOAC. Instead, the Comet 4 series, incorporating the structural data learned from the 1954 accidents and with increased dimensions was designed and produced. BOAC ordered 19 Mk 4s and the first flight was made on April 27, 1958. The airline reintroduced jet service on October 4, 1958 when a Comet 4 flew from London - New York, three weeks ahead of Pan American's Boeing 707s on the same service. The maximum capacity of the Comet 4 was approximately 100 passengers while the Boeing 707s and DC-8s could both carry 180 passengers. Not surprisingly, the Comet's operating economics were unattractive to long haul airlines and although a short haul version was produced for BEA, Comet 4 production totalled only 74 aircraft. In all, 116 Comets were produced plus two unsold Comet 4C airframes which were rebuilt to become the proto-types for the RAF's marine reconnaissance/airborne early warning Nimrod. No Comets remain flying.

Aircraft	de Havilland D.H.106 Comet 1A
Year of first flight	1949
Engines	Four de Havilland Ghost 50 turbojets (5,000 lb thrust)
Wingspan	115 ft 0 in
Length	96 ft 0 in
Height	29 ft 6 in
Weight emtpy	60,000 lb
Maximum take-off weight	115,000 lb
Cruising speed	490 mph
Range	2,000 miles
Crew	4
Passengers	44

▲ Taking on fuel at London's Heathrow Airport, D.H.106 Comet 1A CF-CUN *Empress of Hawaii* is seen immediately prior to its departure for Sydney on March 1, 1953. On the left is a British European Airways' Airspeed Ambassador and on the right is a Swiss Air Convair. The weather appears to be suitably sombre.

85

During 1937 Curtiss-Wright had discussions with several American airlines concerning a pressurized twin engined aircraft which would be larger than the DC-3 and carry 36 passengers. From these meetings, the company designed the CW-20T which made its first flight on March 26, 1940 at St. Louis and was, at that time, the largest twin engined aircraft in the world. The prototype had the typical double bubble design of the C-46, the upper portion of which was designed to be pressurized but never was. It also had a twin tail and was equipped with 1,700 hp Wright Cyclones. Unfortunately, this private venture received no orders from the airlines but the U.S. forces saw the merits of the design as a military transport and ordered 25 C-46s fitted with a single fin and powered by Pratt & Whitney 2,000 hp Double Wasps. This version was designed to carry 50 troops or 33 stretcher cases or 10,000 lb. cargo. The prototype CW-20T was fitted with a single fin and sold to BOAC in late 1941 and operated with the airline as a transport aircraft for two years. Appropriately, it was named *St. Louis.*

Production of the C-46 totalled 3,180 aircraft of which 1,518 were C-46As which was the cargo version with a single loading door. The C-46D was a troop transport fitted with double doors and 1,410

examples were constructed. With a cargo capacity of 16,000 lb., the C-46 was a useful freighter and the type served in all the major areas of conflict during the war. Perhaps it is best known for its service during the airlift to China flying over the Himalayas from Assam in northeastern India to supply the Chinese Nationalist forces of Chiang Kai-shek. This service required operations at up to 25,000 ft. with a full load and the C-46 proved up to the task flying for long periods under some of the worst conditions in the world.

The C-46 entered airline service on October 1, 1942 serving with the Military Transport Division of Eastern Airlines. This service was exclusively for military personnel and the airline operated the aircraft for the forces. After the war, a civil version — the CW-20E — was planned as a 36 passenger airliner, powered by 2,100 hp Wright Duplex Cyclones but Eastern Airlines cancelled the order it had placed and the project was dropped. When hostilities ceased, many surplus C-46s became available but at first sales were slow because of difficulties in meeting FAA conditions for maximum operating weights. The U.S. Civil Aeronautics Authority only granted a domestic civil airworthiness certificate and, because of this, C-46s were primarily restricted

to use in North and South America.

The Distant Early Warning (DEW) line was chief reason for the C-46 coming to Canada. This is a line of radar stations which eventually was constructed from the Aleutians to Greenland, across Alaska and northern Canada. The Canadian sector was constructed between 1954 and 1957 and CPAL purchased eight C-46s from a variety of sources to supply the construction sites. Fort Nelson was selected as the main operating base for the C-46 fleet because of the all weather Alaska Highway connecting Fort Nelson with the outside world and heated hangar space being available. At each radar site a 6,000 ft. gravel landing strip was constructed and the C-46 fleet hauled the freight from Ft. Nelson and Norman Wells directly to the sites. The bulk of the work by CPAL was handled between March 1955 and October 1956 and during this time the airline transported over 12,500 tons of freight. Following the completion of the contract, the aircraft were available for general charter work but in 1958 four were upgraded to Super 46 standards involving aerodynamic refinements and the installation of an improved exhaust systems equipped with thrust augmentor tail pipes. Two of these aircraft remained in cargo service and two were converted into 44

▲ An unidentified Curtiss C-46 is seen about to unload its cargo on DEW Line service in the mid-1950s. CPAL assigned its eight C-46s together with five DC-3s and two DC-4s to the DEW Line contracts. Primarily, CPAL was in charge of delivery fuel to airstrips throughout the western and central Arctic.

passenger aircraft. All four were disposed of on July 21, 1959 to Pacific Western Airlines. The last C-46 was disposed of in mid-1963.

Aircraft	Curtiss C-46
Year of first flight	1940
Engines	Two Pratt & Whitney Double Wasps (2,000 hp)
Wingspan	103 ft 0 in
Length	76 ft 4 in
Height	21 ft 9 in
Weight empty	29,100 lb
Maximum take-off weight	48,000 lb
Cruising speed	227 mph
Range	1,800 miles
Crew	2
Passengers	44 but primarily a cargo aircraft

As the Norseman program was phased out in the mid-1950s, CPAL required two new aircraft for its remaining bush services operating in the Northwest Territories. Rather than purchase further obsolescent Norseman aircraft, Canadian Pacific opted for two de Havilland Otters and these were delivered in 1955. The Otter was a direct descendant of the de Havilland Chipmunk and Beaver. The former was the Canadian subsidiary's first design and had earned an excellent reputation as a military basic trainer. Following on from the company's experience with this aircraft, the Beaver was designed as a seven seat utility transport to replace such aircraft as the Norseman and the Fairchild 82. It made its first flight on August 16, 1947 and was an immediate success with civilian and military operators. Large orders were received from the United States Army and other military users for this high-wing, all metal aircraft which operated so successfully in the development of northern Canada. By the time production ceased, 1,692 examples, including turbine-powered versions, had been constructed.

Such was the success of the Beaver with its 450 hp Pratt & Whitney Wasp engine, that the Ontario Provincial Air Service, which had played an important part in the design of the Beaver, indicated that if de Havilland were to build a similar aircraft with twice the capacity, it would purchase 20 of them. At first the lack of a suitable power plant was a problem but the Canadian subsidiary of Pratt & Whitney agreed to produce a 600 hp Wasp and the 11 seat Otter made its first flight at Downsview, Ontario on December 12, 1951. The Otter received its certificate of airworthiness on November 5, 1952 and quickly obtained the reputation of a rugged, dependable workhorse. Capable of air lifting one and a half tons of freight over 200 miles, the Otter has been used throughout Canada, supplying remote work sites and isolated villages. With a large freight door on the left side, it is possible to get bulky items into the Otter's cabin. The aircraft's ability to operate from 1,000 ft. air strips has provided air access into remote areas with only minimal ground preparation. Furthermore, the Otter can be operated on floats, wheels or skis and, with extra large low pressure tires, is capable of operating from rudimentary airstrips.

The U.S. military ordered a total of 223 Otters and other military customers include Canada, with 69 aircraft of this type, Britain, Australia, India,

CPAL

Ghana and Norway. Civilian operators, apart from CPAL, have included many of the smaller Canadian operators and bush flyers as well as Qantas which used the Otter in New Guinea. The Ontario Provincial Air Service has used the Otter as a water bomber in fighting forest fires and the U.S., Britain and Belgium used the type in Antarctica on exploratory work. Production ceased in 1967 when 466 Otters had been produced but many remain at work in the more remote areas of Canada doing what they were designed to do—providing dependable service under often severe climatic conditions over lengthy periods.

CPAL's two Otters, CF-CZO and CF-CZP, were obtained from de Havilland on April 1, 1955 and were sold to Pacific Western Airlines on February 23, 1959. They were CPAL's last bush aircraft.

▲ DHC-3 Otters CF-CZO and CF-CZP seen in March 1955 ready for delivery to CPAL. They were the airline's final bush aircraft and were sold to Pacific Western Airlines in February 1959.

Aircraft	DHC-3 Otter
Year of first flight	1951
Engine	Pratt & Whitney Wasp (600 hp)
Wingspan	58 ft 0 in
Length	41 ft 10 in
Height	12 ft 7 in
Weight empty	4,165 lb
Maximum take-off weight	8,000 lb
Cruising speed	138 mph
Range	960 miles
Crew	1
Passengers	11 - 14

▲ CPAL's first truly intercontinental aircraft was the Douglas DC-6 and in this photograph CF-CZQ is seen at Vancouver. It served with the airline from October 1956 until displaced by Boeing 737s on the British Columbia interior routes in mid-1969. More than 60 DC-6s remain in scheduled and charter airline service with a total of 24 operators.

In 1939, TWA and Pan American placed orders for the pressurized, four engined, Lockheed Constellation. Although World War Two intervened, construction of the aircraft continued and it made its first flight on January 9, 1943. With a top speed of 347 mph and the ability to fly much higher than contemporary aircraft because of its degree of pressurization, Douglas anticipated, quite correctly, that their unpressurized DC-4 would be no match for the Constellation after the war when airlines would begin purchasing new aircraft once more. Thus in 1944, Douglas proceeded with a stretch of the DC-4 to be equipped with pressurization and to be known as the DC-6 — the DC-5 having been a

twin engined, high winged, all-metal short haul transport produced in small numbers in 1939 and 1940. As construction of an airliner was impossible because of war time conditions, the new aircraft began life as the military XC-112 project and the first flight was made on February 15, 1946. With so many surplus military aircraft available, Douglas concentrated on the airline market and American Airlines placed an order for 50 DC-6s on June 29, 1946, introducing the type into service on April 27, 1947. Powered by Pratt & Whitney Double Wasp 2,100 hp engines, the DC-6 carried up to 86 passengers at 328 mph over ranges of up to 3,300 miles. The fuselage was similar to that of the DC-4

but had been stretched by 6 ft. 8 in. and was equipped with square rather than round windows. A total of 175 aircraft of this type was built, serving with United, Delta and National in the United States and SAS, KLM and Sabena in Europe. Production of the original model ceased in May 1952. However, the type continued in production as a stretched version of the aircraft had been flown on September 29, 1949. Featuring a five foot stretch of the fuselage and originally only available as a cargo aircraft, this was the DC-6A. Equipped with a strengthened floor, enlarged doorways and with plugs fitted over the windows, the DC-6A entered service on April 16, 1951. Subsequently, a convertible cargo/pas-

Nicholas Morant for CPAL

senger version, the DC-6C, was made available. In total, 240 DC-6A and DC-6Cs were produced, including 166 C-118s for the U.S. forces.

The final development of the series was the DC-6B which was the passenger version of the DC-6A with a 13 in. fuselage stretch without the large cargo doors. It was powered by either 2,400 or 2,500 hp Double Wasps and made its first flight on February 2, 1951, entering service with American the following April 29th. It soon built up an outstanding reputation for economical and reliable operation and production totalled 287 when the last one was completed in 1958. Up to 102 passengers could be carried and long after its main

competitor, the Lockheed Constellation had been retired from airline service, the DC-6B remained in service with secondary and cargo airlines.

CPAL operated a mixed fleet of DC-6A and DC-6Bs between January 1953 and 1969. In all, 20 aircraft of these types were obtained and operated on the airlines long haul, international routes until they were replaced by Britannias and DC-8s. Their final use by the airline was on the interior routes of British Columbia.

Aircraft	Douglas DC-6B
Year of first flight (XC-112)	1946
Engines	Four Pratt & Whitney R-2800 Double Wasps (2,500 hp)
Wingspan	117 ft 6 in
Length	105 ft 7 in
Height	29 ft 3 in
Weight empty	54,148 lb
Maximum take-off weight	107,000 lb
Cruising speed	307 mph
Range	3,300 miles
Crew	4
Maximum passenger capacity	102

▲ On the international routes the DC-6s were displaced by the turbo-prop powered Bristol Britannias. In this photograph, taken at Vancouver, DC-6 CF-CZY is seen beside Britannia CF-CZC.

▲ An unidentified CPAL Bristol Britannia is towed out for service at Vancouver immediately prior to the start of the airline's transcontinental service in May 1959. Such was the speed of the Britannia that even with stops at Winnipeg and Toronto, it could cut one hour, 25 minutes off the existing transcontinental flying time.

Like the Comet (page 84), the Britannia was the result of the deliberations of the Brabazon Committee which, in November 1944, issued its specifications for a medium range airliner for use on BOAC's Empire routes. In 1946, Bristol Aircraft Ltd. proposed acquiring Lockheed L.749 Constellations to be re-engined with Bristol Centaurus 660 radial engines but, in the postwar period of recovery, the British Treasury would not approve the expenditure of U.S. dollars and in 1947 the Ministry of Supply issued specification C2/47 for the proposed design. Five companies submitted eight designs but only the Bristol 175, a 32 to 36 passenger aircraft powered by four Bristol Centaurus piston engines, offered the best prospect of meeting the requirements. Discussions with BOAC in October 1947 led to the capacity being increased to 48 passengers and the

gross weight increased from 94,000 to 103,300 lb. The Centaurus radial engines were expected to provide a cruising speed of 310 mph.

On July 5, 1948 the Ministry of Supply ordered three prototype Britannias with Centaurus engines though it was specified that the second and third prototypes would be convertible to Bristol Proteus turbo-prop power with the third aircraft to be completed to full airline standards. Entry into service was forecast for 1954. In October 1948, BOAC decided that the turbo-prop Proteus powered model offered a better alternative and on July 28, 1949 the company ordered 25 Britannias. Of these, the first six would have Centaurus engines while the remaining 19 aircraft would be equipped with Proteus engines. During this delay the Britannia had again increased in size and could carry 83 passengers across the

North Atlantic.

Initial success with the Proteus engine led to the abandonment of the Centaurus project and the prototype made its first flight on August 16, 1952 powered by Proteus 625s. This was followed by the second prototype on December 23, 1953 which was powered by Proteus 705s and had an all-up weight of 155,000 lb. BOAC then amended its order to 15 Series 102 aircraft basically similar to the second prototype and 18 Series 312 Britannias incorporating a 10 ft. 3 in. (3.1m) stretch to the fuselage. Because of continuing problems with the Proteus engines which flamed-out repeatedly, the entry of the Britannia 102 into airline service was delayed for almost a year and the first revenue flight did not take place until February 1, 1957 when the type entered service between London

Nicholas Morant for CPAL

and Johannesburg.

The stretched 300 series prototype G-ANCA did not fly until July 31, 1956. This aircraft had a total weight of 175,000 lbs. and with a range of over 4,000 miles, could carry up to 139 passengers across the North Atlantic at 357 mph. BOAC started trans-Atlantic service with Britannia 312s on December 19, 1957 — less than a year before pure-jet service commenced on this route and, as a result, the Britannia was to have an extremely short life as front line equipment. CPAL acquired its first of six Series 314 Britannias on April 1, 1958 and the last was delivered by July 3, 1958. They soon displaced the DC-6Bs on the majority of the long haul routes and quickly established a reputation for quietness and comfort. Being 50 mph faster than the DC-6B, schedules could be improved slightly but because

of the unreliable electrical systems in the Britannias, service delays were frequent. CPAL leased two Britannia 324s in late 1959 to provide additional capacity on its international routes but these were returned to Britain in early 1961 when the first DC-8-43s were obtained. CPAL's Britannia 314s were quickly displaced from the main routes as the DC-8s became available. Attempts were made to utilize them on the airline's northern routes but they proved to be unsuitable. On the transcontinental service, the Britannia simply could not compete with Trans-Canada Air Lines' DC-8s and the last 314 was sold in February 1966 soon after BOAC withdrew the last of its Britannias. Because of indecision and delays, this fine aircraft had appeared too close to the start of the pure jet era and only 85 Britannias were built. Several aircraft of this type are still

flying in freight service, primarily in the Caribbean area.

Aircraft	Bristol Britannia 314
Year of first flight	1952
Engines	Four Bristol Proteus 761 turbo-props (4,450 ehp)
Wingspan	142 ft 3 in
Length	124 ft 3 in
Height	37 ft 6 in
Weight empty	92,000 lb
Maximum take-off weight	180,000
Cruising speed	357 mph
Range	4,268 miles
Crew	3
Passengers	139 (89 in CPAL service)

▲ Bristol Britannias CF-CZB *Empress of Vancouver* and CF-CZA *Empress of Buenos Aires* seen inside the newly constructed Britannia Hangar at Vancouver in May 1958. Although initially numbered in the 420 series, the Britannias were later renumbered from 522 to 528.

▲ Two DC-8-43s seen at the old Vancouver Airport Terminal in 1961. DC-8-43 CF-CPG, delivered to CPAL on November 11, 1961 was the first commercial aircraft to exceed the speed of sound which it achieved while being tested by Douglas personnel prior to delivery to CPAL.

In 1952, Boeing decided to proceed with a civil passenger jet aircraft and this caused much concern at Douglas which had been preparing jet transport proposals since 1947. With the DC-6 and DC-7 selling well, and the possibility of re-engining the latter with turbo-prop engines, the Company did not want to engage in what could prove to be a costly mistake. However, by 1955 all signs were that Boeing had designed and constructed an excellent aircraft and on June 7, 1955 Douglas announced that the organization was preparing designs for a jetliner. In August, these designs were unveiled showing an aircraft very similar in general concept to the Boeing 707 except that the 30 degree wing sweepback was five degrees less than that of the 707. On October 13, 1955 Pan American ordered 20 DC-8s and 20 Boeing 707s and the race was on!

Douglas just managed to find the $25 million necessary for the prototype and, with progress payments from customers, had sufficient financing to take the DC-8 through to certification. Because of Boeing's lead-time, the first DC-8 did not become available until about a year after the first 707s. Nevertheless, Douglas offered both domestic and

intercontinental versions from more or less the beginning of the project and in this way the company picked up many orders which might have otherwise gone to Boeing. The first domestic DC-8 — the Series 10 — had its initial flight on May 30, 1958, was certificated on August 31, 1959 and almost immediately began service with Delta and United. With a range of 4,300 miles, the Series 10 could cross the Atlantic non-stop from east to west if weather conditions were suitable but it was not until Douglas introduced the Series 30 with a range of 5,970 miles that the Company had a truly intercontinental airliner. This variant first flew on February 21, 1959 and received its certificate of airworthiness on February 1, 1960 just before joining Pan American.

The DC-8-40 had the same airframe as the DC-8-30 except that the Pratt & Whitney JT4A-11 turbojets were replaced with Rolls-Royce Conway 509 turbofans — the first application of the turbofan to an airliner. This series made its first flight July 23, 1959 and proved to be quieter, more powerful and more economical than earlier DC-8s. Despite these attractive features, sales of the Series 40 were limited

to CPAL, Air Canada and Alitalia and consequently only 32 aircraft of this type were built. No doubt the new technology combined with a non-American engine builder discouraged American airlines from purchasing the series. CPAL obtained six DC-8-43s between February 1961 and October 1965. One of these, CF-CPG, was the first commercial aircraft to exceed the speed of sound when it was being tested by Douglas personnel prior to delivery in November, 1961. The DC-8-43s served on all CPAL's international and transcontinental routes and were operated for 20 years until they were sold off because their fuel consumption did not compare favourably with later generation competitors.

The Series 40 DC-8 was followed by the Series 50. Equipped with the Pratt & Whitney JTD-3 turbofan, this version made its first flight on December 20, 1960, receiving certification on May 1, 1961. A total of 141 Series 50 DC-8s was produced and CPAL operated three of these aircraft. DC-8-53 CF-CPM was purchased to replace Series 43, CF-CPK which had been written off in Tokyo Bay on March 4, 1966. Series 51, CF-CPN was leased for a 12 month period from October 1, 1966 to handle

increased traffic and, when this aircraft was returned, it was replaced with DC-8-55F CF-CPT. With a redesigned wing, Series 50 aircraft had considerably less drag than earlier DC-8s and the range of later models in the series was 7,000 miles.

Until 1966, all DC-8s had the same fuselage dimensions capable of seating up to 179 passengers. While Douglas had accommodated prospective customers in regard to engines, it had not altered the basic design of the aircraft's body and, as a result, sales were lost to Boeing which was offering the 707 in various configurations. Passenger traffic was increasing and airlines were demanding aircraft capable of carrying greater passenger loads and on April 5, 1965 Douglas announced plans for a stretched version of the DC-8, to be known as the Super Sixty series. Douglas had established an excellent reputation for successfully stretching its aircraft, a technique dating back to the DC-2 which had evolved into the DC-3 in this manner. It is therefore surprising that it took so long to accomplish the stretch of the DC-8. The first lengthened aircraft was a DC-8-61 which made its initial flight on March 14, 1966. This version was 36 ft. 8 in. (11.2m) longer

than the standard DC-8 which permitted passenger accommodation to be increased to 259 seats. This was followed by the Series 62 which had only a 6 ft. 8 in. (2.03m) stretch but was fitted with redesigned wings and an increased fuel capacity. The final DC-8 was the Series 63 which was a marriage of the Series 61 fuselage and the Series 62 wings. This type made its first flight on April 10, 1967 and five were acquired by CPAL between January 1968 and November 1972. In spite of being extremely noisy and requiring a longer runway than its contemporaries, the Series 63 aircraft proved to be efficient movers of large numbers of passengers until rising fuel costs rendered them uneconomic. CP Air's five Series 63s served into the 1980s and the first to be sold was CF-CPL which went to Commacorp in April 1982. This organization has re-equipped a total of 110 Super Sixty DC-8s with fuel efficient CFM56 turbofans which considerably reduce the take-off run of the aircraft while creating less noise. CP Air sold its remaining DC-8s to Worldways, a charter flight organization operating from Toronto, in May and June 1983.

Considering the fact that the Boeing 367-80, the

fore-runner of the 707 was rolled out over a year before Douglas committed itself to the DC-8 project, the company did well to produce and sell a total of 556 DC-8s. The aircraft built a solid reputation for dependability and the airframe was extremely strong when compared with other airliners.

▲ Douglas DC-8-63 CF-CPP at Vancouver's new terminal. This aircraft was obtained on January 31, 1968 and served with CPAL until May 1983 when it was sold to Worldways of Toronto. A total of 233 DC-8s were in airline service in late 1986.

Aircraft	Douglas DC-8 Srs 43	Douglas DC-8 Srs 63
Year of first flight	1959	
Engines	Four Rolls-Royce Conways (17,500 lb thrust)	Four Pratt & Whitney JT3Ds (19,000 lb thrust)
Wingspan	142 ft 5 in	148 ft 5 in
Length	150 ft 6 in	187 ft 5 in
Height	42 ft 4 in	42 ft 5 in
Weight empty	132,425 lb	141,900 lb
Maximum take-off weight	315,000 lb	350,000 lb
Cruising speed	580 mph	583 mph
Range with maximum payload and no reserves	6,100 miles	4,500 miles
Crew	4	4
Maximum passenger capacity	179	259

▲ Boeing 707-138B N791SA was wet leased from Standard Airways of Seattle on October 15, 1967. Because CPAL had no flight crews cleared to fly the 707, only the cabin crew was provided by the airline. The aircraft was written off at Vancouver on February 7, 1968.

The early success of the de Havilland Comet convinced the Boeing Airplane Company that its future lay not with developed versions of its Stratocruiser but with an entirely new airliner of advanced design and powered by four turbojets. After considerable research to decide the best design for a new aircraft, on May 20, 1952 Boeing announced that it would build the 367-80 aircraft powered by four turbojets slung below 35 degree swept back wings. The prototype was expected to cost $20 million which, at that time, was the largest financial risk ever undertaken by an aircraft constructor.

Roll out of the 367-80 was at Renton, Washington on May 14, 1954 and the first flight took place on July 15th. During taxiing trials, part of the main undercarriage broke through the wing, thus delaying the first flight but, apart from this, development proceeded smoothly and the USAAF ordered 29 tanker aircraft of this design. The first commercial order was announced on October 13, 1955 when Pan American ordered 20 Boeing 707s and 20 DC-8s but, after the order was announced, Boeing decided to redesign the body of the aircraft to provide an increased diameter of four inches—thus providing minimal space for six abreast economy seating. Airlines were able to specify either the standard cabin length of 144 ft. 6 in. (44m) or the slightly shorter cabin of 134 ft. 6 in. (41m). These versions were known respectively as the 707-120 and the 707-138. In the event, only Qantas selected the shorter version and it was one of these which Canadian Pacific Air Lines leased from Standard Airways in 1967.

Because the USAAF had ordered its KC-135 tanker aircraft ahead of Pan American, deliveries of the first 707s were slow and the first 707-121 did not fly until December 20, 1957. Although intended for domestic service, Pan American introduced the 707-120 to service on the New York - Paris route on October 26, 1958. With a full payload of 181 passengers and no reserves, the 707-120 had a maximum range of 3,217 miles (5,177 km). The 707-320 was the intercontinental version of the aircraft and this made its first flight on January 11, 1959. It had an 8 ft. 5 in. stretch to the fuselage, greater wingspan and uprated JT4A series engines. The 320 was followed by the 420, powered by Rolls Royce Conway turbofans and it entered service with BOAC in May 1960. The 320B was fitted with JT3D turbofans as was the final 707 version, the 320C which was a convertible passenger/cargo aircraft equipped with a large cargo door forward on the left side. When production ceased in 1980, a total of 962 Boeing 707s had been constructed.

Aircraft	Boeing 707-138
Year of first flight (707-138)	1959 (First 707 flight 1957)
Engines	Four Pratt & Whitney JT3Cs (13,000 lb thrust)
Wingspan	130 ft 10 in
Length	134 ft 6 in
Height	38 ft 4 in
Weight empty	120,000 lb
Maximum take-off weight	240,000 lb
Cruising speed	590 mph
Range with maximum payload and no reserves	3,217 miles
Crew	4
Maximum passenger capacity	181

CPAL

▲ CP Air's first aircraft to be delivered in orange livery was Boeing 737 CF-CPB which was accepted on October 22, 1968. This photograph shows Boeing 737-217 CF-CPU prior to its delivery to People Express in May 1983. In 1985, the Boeing 737 achieved sales of 282 aircraft or 44% of all large aircraft ordered by airlines in the western world. A further 216 were ordered in 1986 and within the next year or so the 737 will surpass the Boeing sales record of 1831 examples and become the best selling commercial jet aircraft of all time.

▲ Boeing 737-2A3 C-FEPO was purchased by Eastern Provincial Airways in 1970. This livery has now been replaced by Canadian Pacific Air Lines' blue, white and red colour scheme.

When the Boeing 737 was first announced in February 1965 its main competitors, the BAC One Eleven and the Douglas DC-9, were well ahead of it in the race for sales. Indeed, the One Eleven was about to enter commercial service and the DC-9 was on the verge of making its maiden flight. However, Boeing made the decision to go ahead with the short haul jet and, since then, sales of over 1,600 of the various versions of the 737 have been made.

In order to provide as much commonality with the Boeing 707 and 727, the 737 was designed with a fuselage having the same overall width as these aircraft. It was thus the first short haul jet to feature six abreast seating and allowed airlines to standardize on seats, galleys, etc. For the first time in U.S. aircraft history a non-American airline was the launch customer — this being Lufthansa which ordered 21 of what became the 737-100. Originally, Boeing had proposed seating for 60 to 85 passengers but at Lufthansa's request had stretched the design

to hold 100 seats and this gave the aircraft a greater capacity than either the One Eleven or the DC-9 models then available. The first American order was announced on April 5, 1965 when United Airlines contracted for 40 of the 200 series which first flew on August 18, 1967. In this version the fuselage was lengthened by 6 ft. 4 in. (1.9m) which allowed up to 119 passengers to be carried. In the high density configuration, 130 passengers can be carried.

The 737-100 and 200 versions obtained type certification in December 1967 and Lufthansa introduced the type into service on its European routes on February 10, 1968. Only 30 of the 100 series were constructed and the majority of the 737s in service are various versions of the 200 series. United Airlines placed the -200 in service on April 28, 1968. Later the same year the 737-200C, a convertible passenger/cargo version capable of carrying the same size pallets as the 707 and 727, made its first flight and a 737-200 QC "quick change"

version was made available. In late 1969, the Advanced 737-200 with redesigned leading edge slats and flaps for improved take-off and landing performance, together with more powerful 15,500 lb. thrust. JT8D-15 engines and fully automatic brakes, was announced. This type made its first flight on April 15, 1971 and was introduced to service by All Nippon Airways of Japan. In addition, an extended range 737-200 ER with 15 percent more fuel capacity was introduced having a range of 2,340 miles with maximum load.

A later development of the 737 is the 300 series which incorporates a further fuselage stretch of 8 ft. 8 in. (2.6m) allowing an additional 20 passengers to be carried. Powered by two 20,000 lb. thrust CFM56-3 turbofans and with a full load range of 2,540 miles, Boeing initiated the 737-300 in March 1981 and the maiden flight was made in February 1984. Airline deliveries commenced in November 1984. By October 1986, Boeing had received orders for 1,130 737-100s and 200s of which 1,125 had

been delivered. Because many airlines had standardized on the 737-200, this model remains in production at a rate of one and a half aircraft a month. A further 491 Boeing 737-300s had been ordered and 153 had been delivered. Boeing is producing twelve 737-300s a month. The latest development of the Boeing 737 is the 400 series aircraft. This is a further stretch of the fuselage by 114 in. and the aircraft will carry up to 156 passengers in an all-economy layout. First flight is expected in early 1988 and Boeing has 60 firm orders for the type.

CP Air took delivery of its first Boeing 737 CF-CPB on October 22, 1968. This was the first aircraft in the airline's orange livery and CP Air was the first Canadian airline to introduce the 737-200 into revenue service. Since then, a further 24 737-200s of various types have been acquired and the mergers with Eastern Provincial Airways and Nordair have brought in a further 16 737-200s into the fleet. Nordair has three leased 737-200s and CP Air leased

two 737-200s in late 1985.

In 1983, the airline re-negotiated an alteration to a previous order for four Boeing 767s. Under this revision, CP Air was allowed to cancel its order for the 767s and to replace this with an order for ten 737-300s. The first of these, C-FCPG, was received from Boeing on April 12, 1985 and entered service on April 17th between Vancouver and Edmonton. Two other 737-300s were received in 1985 and two more were delivered in April 1986. However, the airline has now decided to standardize on the 737-200 to operate its domestic services and the five Boeing 737-300s left the fleet by the end of 1986.

▲ Boeing 737-317 C-FCPI was the second 300 series 737 to be delivered to CP Air. In this scene it is shown in the short-lived Attaché livery of ivory and grey. In June 1986, the aircraft was sold to the GPA Group of Shannon, Ireland.

Aircraft	Boeing 737-200 ER	Boeing 737-242C	Boeing 737-300
Year of first flight	1967	1968	1984
Engines	Two Pratt & Whitney JT8D	Two Pratt & Whitney JT8D	Two CFM56-3
	(16,000 lb thrust)	(14,500 lb thrust)	(20,000 lb thrust)
Wingspan	93 ft 0 in	93 ft 0 in	94 ft 9 in
Length	100 ft 0 in	100 ft 0 in	109 ft 7 in
Height	37 ft 0 in	37 ft 0 in	36 ft 6 in
Weight empty	66,700 lb	63,700 lb	72,100 lb
Maximum take-off weight	124,500 lb	117,000 lb	135,000 lb
Cruising speed	480 mph	480 mph	495 mph
Range	2,400 miles	2,600 miles	2,540 miles
Crew	2	2	2
Passengers	109	120	138

▲ CP Air operated four Boeing 727-117s between 1970 and 1977. In this shot the first 727, CF-CPN is seen prior to its delivery to Vancouver in March 1970. It was sold to National Aircraft Leasing of Los Angeles in May 1977.

In February 1956, the Boeing Airplane Company began project studies to develop a short to medium range jet aircraft to be a partner for the long range Boeing 707. From the beginning, it was decided to provide maximum commonality with the 707 and the design was finalized on September 18, 1959. The launch of the 727 was announced on December 5, 1960 with initial orders of 40 aircraft each for Eastern and United Airlines. The first production aircraft flew on February 9, 1963 and was certificated on December 24, 1963. Eastern Airlines flew the first commercial flight on February 1, 1964 and the 727-100 soon developed a reputation for reliability and economy of operation. Such was the popularity of the 727 that approximately 100 aircraft were

built each year and the one thousandth 727 was delivered on January 4, 1974 — just less than ten years after the type entered service. This was the first time that a purely commercial jet aircraft had reached such a sales figure although the 707 had sold far more than this if military variants are taken into account.

The 727-100 could operate over stage routes of up to 1700 miles with 131 passengers and was soon joined by the 727-100C convertible passenger/ cargo version. This had a strengthened floor and first flew on December 30, 1965. A 727-100QC version which could be "quick changed" from cargo to passenger configuration in 30 minutes was also

supplied. With increasing passenger traffic there was a requirement for a larger capacity 727 and in August 1965 the company announced that a 727-200 with seating for up to 189 passengers would be produced. The fuselage on the new model was lengthened by 20 ft. (6.1m) and this was achieved by inserting equal length sections fore and aft of the wings. Northeast Airlines was the first customer for the 200 which flew for the first time on July 27, 1967. It entered service with Northeast Airlines on the Montreal-New York-Miami route on December 14, 1967.

Development of the 727 continued with the introduction of the Advanced 727-200 in 1970. This

series was equipped with additional fuel capacity, improved noise suppression and the "wide body" look in the cabin. Subsquently, it was planned to develop a 727-300 with a fuselage stretch of a further 18 ft. 4 in. (5.6m) but this proposal was replaced by the decision to proceed with the completely new Boeing 757 in 1975. Nevertheless, the Boeing 727 has had an amazing production history. The last 727 rolled off the production line in 1984, twenty years after the type had first entered service. By then, sales had totalled 1831 aircraft of which 407 were 727-100s. In addition, one 727-100 test aircraft was constructed.

With such an illustrious career with many of the better known airlines in the world, it is rather strange that the 727 did not have a more distinguished record with CP Air. Four 727-117s were delivered in 1970 and 1971 but all were disposed of in 1977. As the 117s left the fleet, two 727-217s were received but by 1982 these aircraft were being leased to other operators. Both were then sold to the U.K. operator Dan Air. The 727 did not suit Canadian Pacific's route network and they were relatively fuel inefficient. They did not have the range and carrying capacity for the airline's international routes and yet they were too large for the company's domestic services. Because of these factors, it was decided to dispose of the 727s and to standardize on the Boeing 737 on the domestic network.

Aircraft	Boeing 727-100	Boeing 727-200
Year of first flight	1963	1967
Engines	Three P & W	Three P & W
	JT8D-9A	JT8D-17
	(14,500 lb thrust)	(17,400 lb thrust)
Wingspan	108 ft 0 in	108 ft 0 in
Length	133 ft 2 in	153 ft 2 in
Height	34 ft 0 in	34 ft 0 in
Operating weight empty	87,600 lb	100,000 lb
Weight maximum take-off	169,000 lb	209,500 lb
Cruising speed	605 mph	599 mph
Range	1,900 miles	2,800 miles
Crew	3	3
Passengers	131	189

▲ Boeing 727-217 C-GCPA was one of two examples acquired in 1975. Like the 727-117s, they proved unsuitable to CP Air's route network and C-GCPA was leased to the British operator Dan Air in March 1982 and sold to that airline on December 1, 1983. At the end of 1986, nearly 1700 Boeing 727s remain in airline service.

▲ CP Air's first Boeing 747 CF-CRA seen flying off Seattle prior to its delivery to the airline on November 16, 1973. Note the original registration letters. Soon after commencing service, it became C-FCRA and subsequently was renamed *Empress of Japan*.

Long haul airline travel was changed dramatically by the April 13, 1966 announcement by Boeing that Pan American had signed a $520 million contract for 25 aircraft each capable of carrying between 350 and 490 passengers. The new aircraft — the Boeing 747 — was to have a cabin 20 feet wide, seven feet wider than anything then in existence and yet, with Pratt & Whitney JT9D engines producing 41,000 lb. thrust, the new aircraft would not require a longer runway than that used by a Boeing 707. Although the aircraft could operate from the bulk of the world's major airports, the majority of the airports did not have the facilities to handle aircraft with the capacity of the 747 and the late 1960s and 1970s saw many terminals being ex-

panded to handle the huge surges in passenger traffic which the new aircraft would create.

In order to construct the aircraft, Boeing built a new plant at Everett, Washington, 30 miles north of Seattle but rather surprisingly no prototype aircraft was used. Instead, five development aircraft were built and the first of these was rolled out on September 30, 1968. The maiden flight was originally planned for December 17, 1968, the 65th anniversary of the Wright Brothers first flight but this was delayed and did not take place until February 9, 1969. During the certification program it became apparent that the JT9D engine consumed approximately five percent more fuel than was originally forecasted and attempts to rectify this problem delayed the introduction of the type into commercial service. It was found that, as power was applied, the engines adopted a slightly nose down attitude which caused the turbine blades to rub on the engine casing and this, in turn, led to the ovalization of the engine. Eventually, the problem was solved by moving the

rear attachment point of the engine further forward but by this time more than 20 aircraft had been completed although only the five development 747s were equipped with engines. The aircraft received its certificate of airworthiness on December 30, 1969 and it was decided to release the first 30 Boeing 747s in unmodified form to the airlines and that these would be retroactively fitted with new engine mountings as these became available. Pan American was thus able to introduce the 747 to commercial service between New York and London on January 22, 1970 although the airline experienced considerable difficulties with engines either failing to start or overheating while taxiing. On its first commercial flight with the 747, Pan American suffered from both problems and the flight arrived in London six hours late. The media had a field day but eventually the problems were overcome and after a year in service the 747 had become one of the most reliable aircraft in operation and one with great passenger appeal. True, the fuel price increases have meant that more seats have had to be squeezed

into the available space but many passengers have fond memories of the upstairs bar that some airlines, including CP Air, fitted into their 747s. Canadian Pacific, proud of its railway origins, had the bar in C-FCRA equipped with various items of railway memorabilia. Alas, the price of fuel precludes such luxuries and the lounges were replaced by sleeper seats for 12 first class passengers.

When the 747 had its original faults corrected and it proved to be a reliable aircraft, Boeing began developing the type's full potential. The original design, the 747-100, was certificated at a maximum weight of 710,000 lb. and this was increased to 735,000 lb. with the 63rd aircraft to be constructed. The 747B, with more powerful engines, increased range and an all-up weight of 775,000 lb., but with the dimensions of the 747-100, flew for the first time on October 11, 1970 and as the 747-200 was introduced into commercial service by KLM in early 1971. At the same time, the 747SR was introduced for high density, short range routes, a 747-200F

was available for freight service and the 747-200C was a convertible passenger/cargo aircraft. The 747-200B became the standard aircraft and was at first powered by Pratt & Whitney JT9D 45,000 lb. thrust engines but subsequently became available with General Electric CF6-50D 51,000 lb. thrust engines and the 747 made its first flight with these new engines in June 1973.

In August 1973 Boeing announced the special performance 747SP as an alternative to the long range DC-10-30. With a fuselage 47 feet shorter than the basic 747 and a take-off weight of only 660,000 lb. the SP is capable of flying extremely long range sectors non-stop. It first flew on July 4, 1975, was certificated on February 4, 1976, and on its delivery flight to Capetown for South African Airways, one of the 747SPs flew 10,290 miles and landed with more than two hours fuel still aboard.

Other versions of the 747 have included the 200B Combi which entered service in 1974 with passenger accommodation in the forward compartments and cargo in the rear of the main cabin. This was followed in 1976 by the first 747-200B with Rolls Royce RB-211 engines offering initially 48,000 lb. thrust and allowing the Jumbo to be certificated for a take-off weight of 820,000 lb. Subsequently, the introduction of 53,000 lb. thrust engines enabled Boeing to increase take-off weight to 833,000 lb. and this led to the development of the 747-300 with the stretched upper deck. By extending the "bubble" rearwards by 23½ feet, it has been possible to increase the maximum capacity from 32 to 69 passengers and thus improve capacity of the aircraft by almost 10 percent for only a two percent increase in weight. The new 747 flew for the first time in October 1982 and was certificated on March 4, 1983. Currently, Boeing is developing the 747-400 which is a long range version of the 747-300 capable of carrying 412 passengers, non-stop from London to Singapore or Tokyo to London. On a seat mileage basis, aerodynamic refinement will allow the 747-400 to operate 13 - 15 percent more economically than the 747-300 and 18 to 21 percent more efficiently than the 747-200. First flight of the 747-400 is scheduled for the last quarter of 1987. By October 1986, orders for all models of the 747 totalled an appropriate 747 of which 635 had been delivered. The current production rate is three aircraft per month.

CP Air purchased four 747-200s from Boeing and these were delivered between November 1973 and December 1974. They operated primarily on the airline's long haul services to Amsterdam, Tokyo, Hong Kong and Sydney but in October 1985 it was announced that the 747s were being sold to Pakistan International Airlines and in return CPAL acquired this carrier's four DC-10-30s. The first 747, C-FCRE, was handed over to its new owners on December 18, 1985. At the same time, DC-10-30 PK-BBL was obtained. C-FCRB left CPAL service on May 1, 1986, C-FCRA was transferred on September 20th and the last 747, C-FCRD was exchanged on October 25, 1986.

▲ Boeing 747-217B C-FCRD *Empress of Canada* at Vancouver in late 1985 showing the airline's Expo 86 livery. In addition to the *Empress of Canada*, Boeing 737 C-FCPV, the *Empress of Vancouver*, McDonnell Douglas DC-10-10 N1836U, the *Empress of Santiago* and DC-10-30 C-GCPD the *Empress of British Columbia* were given this special livery to publicize British Columbia's World Fair.

Aircraft	Boeing 747-200B
Year of first flight (747B)	1970
Engines	Four Pratt & Whitney JT9D (47,670 lb thrust)
Wingspan	195 ft 8 in
Length	231 ft 4 in
Height	63 ft 5 in
Weight empty	370,100 lb
Maximum take-off weight	776,500 lb
Cruising speed	550 mph
Range	5,990 miles
Crew	3
Passengers	409

▲ Prior to deciding to concentrate on the Boeing 737 for domestic services and the McDonnell DC-10-30 on international routes, CP Air cross-leased three DC-10-30s with United Air Lines for three DC-10-10s for use within Canada. As can be seen, the UAL DC-10-10s retained their U.S. registrations. Currently they are being used primarily on the shorter north-Atlantic services and between Vancouver and Honolulu.

The origin of the Douglas DC-10 can be traced back to April 1966 when American Airlines circulated to seven American aircraft manufacturers an outline specification for an aircraft which market research indicated would be required in the 1970s. This exercise led to the development of the DC-10 and the Lockheed Tristar. American Airlines originally envisaged a twin engined design but with the advent of the DC-10 program in 1968, both American and United ordered a total of 55 three-engine jets. The

design was unusual in that the third engine was faired into the tail near the base of the fin.

The construction of five development aircraft started at the Douglas factory in January 1969 and the prototype flew for the first time at Long Beach on August 10, 1970. This was a DC-10-10 designed to operate over stage lengths of between 300 and 3600 miles and by mid-1971 all five development aircraft were flying. The first deliveries were made to American and United Airlines on July 29, 1971, the day the aircraft was certificated, and both airlines commenced service with this type in mid-August 1971. The aircraft, with its accommodation for just over 200 persons, soon became known for its quietness and smoke-free operation, unlike many of the first generation jets.

As with the DC-8, Douglas made long range versions of the DC-10 from early in the project's life and to this end the series 30 and 40 models were turbofan powered by General Electric CF6-50 and Pratt & Whitney JT9D, respectively. In addition to

their uprated engines, these long range versions had an extended wingspan, carried more fuel and their all up weight was increased from the original 386,500 lb. of the DC-10-10 to 572,000 lb. To support this increased weight, additional landing gear was fitted in the belly of the aircraft. The Series 40 flew for the first time on February 28, 1972 and the Series 30 prototype made its maiden flight on June 21, 1972. The future for the DC-10 looked assured. However, in November 1971 as a DC-10-10 left Buffalo, a cargo door blew open. Despite critical damage to the aircraft, the captain's judicious use of the engines enabled him to land safely. Then, on March 3, 1974 a DC-10-10 of THY, the Turkish airline, crashed at Ermononville, outside Paris when "... in flight depressurization" destroyed the controls and all aboard perished. Finally, an American Airlines DC-10-10 shed an engine on take off from Chicago on May 25, 1979, following which all DC-10s were grounded by the U.S. Federal Aviation Authority until the cause of that crash was determined. This grounding lasted 36 days and it was established

that faulty installation procedures for replacing engines had been implemented and DC-10s were cleared to resume operations. Understandably, many passengers showed reluctance to fly on any DC-10 even though the problems related only to the DC-10-10. To foster passenger confidence, operators of the long range versions had their cabin attendants identify their aircraft specifically as DC-10-30s or DC-10-40s. Once the problems with cargo doors and engine mountings were solved, DC-10s of all types have proven to be safe, reliable and comfortable aircraft.

KLM introduced the DC-10-30 into service in 1973 and development of the type continued. During 1973, the series 10CF and 30CF convertible passenger/freight versions became available, capable of carrying 155,700 lb of freight. These aircraft are fitted with a large cargo door forward of the wing on the left side of the plane. The development of the 30CF series was extremely important to McDonnell Douglas as the USAF was looking for an Advanced Tanker/Cargo Aircraft to supplement its

large fleet of KC-135 tanker aircraft. As a freight version of the Lockheed L-1011 was not produced and the Galaxy C-5A was out of production, the choice was between the DC-10 and the Boeing 747. On December 19, 1977 the DC-10 was announced as the successful contender and on November 20, 1978 the first two KC-10A Extenders were ordered. Originally it was intended to order 36 aircraft of this type but additional orders in November 1979, February 1981 and January 1982 were placed for four, six and four aircraft, respectively. At the end of 1982 it was decided to expand the program to a total of 60 Extenders. The first KC-10A flew at Long Beach on April 16, 1980 and the initial aircraft to reach the USAF was delivered on March 17, 1981. With an aircraft of such dimensions it is possible to carry out extemely lengthy missions and in October 1982 one KC-10 accompanied six F-15C Eagles on a non-stop flight of 7,000 miles from Japan to Florida. Each fighter was refuelled seven times while the parent Extender took on fuel from another aircraft of the same type and two KC-135s. The flight took

15 hours to complete and in addition to carrying 59 support personnel as passengers, the KC-10A carried 55,000 lb. of cargo. Although the number of Extenders ordered each year is small, it keeps the DC-10 line open and has allowed the company to solicit orders for the aircraft until the MD-11 becomes available. A total of 385 civil aircraft has been ordered and 379 have been delivered. In addition, 46 KC-10s have been built.

CPAL has recently expanded its DC-10 fleet to 12 aircraft with the exchange of its Boeing 747s for four DC-10-30s from Pakistan International Airlines. As a result, CPAL now shares the distinction with the Brazilian airline Varig of having the world's largest DC-10-30 fleet. However, three of CPAL's DC-10-30s are leased to United Airlines until 1987 and have been replaced by three United DC-10-10s.

▲ The first aircraft to appear in CPAL's new livery was McDonnell Douglas DC-10-30 C-FCRE *Empress of Canada* which formerly served with Pakistan International Airlines. It was obtained on December 17, 1985, refurbished and unveiled in the new livery on January 12, 1986.

The MD-11, which is to replace the DC-10, will make its first flight in 1989. In December, 1986, it was announced that McDonnell Douglas had received 52 firm orders from 12 airlines for the new aircraft which will have a fuselage 18 ft 6 in longer than the DC-10-30, a two man flight deck, revised wings and updated engines. Of the 12 airlines ordering the MD-11, only one does not already operate the DC-10.

Aircraft	McDonnell Douglas DC-10-10	McDonnell Douglas DC-10-30	McDonnell Douglas DC-10-30-ER
Year of first flight	1971	1972	1980
Engines	Three GE CF6 (39,300 lb thrust)	Three GE CF6 (51,800 lb thrust)	Three GE CF6 (53,200 lb thrust)
Wingspan	155 ft 4 in	165 ft 4 in	165 ft 4 in
Length	181 ft 5 in	182 ft 1 in	182 ft 1 in
Height	58 ft 1 in	58 ft 1 in	58 ft 1 in
Weight empty	240,500 lb	270,000 lb	273,900
Weight maximum take-off	440,000 lb	572,000 lb	590,000 lb
Cruising speed	542 mph	549 mph	549 mph
Range	3,915 miles	6,702 miles	7,140 miles
Crew	3	3	3
Passengers	259	281	281

The British Aerospace 748 was the last design of the A.V. Roe and Company Limited, the makers of the Anson, Lancaster, Vulcan and other famous military aircraft, before Avro became part of Hawker Siddeley in 1963. Subsequently, Hawker Siddeley was incorporated into British Aerospace but the aircraft has been made by all three manufacturers and the Avro, Hawker Siddeley and British Aerospace 748s are all basically the same aircraft although much development has been undertaken since the first production Avro 748 made its initial flight on June 24, 1960. Avro had elected to re-enter the commercial aircraft manufacturing field after the infamous Sandys White Paper of 1957 indicated that the RAF would require no more new manned war planes. Avro decided to design a short-haul, twin turbo-prop, pressurized commercial transport as a suitable replacement for the DC-3. To keep costs down, as Avro had no government funding, and to ensure that the resulting aircraft would have the highest possible utilization, the company,

wherever possible, incorporated parts that had been already proven in other aircraft. Thus the Rolls Royce Dart turboprop was incorporated into the low wing, 36 passenger design. The second prototype flew on April 10, 1961 and British certification for the Series 1 production model was awarded in January 1962 with the type going into commercial service with Skyways Coach Air on its short routes across the English Channel shortly afterwards.

The company perceived a need for the 748 to be cleared for higher gross weights than that offered by the Series 1 aircraft which was powered by 1880 ehp Darts and eventually approved for an operating weight of 39,500 lb. On November 6, 1961 the second prototype re-engined with 2,150 ehp Dart engines made its first flight and it subsequently was approved for operation at weights of up to 44,495 lb. After 18 Series 1 production aircraft had been built, construction switched to the Series 2 and the first production model of the more powerful

aircraft made its initial flight in August 1962. Improved performance was achieved in 1967 when the Series 2A was introduced powered by 2,280 ehp Darts and in 1977 the Series 2B with a four foot increase in wingspan made its first flight. This model entered production in 1979. Currently, British Aerospace is developing the 748 into the Advanced Turbo Prop airliner capable of carrying 60 passengers.

Licensed production of the 748 has been undertaken by Hindustan Aeronautics of Kanpur, India for the Indian Air Force and Indian Airlines. Total production of all series, including military variants is now over 360 aircraft and the 748 is in worldwide use. Air Maritime had four Series 2As which were used on feeder routes for Eastern Provincial Airway's trunk services. The 748s served Fredericton, Moncton, Saint John, Halifax, Sydney, Charlottetown, St. Pierre and Miquelon.

▲ Air Maritime was founded in 1982 as a wholly-owned subsidiary of Eastern Provincial Airways and operated a fleet of British Aerospace 748s on feeder services to the main EPA trunk routes. Air Atlantic has taken over the Air Maritime services and the 748s are for disposal.

Aircraft	BAe 748 Series 2
Year of first flight (Avro 748)	1960
Engine	Rolls-Royce Dart 532 (2,080 ehp) turbo-props
Wingspan	98 ft 6 in
Length	67 ft 0 in
Height	24 ft 10 in
Operating weight	26,700 lb
Maximum take-off weight	44,495 lb
Cruising speed	278 mph
Range	1,987 miles
Crew	2
Maximum passenger capacity	58

Following World War Two Fokker re-entered the aircraft industry and began refurbishing war surplus DC-3s for airline use. In 1950, the company obtained input from its airline customers on what they wanted for use on their routes. With this information, Fokker designed an aircraft to meet the airlines' requirements and in 1952 outlined the F27 which over the past 30 years has become the non-Communist world's best selling turbo-prop transport aircraft.

The initial F27 design was a circular-section, pressurized fuselage with accommodation for up to 40 passengers. Power was provided by two Rolls-Royce Dart turbo-props and the high-winged aircraft was designed to operate over a range of 300 miles with a full payload. The Netherlands government provided financial assistance for two prototypes and the first of these flew on November 24, 1955 equipped with 1540 ehp Darts. During 1956, a licensing agreement was reached with the Fairchild Engine and Airplane Corporation which subsequently became Fairchild Hiller. This gave the American manufacturer the right to construct F27s for North American customers.

Fokkers' second prototype made its maiden flight on January 31, 1957. This aircraft was powered by 1720 ehp Darts and the fuselage had been stretched by three feet to increase passenger accommodation. It was decided that this would become the standard for subsequent aircraft and the first 36 seat production Friendship flew for the first time on March 23, 1958. In the United States, Fairchild increased the seating capacity to 40 passengers and also increased the fuel capacity to meet North American requirements. The nose was lengthened to accommodate weather radar in the first F27 built at Hagerstown, Pennsylvania which made its maiden flight on April 12, 1958. It received its type certificate on July 16, 1958 and on September 27th the F27 entered service with West Coast Airlines. The first Fokker-built F27 entered service with Aer Lingus on December 15, 1958.

Since then the basic design has undergone continual development but until 1966 all Friendships had the same dimensions and could seat a maximum of 48 passengers. In 1961, Fokker had proposed the Series 500 with a 4 ft. 11 in. fuselage stretch but no orders were realized until 1966 when the French government ordered 15 aircraft to replace DC-3s in the domestic night air mail service. In the meantime, however, Fairchild had proceeded with a stretched version of its own. With a six foot fuselage stretch, the FH227 made its first flight on January 27, 1966. Several secondary airlines in the United States purchased the FH227 and Fairchild produced a total of 79 of these aircraft. In addition, it constructed 128 F27s.

▲ Fairchild Hiller FH-227B C-GNDH seen at Nordair's Montreal base. Nordair has five aircraft of this type which were built in 1966 and 1967.

Aircraft	Fairchild FH-227E
Year of first flight (FH-227)	1966
Engines	Two 2,300 shp Rolls-Royce Dart turbo-props
Wingspan	95 ft 2 in
Length	83 ft 8 in
Height	27 ft 7 in
Weight empty	30,100 lb
Gross weight	45,500 lb
Cruising speed	260 mph
Range	1,350 miles
Crew	2
Passengers	42

To follow on from its very successful Constellation program, Lockheed produced the L-188 Electra which proved to be a financial disaster for the company as the aircraft was introduced at a time when the pure-jet was every major airlines' requirement. The Electra thus became the only major US airliner to date to use turboprop propulsion.

The design originated in 1954 as a result of a request by American Airlines for a short to medium range transport for US operations and having a larger capacity than the very successful Vickers Viscount. Lockheed eventually managed to sell its design to American "off the drawing board" in June 1955 when it was announced that the airline would purchase 35 Electras. Soon afterwards it was announced that Eastern would take another 40 of these 100 seaters and the future looked bright for the aircraft. Other airlines including National, Braniff, Northwest Orient, Western, KLM, Ansett, Trans Australian Airlines and Qantas ordered the Electra and by the time the prototype made its first

flight on December 6, 1957, orders totalled 144. During 1958, three more prototypes joined the testing program and the Electra received type approval on August 22, 1958. Eastern introduced the type to commercial service on January 12, 1959 New York and Miami. American started service with the Electra between New York and Chicago on January 23, 1959. Two basic designs were produced, the L-188A intended primarily for US domestic operations and the L-188C with an additional fuel capacity and designed for long range service.

On March 25, 1960 the Federal Aviation Authority, acting as a result of two Electras losing wings while in flight, restricted the aircraft's top speed to 275 knots and almost immediately afterwards reduced this to 225 knots. Comprehensive investigation revealed that in hard landings the engine mount could be damaged. Engine oscillation could then develop and this could result in complete structural failure. Lockheed obtained FAA approval for its structurally modified aircraft on January 5,

1961 and subsequently modified all Electras already delivered or then on the production line. The modified Electra proved to be a robust, reliable aircraft but further orders were not forthcoming and the final and 170th aircraft was completed in January 1961. One of the original prototypes became the initial P-3 Orion maritime reconnaissance aircraft and Lockheed has enjoyed a long and successful production run with this airplane. Possibly the Electra and Britannia might have enjoyed a far greater acceptance had it not been for the pure-jet aircraft. Passengers very rapidly progressed from showing reluctance to boarding aircraft without propellers to showing disdain for aircraft that had them. As a result, Lockheed gave up passenger aircraft construction and only re-entered this market when conditions appeared favourable for the jet-engined L-1011. Unfortunately for Lockheed, the market was insufficient to support the Boeing 747, the DC-10 and the L-1011 and the Tristar production line has been closed.

▲ Nordair's Lockheed L-188C Electra C-GNDZ is one of two such aircraft operated by the company on ice reconnaissance for Environment Canada over the eastern and northern waters.

Aircraft	Lockheed L-188C Electra
Year of first flight	1957
Engines	Four 3,750 shp Allison 501 turbo-props
Wingspan	99 ft 0 in
Length	104 ft 6 in
Height	32 ft 10 in
Basic operating weight	64,620 lb
Gross weight	116,000 lb
Cruising speed	380 mph
Range	4,300 miles
Crew	3

de Havilland Canada has specialized in the design and construction of STOL aircraft for many years and in January 1968 the first steps that were to lead to the DHC-7 were taken. In the mid-1960s the concept of a quiet STOL airliner operating from inner city airports had begun to receive some support and de Havilland Canada proposed a high-wing, four engined, turbo-prop powered, 39 seat airliner which would operate with low noise levels from a 2,000 foot runway. A full-scale mock-up was built but Hawker Siddeley, which then owned de Havilland Canada, showed relatively little interest in the project as it was already producing the HS748 in Britain and was designing the four-engined, jet powered HS146. Canadian government financial support allowed the DHC-7 project to continue and it was announced on October 16, 1972 that two pre-production aircraft were to be built. A worldwide market survey for the type was undertaken and in October 1973, the name Dash 7 was adopted.

The Canadian government bought de Havilland Canada on May 27, 1974 and the following November it was announced that an initial batch of 25 production aircraft would be built. On February 5, 1975 the first prototype was rolled out and on March 27th it made its maiden flight. The second prototype took to the air on June 26, 1975 and the type certificate was granted by the Canadian authorities on May 2, 1977. The first production aircraft was rolled out in June 1977 and was delivered to Rocky Mountain Airways on November 21, 1977. It entered service in February 1978 operating seven daily round trips between Denver and Aspen. Wardair was the first Canadian operator, purchasing the seventh aircraft to be constructed. This was the first Dash 7 equipped with a large cargo door on the port side of the aircraft ahead of the wing. Such aircraft can be operated in a mixed traffic configuration and Wardair operated C-GXVF, the first passenger/cargo Dash 7, out of Yellowknife, taking delivery of the aircraft on June 8, 1978. Another Dash 7 joined the Wardair fleet in June 1979 but the company then decided to give up its northern Canada charter services and disposed of these aircraft.

In August and September 1979, the Canadian Armed Forces took delivery of two Dash 7s for freight and passenger service to replace two CC-109 Cosmopolitans (see page 109). A Dash 71R was obtained by the Canadian government in 1986 to supplement the two Lockheed Electras (see page 106) on sea ice and iceberg surveys off Canada's east coast. This unique aircraft is fitted with a dorsal observation cabin immediately aft of the flight deck.

The Dash 7 has earned an excellent reputation with charter and second and third tier carriers throughout the world. Although the concept of inter city travel from downtown airports has yet to gain wide acceptance, the Dash 7 has found ready acceptance with commuter airlines and charter companies operating into airports with short runways. AirBC and Air Atlantic both operate Dash 7s.

▲ AirBC's first Dash 7, C-GFEL, was the third aircraft of this type to be built. After three years service with the Spanish charter airline Spantax, the aircraft was returned to de Havilland Canada and purchased by AirBC in July 1983.

Aircraft	de Havilland Canada DHC-7
Year of first flight	1975
Engines	Four Pratt & Whitney PT6A-50 turbo-props (1,120 shp)
Wingspan	93 ft 0 in
Length	80 ft 8 in
Height	26 ft 3 in
Weight empty	27,650 lb
Weight maximum take-off	44,000 lb
Cruising speed	261 mph
Range	1,335 miles
Flight deck crew	2
Passengers	50

Charles Bryant via CPAL

In the 1970s, de Havilland Canada conducted extensive market surveys to determine what type of aircraft was required by second and third tier carriers and which the company could supply by capitalizing on its specialization in STOL airplanes. As a result of these studies, the company designed the quiet, fuel efficient, short haul DHC-8 with accommodation for 36-39 passengers. To be known as the Dash 8, the new aircraft complemented the company's 19 seat Twin Otter and the Dash 7 (described on page 107). The new design was made public in April 1980 and, at the same time, it was announced that NorOntair, the Ontario Northland Transport Commission's airline, would purchase two Dash 8s.

Four prototypes were authorized and the first of these, C-GNDK, made its initial flight on June 20, 1983, two more followed in October/November 1983 and the fourth was airborne in early 1984. The first aircraft to be completed to production standards,

C-GGTO, joined the flight testing program in June 1984 and the Canadian authorities awarded the type certificate on September 28, 1984. The sixth aircraft to be completed was the first of NorOntair's order and was delivered on October 23, 1984 entering service the following December 19th.

The Dash 8 is available in both commuter and corporate versions. Both Air Atlantic and AirBC use the aircraft in connection with CPAL's transcontinental services and other purchasers include Eastern Metro Express, Henson Aviation, Lecward Island Air Transport, Transport Canada and the Canadian Armed Forces. Transport Canada's Dash 8s are for airways calibration service and four of the Canadian Armed Forces aircraft are navigation trainers. The remaining two Dash 8s are for passenger/cargo service in Europe. All six military aircraft are classified as Dash 8M and are equipped with long-range fuel tanks, rough field landing gear and extra-strength floors. Corporate purchasers

include Mobil Oil Canada, Home Oil and the Government of Alberta.

In mid-1985 a stretched Dash 8 with a 10 ft 8 in lengthened fuselage was announced. This will enable 50 passengers to be carried and will compete directly with the Dash 7.

▲ Air Atlantic's Dash 8, C-GAAC, illustrates the commuter airline's livery which complements that of Canadian Pacific Air Lines. The lower fuselage is green and is separated from the sky white upper fuselage by a corporate red cheat line.

Aircraft	de Havilland Canada DHC-8
Year of first flight	1983
Engines	Two Pratt & Whitney PW120 turbo-props (1,800 shp)
Wingspan	84 ft 0 in
Length	73 ft 0 in
Height	25 ft 0 in
Weight empty	20,176 lb
Weight maximum take-off	30,500 lb
Cruising speed	310 mph
Range	1,100 miles
Flight deck crew	2
Passengers	36

The success of the Convair 240, which resulted in 571 examples being built, led to the company designing its Convair 340 with a 13 ft 7 in increase in wingspan and the fuselage lengthened by 4 ft 6 in. This allowed four more passengers to be carried and over 160 aircraft had been ordered by the time the type certificate was issued on March 28, 1952, the day the Convair 340 entered service with United Airlines. Total 340 sales amounted to 311 aircraft. Subsequently, Convair refined the 340 by improving the soundproofing, redesigning the engine nacelles etc. and the new aircraft, known as the Convair 440, made its first flight on October 5, 1955, entering service with Continental Airlines in February 1956. Total production was 179 aircraft.

With the introduction of turbo-prop powered aircraft such as the Vickers Viscount and the Lockheed Electra, piston-engined aircraft rapidly came to be regarded by travellers as "old-fashioned". At the same time, airlines with relatively new piston-powered aircraft sought ways to improve the operating economics of these types and at the same time improve the performance of the aircraft. The obvious course of action was to replace the piston engines with turbo-props but, although this was attempted with several aircraft types, only the Convair 240/340/440 family achieved reasonable success. In 1954, a Convair 340 was equipped with two Napier 3,060 shp Eland turbo-props and the first flight was made on February 9, 1955. Six more conversions were made before development of the Eland ceased but Canadair converted 13 Convair 440s, ten of which served with the RCAF as CC-109 Cosmopolitans. The civil version was known as the Convair 540.

The next conversion was the Convair 580 which was fitted with two Allison 3,750 shp turbo-props and made its first flight on January 19, 1960, entering service with Frontier Airlines in June 1964. In all, 175 Convair 340s and 440s were converted to 580 standards and the type became the primary component of the fleets of several U.S. second tier carriers including Allegheny, with over 40 examples, North Central and Frontier.

The Rolls-Royce powered conversion was the last development of the Convair 240/340/440 family and was the only program in which Convair was involved in directly. Central Airlines ordered ten Convair 240s to be converted to Convair 600s, equipped with Rolls-Royce 3,025 shp Darts. The first flight was made on May 20, 1965 and the type entered service the following November 30th. The Convair 340s and 440s became Convair 640s and Caribair introduced this final development into service on December 22, 1965. A total of 39 Convair 600s and 28 Convair 640s were constructed.

During the 1970s, many of the original purchasers of turbo-prop powered Convairs began upgrading their fleets by introducing jet aircraft such as the Boeing 737 and the various versions of the DC-9. As a result, the Convairs were dispersed to other operators. Of the regional carriers associated with Canadian Pacific Air Lines, Nordair Metro and Quebecair operate Convair 580s and Norcanair has two Convair 640s.

▲ A Nordair Metro Convair 580 at Montreal.

Aircraft	Convair 580	Convair 640
Year of first flight	1960	1965
Engines	Two 3,750 shp Allison turbo-props	Two 3,025 shp Rolls-Royce Dart turbo-props
Wingspan	105 ft 4 in	105 ft 4 in
Length	81 ft 6 in	81 ft 6 in
Height	29 ft 2 in	28 ft 2 in
Weight empty	30,275 lb	30,275 lb
Weight maximum take-off	58,140 lb	55,000 lb
Cruising speed	342 mph	300 mph
Range	1,614 miles	1,230 miles
Flight deck crew	2	2
Passengers	52	52

Norcanair via CPAL

The interest shown in the Fokker F27 (see page 105) encouraged the manufacturer to design the short-haul twin jet F28 which was announced in April 1962. Originally, it was designed as a 50 seat aircraft with two rear mounted Bristol-Siddley turbofans to operate over routes of up to 1000 miles but this was subsequently changed to a 65 seater powered by two Rolls-Royce Spey turbofans. Construction began in 1964 following the granting of financial support by the Netherland's government and risk sharing by Shorts of Belfast together with MBB and VFW of West Germany. Three prototypes were constructed and these made their first flights on May 9, August 3 and October 20, 1967. The first production aircraft was delivered to the West German charter airline, LTU, on February 24, 1969, the day the Netherland's authorities granted the type certificate. The first service flight was made on March 29, 1969 by the Norwegian airline, Braathens SAFE.

The first production version was the MK 1000 which provided accommodation for 65 passengers in a five abreast, all-economy layout at a gross weight of 65,000 lb. As in the case of the F27, orders were for two and three aircraft at a time unlike more recent developments where large numbers of one aircraft have been ordered by individual airlines. In 1967, Fairchild Hiller developed plans to construct a 50 seat US version, the FH-228, but this project was cancelled in 1968. Fokker then designed the MK 2000 with a 7 ft 3 in stretch of the fuselage allowing up to 85 passengers to be carried in high density, 29 inch pitch seating. The prototype, a modified MK 1000 made its initial flight on April 28, 1971 and the first production version was delivered to Nigeria Airways in October 1971. There then followed the MK 5000 and MK 6000 which were to be the equivalents of the MK 1000 and MK 2000 but with the wingspan increased by 6 ft 11½ in and leading edge slats to provide shorter runway performance. The original F28, PH-JGH, was converted to MK 6000 standards and made its first flight in this configuration on September 28, 1973 but little requirement was found for the short airfield capability and the MKs 3000 and 4000 were then designed with the increased wingspan but without the leading edge slats. The first MK 4000 made its maiden flight on October 20, 1976 and this was followed by the initial MK 3000 on December 23, 1976. Since then the larger MK 4000 has consistently outsold the MK 3000, the last example of which was delivered in 1981. Production of the MK 4000 has just terminated with the delivery of the last of 241 F28s. It is being replaced by the larger and more economical Fokker 100 but 57 customers in 37 countries purchased the F28.

Following the deregulation of the US airline industry, many second tier carriers purchased jet aircraft including the F28. In Canada, commuter airlines have tended to restrict themselves to piston and turbo-prop powered aircraft. The main exception is Norcanair with two F28 MK 1000s which operate on its trunk routes and provide a coordinated service with CPAL's flights.

▲ Norcanair's newly acquired Fokker F28 C-GTUU in the airline's new livery. As in the case of CPAL aircraft, the name Canadian Pacific is in English on the left hand side and is in French on the other side.

Aircraft	Fokker MK 1000
Year of first flight	1967
Engines	Two Rolls-Royce Spey turbofans (9,850 lb. thrust)
Wingspan	77 ft 4 in
Length	89 ft 11 in
Height	27 ft 9½ in
Weight empty	35,275 lb
Weight maximum take-off	65,000 lb
Cruising speed	523 mph
Range	1,300 miles
Crew	2
Passengers	65

PWA

▲ Boeing 737-275 C-GNPW of Pacific Western Airlines at Kelowna, British Columbia. Pacific Western Airlines Corporation, which has purchased Canadian Pacific Air Lines, also owns Pacific Western Airlines Ltd. of Calgary. This carrier operates a fleet of 24 Boeing 737-200s throughout western Canada with trunk services to Toronto and Ottawa. The combined fleet of PWA and CPAL now totals 88 aircraft of which 60 are Boeing 737-200s.

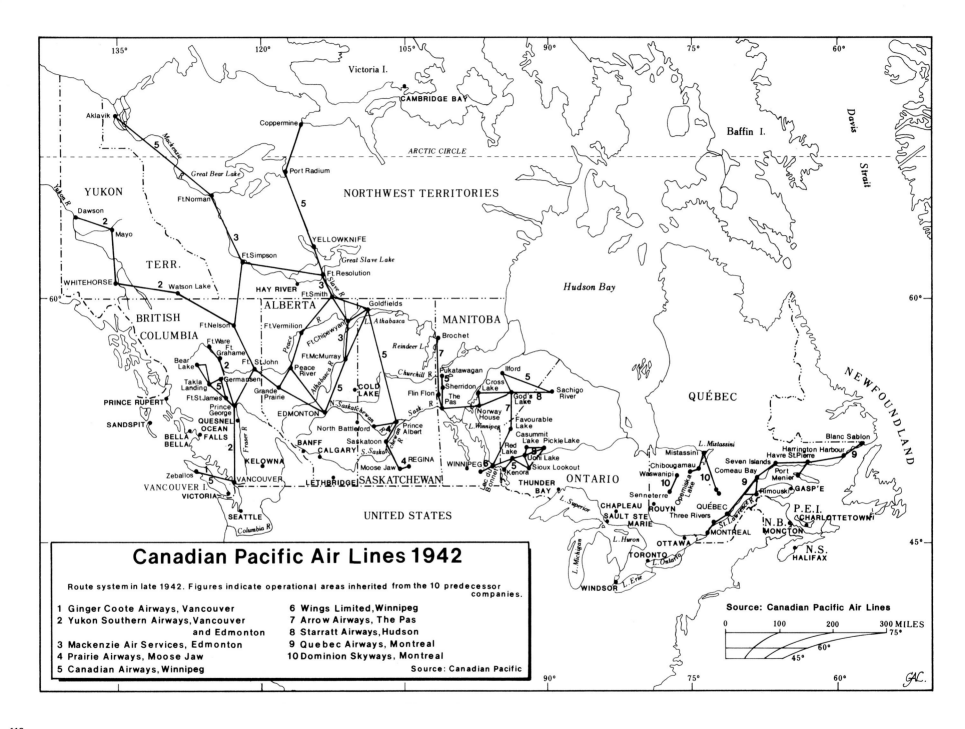

Canadian Pacific Air Lines 1942

Route system in late 1942. Figures indicate operational areas inherited from the 10 predecessor companies.

1 **Ginger Coote Airways, Vancouver**
2 **Yukon Southern Airways, Vancouver and Edmonton**
3 **Mackenzie Air Services, Edmonton**
4 **Prairie Airways, Moose Jaw**
5 **Canadian Airways, Winnipeg**
6 **Wings Limited, Winnipeg**
7 **Arrow Airways, The Pas**
8 **Starratt Airways, Hudson**
9 **Quebec Airways, Montreal**
10 **Dominion Skyways, Montreal**

Source: Canadian Pacific

Source: Canadian Pacific Air Lines

0   100   200   300 MILES

GAC.

Wings

of the World's Greatest Travel System...

Canadian Pacific

≡AIR≡LINES

Half a century ago, the Canadian Pacific linked ocean to ocean across Canada by rail. Now it adds air transport to its rail and steamship facilities. Recently, it consolidated ten Canadian air transport companies running northward like arteries from the main east-west lines of communication...to the borders of the Yukon ...and the shores of the Arctic.

It now operates close to 100 planes, with a flying mileage of more than 5,000,000 plane miles a year. This makes it one of the world's largest commercial air operators. Its routes connect with Trans-Canada Air Lines and the leading American air lines.

For information, rates and reservations, apply to any traffic office of Canadian Pacific Air Lines or to any Canadian Pacific Railway agent.

PASSENGERS - MAIL - EXPRESS

See pages 62 and 63 of this Folder for services operated

◄ Canadian Pacific Air Lines system as illustrated in the Canadian Pacific Railway timetable issued on November 28, 1943. By this time, Boeing 247D CF-BVZ had been owned by the airline for nearly two months though it had been operated by Quebec Airways from May 13, 1942 when it was loaned by RCAF to the airline.

Canadian Pacific AIR LINES

EXECUTIVE OFFICE—WINDSOR STATION, MONTREAL, QUE.
OFFICERS
D. C. COLEMAN, Chairman   L. B. UNWIN, President   W. M. NEAL, Vice-President
GENERAL OFFICES: ROOM 620, DOMINION SQUARE BUILDING, MONTREAL, QUE.
C. H. DICKINS,   D. B. WALLACE,   E. L. SMITH,
Vice-President and General Manager   Assistant to the Vice-President and General Manager   General Traffic Manager

G. W. G. McCONACHIE, General Manager, Western Lines, Municipal Airport, Edmonton, Alta.
O. H. JOHNSTON, Regional Traffic Manager, Municipal Airport, Edmonton, Alta.

VANCOUVER - WHITEHORSE

21 Daily ex. Sun.		TABLE 200 (P.T.) Pacific Time (Y.T.) Yukon Time	22 Daily ex. Sun.		
		A.M.	**P.M.**		
▲ Connections to Fairbanks and other points in Alaska.		9.00 Lv..Vancouver (P.T.)..Ar	6.00	......	......
		ƒ ☉ Ar....Williams Lake....Ar	ƒ ☉	......	......
		11.30 Ar....Prince George....Lv	3.30	......	......
		11.45 Lv....Prince George....Ar	3.15		
		1.00 Ar....Fort St. John....Lv	2.05		
		1.20 Lv....Fort St. John....Ar	1.50		
		2.40 Ar....Fort Nelson....Lv	12.35		
		2.55 Lv....Fort Nelson (P.T.) Ar	12.20		
		MVS	**MVS**		
......	......	3.20 Ar..Lower Post (Y.T.) Ar	10.00		
		Ar....Watson Lake....Lv			
		3.35 Lv....Watson Lake....Ar	9.45		
......	......	ƒ ☉ Ar......Teslin......Ar	ƒ ☉	......	......
......	......	5.00 Ar ▲Whitehorse (Y.T.) Lv	8.30	......	......
		P.M.	**A.M.**		

VANCOUVER - VICTORIA

9 Daily	7 Daily exSun.	5 Daily	3 Daily	1 Daily exSun.	TABLE 201 Pacific Time	2 Daily exSun.	4 Daily	6 Daily	8 Daily exSun.	10 Daily
P.M.	**P.M.**	**P.M.**	**A.M.**	**A.M.**		**A.M.**	**P.M.**	**P.M.**	**P.M.**	**P.M.**
3.00	2.00	1.00	11.00	9.00	Lv....Vancouver....Ar	10.30	12.30	2.30	3.30	4.30
3.30	2.30	1.30	11.30	9.30	Ar....Victoria....Lv	10.00	12.01	2.00	3.00	4.00
P.M.	**P.M.**	**P.M.**	**A.M.**	**A.M.**		**A.M.**	**P.M.**	**P.M.**	**P.M.**	**P.M.**

VANCOUVER - ZEBALLOS

15 Saturday		TABLE 202 Pacific Time	16 Saturday		
		A.M.	**P.M.**		
......	......	10.00 Lv....Vancouver....Ar	3.30	......	......
		ƒ Ar....Tofino....Ar	ƒ		
		12.01 Ar...Zeballos....Lv	1.30		
		P.M.	**P.M.**		

VANCOUVER - PORT ALICE

17 Mon.& Fri.		TABLE 203 Pacific Time	18 Mon.& Fri.		
		A.M.	**P.M.**		
....	......	10.00 Lv....Vancouver....Ar	4.00	......	......
		ƒ Ar....Alert Bay....Ar	ƒ		
		12.30 Ar....Port Alice....Lv	1.30		
		P.M.	**P.M.**		

EDMONTON - WHITEHORSE

23 Daily ex. Sun.		TABLE 204 (M.T.) Mountain Time (P.T.) Pacific Time (Y.T.) Yukon Time	24 Daily ex. Sun.		
		A.M.	**P.M.**		
▲ Connections to Fairbanks and other points in Alaska.		7.00 Lv..Edmonton (M.T.)..Ar	10.45	......	......
		7.30 Ar Grand Prairie (P.T.) Lv	8.15	......	......
		7.45 Lv....Grand Prairie....Ar	8.00	......	......
		@ ☉ Ar....Peace River....Ar	@ ☉		
		ƒ ☉ Ar...Dawson Creek...Ar	ƒ ☉		
		8.35 Ar...Fort St. John...Lv	7.10		
		9.00 Lv...Fort St. John...Ar	6.50		
		10.20 Ar...Fort Nelson...Lv	5.35		
		10.35 Lv...Fort Nelson (P.T.) Ar	5.20		
		MVS	**MVS**		
......	......	11.00 Ar..Lower Post (Y.T.) Ar	3.00		
		Ar....Watson Lake....Lv			
		11.15 Lv....Watson Lake....Ar	2.45		
......	......	ƒ ☉ Ar......Teslin......Ar	ƒ ☉	......	......
......	......	12.30 Ar ▲Whitehorse (Y.T.) Lv	1.30	......	......
		P.M.	**P.M.**		

WHITEHORSE - DAWSON CITY

25 Tue.Fri.		TABLE 205 Yukon Time	26 Tue. Fri.		
		A.M.	**P.M.**		
......	......	9.15 Lv....Whitehorse....Ar	4.40	......	......
......	......	11.40 Ar......Mayo......Lv	2.30	......	......
......	......	11.55 Lv......Mayo......Ar	2.20	......	......
......	......	12.45 Ar....Dawson City....Lv	1.30	......	......
		P.M.	**P.M.**		

EDMONTON - NORMAN WELLS

47 Tue.Thur. Sat.	43 Thur.	41 Mon.Tue. Wed.Fri. Sat.	TABLE 206 (M.T.) Mountain Time (P.T.) Pacific Time	42 Sun.Tue. Wed.Thur. Sat.	44 Fri. Sat.	48 Tue.Thur. Sat.
A.M.	**A.M.**	**A.M.**		**P.M.**	**P.M.**	**P.M.**
9.00	9.30	6.00	Lv....Edmonton (M.T.)..Ar	9.15	5.30	5.40
10.45	11.15		Ar....McMurray....Lv		3.45	3.55
11.05	11.45		Lv....McMurray....Ar		3.15	3.35
12.50	1.30		Ar....Fort Smith....Ar		1.30	1.40
P.M.	2.00		Lv....Fort Smith....Ar		1.00	......
......	3.00		Ar....Hay River....Lv		12.00	......
......	3.15		Lv....Hay River....Ar		11.45	......
......	3.45		Ar....Providence....Lv		11.15	......
......	4.00		Lv....Providence (M.T.) Ar		11.00	......
......		6.50	Ar Grand Prairie (P.T.) Lv	6.4ƒ.		
......		7.05	Lv...Grand Prairie....Ar	6.30		
......		7.55	Ar....Fort St. John....Lv	5.45		
......		8.15	Lv....Fort St. John....Ar	5.30		
......		9.45	Ar....Fort Nelson....Lv	4.15		
......		10.00	Lv....Fort Nelson....Ar	4.00		
......	4.05 Fri.	12.00	Ar.Fort Simpson (P.T.) Lv	2.00	9.00 Fri.	......
	A.M.				**P.M.**	
10.00	12.30		Lv....Fort Simpson....Ar	1.45	3.30	......
ƒ	ƒ		Ar....Wrigley....Ar	ƒ	ƒ	
12.15	3.00		Ar Norman Wells (P.T.) Lv	11.20	1.15	......
P.M.	**P.M.**			**A.M.**	**P.M.**	

EXPLANATION OF SIGNS—THIS PAGE

ƒ Flag stop.   MVS Via Motor Vehicle Service.   ☉ Subject to landing conditions.   @ Scheduled off line point.

◄ Canadian Pacific Air Line's first timetable issued as part of the Canadian Pacific Railway timetable on November 28, 1943.

Canadian Pacific AIR LINES

FORT SMITH - YELLOWKNIFE - PORT RADIUM

TABLE 207 — Mountain Time

51 Friday	45 Tue., Thu., Sat.		46 Tue., Thu., Sat.	52 Saturday
A.M.	P.M.		P.M.	P.M.
......	1.30	Lv....Fort Smith....Ar	12.15	......
......	a 2.15	Ar....Rocher River....Lv	d 11.30	......
......	a 2.30	Lv....Rocher River....Ar	d 11.15	......
......	d 2.15	Ar....Resolution....Lv	a 11.30	......
......	d 2.30	Lv....Resolution....Ar	a 11.15	......
......	f	Ar....Outpost Island....Ar	f	......
......	3.30	Ar....Yellowknife....Lv	10.00	......
10.30	......	Lv....Yellowknife....Ar	......	4.30
2.30	......	Ar....Port Radium....Lv	......	12.30
P.M.			A.M.	A.M.

REGINA - MOOSE JAW - NORTH BATTLEFORD

TABLE 208 — Mountain Time

63 Daily ex. Sun.	61 Daily		62 Daily	64 Daily ex. Sun.
P.M.	A.M.		P.M.	A.M.
▼12.20	♣8.00	Lv....Regina....Ar	5.40	11.45
12.40	8.20	Ar....Moose Jaw....Lv	5.20	11.25
12.50	8.30	Lv....Moose Jaw....Ar	5.10	11.15
1.50	9.35	Ar....Saskatoon....Lv	4.10	10.20
......	9.45	Lv....Saskatoon....Ar	4.00	......
......	10.25	Ar....Prince Albert....Lv	3.20	......
......	10.35	Lv....Prince Albert....Ar	3.10	......
......	11.25	Ar....North Battleford....Lv	2.20	......
P.M.	A.M.		P.M.	A.M.

▼ Will hold one half hour for connection with T.C.A. Eastbound Trip 2.
♣ Will hold at Regina for arrival of T.C.A. Westbound Trip 3 until 9.30 a.m.

WINNIPEG - FAVOURABLE LAKE - GOD'S LAKE

TABLE 209 — Central Time

85 1st & 3rd Wed.	83 Tue., Fri.		84 Tue., Fri.	86 1st & 3rd Thur.
A.M.	A.M.		P.M.	P.M.
......	MVS 8.00	Lv....Winnipeg....Ar	MVS6.00	MVS6.00
......	MVS10.00	Ar...Lac du Bonnet....Lv	MVS4.00	MVS4.00
9.00	10.30	Lv....Lac du Bonnet....Ar	3.45	3.50
10.20	f	Ar Little Grand Rapids Lv	f	@
10.30		Lv Little Grand Rapids Ar		2.10
......		Ar....Berens River....Lv		2.00
......		Lv....Berens River....Ar	1.30	f
......	12.45	Ar....Favourable Lake....Lv		......
......		Lv....Favourable Lake....Ar		......
12.00		Ar....Island Lake....Lv	P.M.	P.M.
12.10		Lv....Island Lake....Ar		
12.45		Ar....God's Lake....Lv		11.00
P.M.	P.M.			A.M.

WINNIPEG - BERESFORD - BISSETT

TABLE 210 — Central Time

81 Mon. Wed. Sat.		82 Mon. Wed. Sat.
A.M.		P.M.
MVS 8.00	Lv....Winnipeg....Ar	MVS3.00
MVS10.00	Ar...Lac du Bonnet....Lv	MVS1.00
10.30	Lv....Lac du Bonnet....Ar	12.45
m 11.15	Ar....Beresford Lake....Lv	↑
11.25	Lv....Beresford Lake....Ar	
11.40	Ar....Bissett....Lv	12.01
A.M.		P.M.

WINNIPEG - McKENZIE ISLAND - RED LAKE

TABLE 211 — Central Time

87 Daily ex. Sun.		88 Daily ex. Sun.
A.M.		P.M.
MVS 8.00	Lv....Winnipeg....Ar	MVS4.00
MVS10.00	Ar...Lac du Bonnet....Lv	MVS2.00
10.15	Lv....Lac du Bonnet....Ar	1.45
@	Ar....Beresford....Lv	@
11.30	Ar...McKenzie Island....Lv	......
11.45	Lv...McKenzie Island....Ar	f
12.01	Ar....Red Lake....Lv	12.30
MVS1.00	Lv....Red Lake....Ar	MVS9.30
MVS1.30	Ar....Madsen....Lv	MVS9.00
P.M.		A.M.

KENORA - RED LAKE - McKENZIE ISLAND

TABLE 212 — Central Time

89 Daily ex. Sun.		90 Daily ex. Sun.
A.M.		P.M.
9.15	Lv....Kenora....Ar	12.01
f	Ar....Minaki....Ar	
10.15	Ar....Red Lake....Lv	
10.30	Lv....Red Lake....Ar	
10.40	Ar McKenzie Island Lv	11.00
A.M.		A.M.

SIOUX LOOKOUT - PICKLE LAKE

TABLE 213 — Central Time

93 Daily ex. Sun.		94 Daily ex. Sun.
A.M.		A.M.
8.30	Lv...Sioux Lookout...Ar	11.15
f	Ar....Hudson....Ar	
f	Ar....Doghole Bay....Ar	
9.45	Ar....Pickle Lake....Lv	10.00
A.M.		A.M.

MONTREAL - QUEBEC - SAGUENAY

TABLE 214 — Eastern Time

102 Daily ex. Sun.	104 Daily		101 Daily ex. Sun.	103 Daily
P.M.	A.M.		P.M.	P.M.
1.00	9.00	Lv....Montreal....Ar	1.45	6.10
f ⊙		Ar....Three Rivers....Ar	f ⊙	5.00
2.10	10.05	Lv....Quebec....Ar	12.40	5.00
2.25	10.15	Lv....Quebec....Lv	12.25	4.40
3.20	11.10	Ar....★Saguenay....Lv	11.30	3.45
P.M.	A.M.		A.M.	P.M.

★ SERVING

ARVIDA	KENOGAMI
CHICOUTIMI	PORT ALFRED
JONQUIERE	BAGOTVILLE

QUEBEC - RIMOUSKI and NORTH SHORE

TABLE 215 — Eastern Time

108 Monday Thursday		107 Wednesday Saturday
A.M.		P.M.
10.30	Lv....Quebec....Ar	4.45
12.15	Ar....Rimouski....Lv	2.30
P.M.		P.M.

116 Daily ex. Sun	114 Daily ex. Sun		113 Daily ex. Sun	115 Daily ex. Sun
P.M.	A.M.		P.M.	P.M.
12.30	8.30	Lv....Rimouski....Ar	12.01	4.15
f	9.00	Lv....Mont Joli....Ar	f	f
1.00	9.00	Lv....Baie Comeau....Lv	11.30	3.45
2.30	9.20	Lv....Baie Comeau....Ar	11.00	1.50
f		Ar....Godbout....Ar		f
f		Ar....Trinity Bay....Ar		f
4.30	11.20	Ar....Seven Islands....Lv	9.00	11.50
P.M.	A.M.		A.M.	A.M.

EXPLANATION OF SIGNS—THIS PAGE

f Flag stop.
MVS Via Motor Vehicle service.
⊙ Subject to landing conditions.
@ Scheduled off line point.
E.T. Eastern Time.
C.T. Central Time.   a Saturday.
M.T. Mountain Time.   d Thursday.
P.T. Pacific Time.   m Monday.
Y.T. Yukon Time.

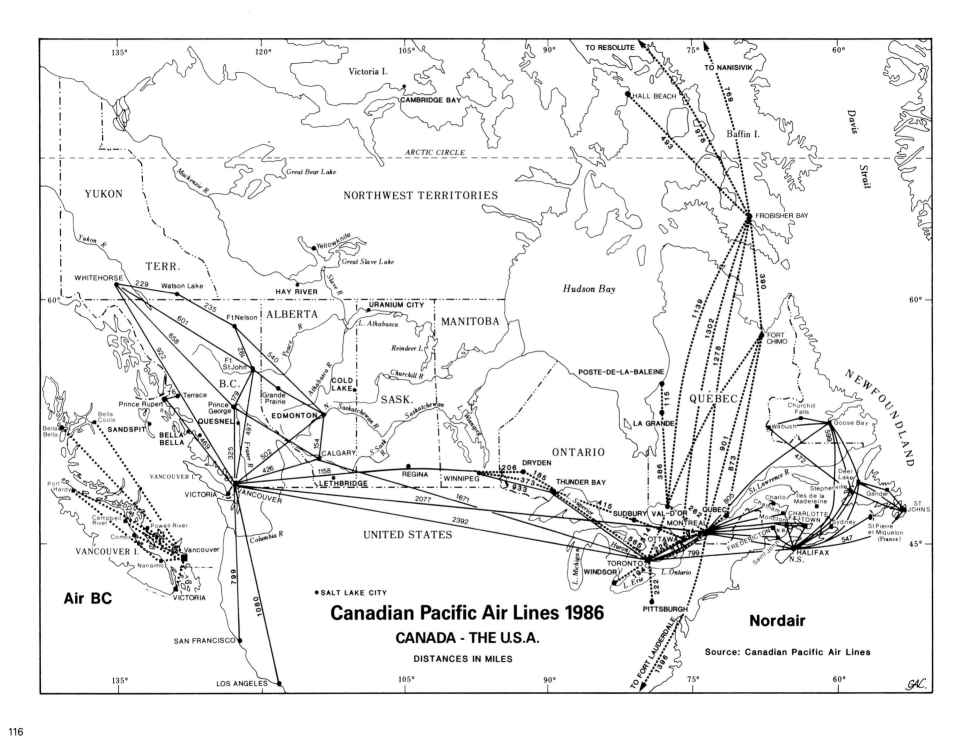

Canadian Pacific Air Lines 1986
CANADA - THE U.S.A.
DISTANCES IN MILES

Air BC

Nordair

Source: Canadian Pacific Air Lines

116

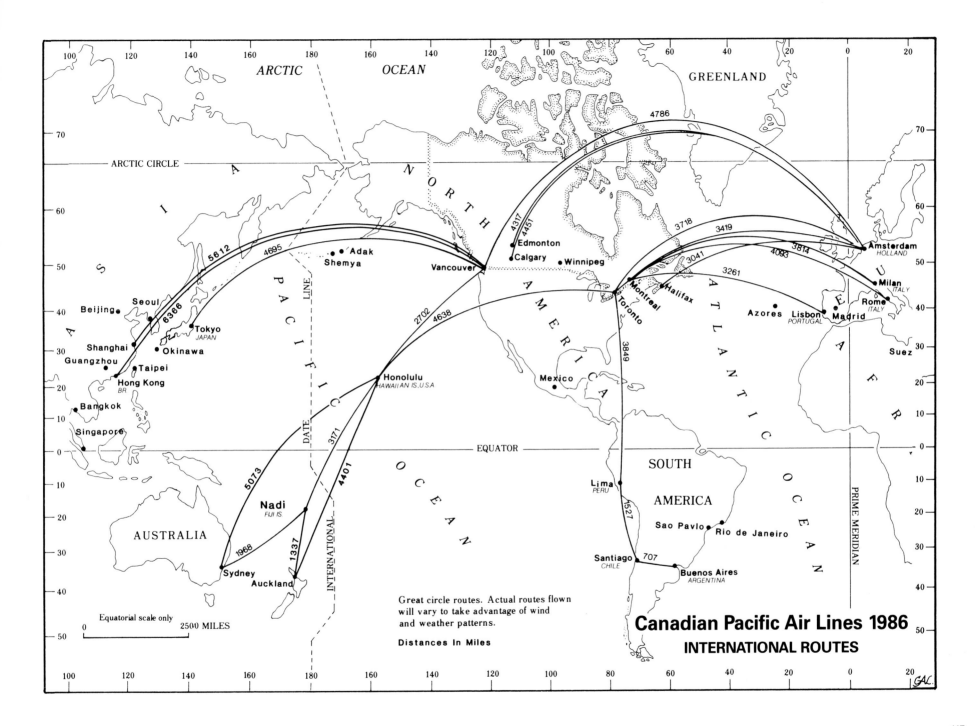

Canadian Pacific Air Lines 1986

INTERNATIONAL ROUTES

Great circle routes. Actual routes flown will vary to take advantage of wind and weather patterns.

Distances In Miles

117

Aircraft of the Constituent Companies on July 1, 1942

Table 1

Regn.	Type	Constructor	Year Built	Constr. Number	Acquired From	Date Registered by CPAL	CPAL Fleet Number	Disposition	Disposition Date	Comments
CF-AAL	Lockheed Vega 1	Lockheed	1929	30	Canadian Airways			International Aviation Enterprises, N.Y.	9 6 44	
CF-AEJ	Travel Air SA-6000-A	Travel Air	1929	1040	Starratt Airways	29 4 44		G.W. Campbell, Red Lake, Ontario	31 5 46	
CF-AGX	D.H.60M Moth	de Havilland	1930	943	Starratt Airways	2 12 43		H.A. Hennesy, Toronto	25 1 45	
CF-AHG	Fairchild FC-2W2	Fairchild	1928	138	Dominion Skyways			Keystone Fisheries, Manitoba	21 12 46	Converted to 71C by de Havilland 13/1/41
CF-AJB	Fokker Super Universal	Canadian Vickers	1929	CV-137	Starratt Airways			WFU and RTS	6 11 42	
CF-AKT	Fairchild 71C	Fairchild	1928	516	Canadian Airways			DBR 40 mi. N.W. Watson Lake, Y.T.	20 8 43	Overturned in forced landing
CF-AMO	Bellanca CH-300 Pacemaker	Bellanca	1930	177	Wings Ltd.			Austin Airways, Toronto	30 8 44	
CF-AMZ	Junkers W-34f	Junkers	1930	2588	Canadian Airways	42		WFU and RTS for CF-AQW	11 1 45	
CF-ANW	Stinson SR-5A Reliant	Stinson	1935	9321-A	Starratt Airways			T. Lamb, The Pas, Manitoba	20 10 42	
CF-APG	D.H.83 Fox Moth	de Havilland	1933	4038	Canadian Airways			WFU and RTS	24 9 42	SD in windstorm at Cartierville, Quebec
CF-APJ	D.H.84 Dragon	de Havilland	1933	6024	Canadian Airways			RTS and used to recondition CF-AVD	23 10 42	
CF-AQW	Junkers W-33f fi	Junkers	1931	2587	Canadian Airways	42		Central B.C. Airways, Ft. St. James, B.C.	20 10 47	Converted to W-33/34 on 19/5/36
CF-ARM	Junkers Ju-52/cao	Junkers	1931	4006	Canadian Airways		1	WFU, certificate lapsed	43	Considered re-engining with RR Merlin — scrapped 16/5/47
CF-ASN	Junkers W-34fi	Junkers	1933	2731	Canadian Airways	42		Central B.C. Airways, Prince George, B.C.	4 9 46	
CF-ATF	Junkers W-34f fi	Junkers	1931	2718	Canadian Airways	42		Central B.C. Airways, Prince George, B.C.	4 9 46	Preserved in Nat. Av. Museum, Ottawa
CF-ATZ	Fairchild 71C	Canadian Fairchild	1933	17	Canadian Airways	22 5 44	7	A.M. Berry, Edmonton	12 7 47	
CF-AVD	D.H.84 Dragon II	de Havilland	1934	6086	Canadian Airways			DBR at Baie Comeau, Quebec	26 5 44	
CF-AWK	Waco YKC-S	Waco	1935	4239	Dominion Skyways			Spilsbury and Hepburn, Vancouver	6 11 43	
CF-AWL	Waco YKC-S	Waco	1935	4238	Ginger Coote Airways			P. Sigurdson, Winnipeg	18 2 43	Sold for spares
CF-AWR	Bellanca 66-70 Air Cruiser	Bellanca	1935	719	Canadian Airways		21	DBR 130 mi. N.E. Sioux Lookout, Ontario	24 1 47	Forced landing because of fuel starvation
CF-AWV	Fairchild 71C	Canadian Fairchild	1934	31	Canadian Airways	25 11 43		Fletcher Air Transport, Ontario	20 6 47	
CF-AWX	Fairchild 71C	Canadian Fairchild	1935	33	Wings			DBR at Deschambault Lake, Saskatchewan	4 7 43	Floats collapsed on landing after engine failure
CF-AXA	Fairchild 82	Canadian Fairchild	1935	35	Yukon Southern Air Transport			SD at Anishanabi Lake, Ontario	16 3 44	WFU and RTS
CF-AXE	Fairchild 82A	Canadian Fairchild	1936	40	Canadian Airways	17 10 44	11	Central Northern Airways, Winnipeg	29 5 47	
CF-AXF	Fairchild 82A	Canadian Fairchild	1936	41	Wings Ltd.	42		DBR at Lake Pipmaukin, Quebec	12 9 42	Leased to Dominion Skyways
CF-AXG	Fairchild 82A	Canadian Fairchild	1936	42	Starratt Airways	42		DBR at Abram Lake, Ontario	2 11 42	Hit shore after engine stalled on take-off
CF-AXL	Fairchild 82A	Canadian Fairchild	1937	61	Starratt Airways		12	Ontario Central Airlines, Kenora, Ontario	3 2 47	Donated to The Nat. Av. Museum, Ottawa by CPAL in 1966
CF-AXM	Fairchild 82B	Canadian Fairchild	1937	62	Mackenzie Air Service	30 6 44	14	Ontario Central Airlines, Kenora, Ontario	3 2 47	
CF-AXQ	Fairchild 82D	Canadian Fairchild	1939	69	Mackenzie Air Service	42		Waite Fisheries, Big River, Saskatchewan	3 12 46	
CF-AYE	D.H.89 Dragon Rapide	de Havilland	1936	6304	Quebec Airways	42	200	Central Northern Airways, Winnipeg	31 7 47	
CF-AYO	Noorduyn Norseman 1	Noorduyn	1935	1	Dominion Skyways	42	31	Cap Airways, Cap de la Madeleine, Quebec	27 3 47	The original Norseman — crashed 28/8/53
CF-AYS	Waco YKC-S	Waco	1935	4267	Arrow Airways	42		P. Sigurdson, Winnipeg	11 8 42	
CF-AYT	Waco YKS-6	Waco	1936	4450	Wings Ltd.	42		SD on flight to Cooking Lake, Alberta	13 7 43	Ran out of fuel. Frame sold to P. Sigurdson, Winnipeg
CF-AZP	Waco ZQC-6 Custom	Waco	1936	4481	Wings Ltd.	2 8 44		P. Sigurdson, Winnipeg	11 8 44	
CF-AZV	Stinson SR-8CM Reliant	Stinson	1936	9733	Canadian Airways	42		W.C. Plummer, Flin Flon, Manitoba	28 9 44	
CF-AZX	Stinson SR-8CM Reliant	Stinson	1936	9749	Canadian Airways			K. Johannesson, Winnipeg	10 44	
CF-BAU	Noorduyn Norseman IV	Noorduyn	1936	6	Canadian Airways	42	36	Central Northern Airways, Winnipeg	28 6 47	
CF-BAW	Noorduyn Norseman IV	Noorduyn	1937	9	Arrow Airways	42	40	DBF at Yellowknife, N.W.T.	3 1 44	Caught fire in nose hangar
CF-BBC	D.H.89 Rapide	de Havilland	1936	6307	Quebec Airways		201	DBR at Mont Joli, Quebec	16 12 46	Forced landing on floating ice on St. Lawrence River
CF-BBH	D.H.89A Rapide	de Havilland	1937	6370	Canadian Airways	42	202	DBR at Pentecost, Quebec	19 3 47	Stalled on takeoff because of sticky snow
CF-BBO	Waco ZQC-6 Custom	Waco	1936	4497	Wings Ltd.	14 9 43		B.C. Airlines, Victoria, B.C.	8 9 44	
CF-BBR	Waco ZQC-6 Custom	Waco	1936	4542	Dominion Skyways	42		DBR 40 mi. south of Senneterre, Quebec	18 3 44	Engine stalled after takeoff
CF-BDC	Noorduyn Norseman IV	Noorduyn	1937	10	Canadian Airways	42	41	Central Northern Airways, Winnipeg	28 6 47	
CF-BDD	Noorduyn Norseman IV	Noorduyn	1937	11	Canadian Airways	42		DBR at Tofino, B.C.	29 12 46	Floats torn off on landing
CF-BDF	Noorduyn Norseman IV	Noorduyn	1937	13	Canadian Airways	42	42	Peace River Northern Air Lines	13 8 47	
CF-BDJ	Waco ZQC-6 Custom	Waco	1937	4543	Prairie Airways			P. Sigurdson, Winnipeg	19 1 45	
CF-BDK	Waco ZKS-6	Waco	1937	4269	Wings	42				
CF-BEB	Stinson SR-9DM Reliant	Stinson	1937	5222-S	Canadian Airways	41		SD at Edmonton	19 8 43	Nosed over because of excessive braking
CF-BFA	Bellanca CH-300 Pacemaker	Bellanca	1930	189	Quebec Airways			DBR at Baie Comeau, Quebec	23 12 42	Took off in strong cross wind — drifted into bush
CF-BFE	Cessna C-37 Airmaster	Cessna	1937	354	Prairie Airways	41		DBR at Stalwart, Saskatchewan	17 3 43	Propeller broke off in flight
CF-BFP	D.H.89A Rapide	de Havilland	1938	6374	Quebec Airways			DBF at Walker Lake, Quebec	5 7 45	Port engine caught fire while starting
CF-BIF	Beechcraft C-17-R	Beech	1937	120	Starratt Airways	42		C.A. Martin, Fairbanks, Alaska	5 44	
CF-BJE	Fairchild 71C	Canadian Airways	1938	1203	Canadian Airways	42		DBF at Franquelin, Quebec	4 1 43	Ran out of fuel and forced to land in trees
CF-BKN	Beechcraft 18D	Beech	1938	177	Prairie Airways	42		T.A.C.A. (Venezuela)	44	
CF-BKO	Beechcraft 18D	Beech	1938	178	Prairie Airways	42		T.A.C.A. (Venezuela)	44	
CF-BKP	Fairchild 71C	Canadian Fairchild	1938	68	Canadian Airways	42		Aero Tool Works, Toronto	26 7 47	Constructed using parts from CF-AIW
CF-BKV	Bellanca 66-76 Aircruiser	Bellanca	1938	722	Mackenzie Air Service	42	22	Central Northern Airways, Winnipeg	18 7 44	
CF-BLU	Beechcraft D-17-S	Beech	1938	238	Yukon Southern Air Transport	42		DBR at Camp Canol, N.W.T.	16 8 42	Turned over on takeoff after hitting sandbar
CF-BLV	Barkley-Grow T8P-1	Barkley-Grow	1938	3	Yukon Southern Air Transport	23 12 43	212	H.R. Peets, Edmonton	29 11 49	Scrapped at Peace River, Alberta in 1960
CF-BMG	Barkley-Grow T8P-1	Barkley-Grow	1939	4	Yukon Southern Air Transport	5 5 43	211	DBR at Port Alberni, B.C.	1 2 47	Overturned at moorings
CF-BMW	Barkley-Grow T8P-1	Barkley-Grow	1939	6	Yukon Southern Air Transport	8 1 43	213	Associated Airways, Edmonton	8 12 49	
CF-BND	D.H.89A Rapide	de Havilland	1939	6375	Quebec Airways		203	Central Northern Airways, Winnipeg	2 6 47	
CF-BNE	D.H.89A Rapide	de Havilland	1939	6376	Quebec Airways			DBR at Lake George, Manitoba	3 12 43	Broke through ice and sank
CF-BNG	D.H.89A Rapide	de Havilland	1940	6472	Ginger Coote Airways	42		DBF at Great Lake, Quebec	9 3 46	Caught fire in air and forced landed on St. Lawrence
CF-BPD	D.H.90 Dragonfly	de Havilland	1937	7538	Ginger Coote Airways	42		DBR at Edmonton	13 4 43	Groundlooped on takeoff
CF-BQG	Beechcraft A-18A	Beech	1940	291	Canadian Airways	42	216	Rimouski Airlines, Rimouski, Quebec	10 3 48	
CF-BQH	Beechcraft A-18A	Beech	1940	318	Canadian Airways	42	217	H.R. McConachie, Ft. St. James, B.C.	29 6 48	
CF-BQM	Barkley-Grow T8P-1	Barkley-Grow	1940	8	Mackenzie Air Service	42	214	Associated Airways, Edmonton	20 3 50	

DBF = Destroyed by fire   DBR = Damaged beyond repair   RTS = Reduced to spares   SD = Severely damaged   WFU = Withdrawn from use

Aircraft of the Constituent Companies on July 1, 1942

Table 1

Regn.	Type	Constructor	Year Built	Constr. Number	Acquired From	Date Registered by CPAL	CPAL Fleet Number	Disposition	Disposition Date	Comments
CF-BQQ	Beechcraft A-18A	Beech	1939	290	Canadian Airways	42		Northern Wings, Quebec City, Quebec	16 11 46	
CF-BTW	Bellanca 66-75 Aircruiser	Bellanca	1938	721	Mackenzie Air Service	9 9 43	23	Central Northern Airways, Winnipeg	19 5 47	
CF-BTX	Barkley-Grow T8P-1	Barkely-Grow	1940	11	Mackenzie Air Service	2 12 43	215	DBR at Lake Porcupine, Alberta	19 10 45	Engine failure after takeoff
CF-BVE	Barkley-Grow T8P-1	Barkely-Grow	1937	1	Prairie Airways	2 11 42		F. Ambrose, Long Island, N.Y.	2 45	
CF-BVI	Fairchild 71	Fairchild	1930	674	Wings	42		Austin Airways, Toronto	19 2 44	
CF-BVJ	Fairchild 71	Fairchild	1930	690	Wings	42		H.A. Hennessy, Toronto	24 8 44	
CF-BVK	Fairchild 71C	Fairchild	1929	625	Dominion Skyways			Trans-American Mining, Yellowknife, N.W.T.	7 12 46	
CF-BVS	Fairchild 71B	Canadian Fairchild	1931	FAC-7	Canadian Airways	42		DBR at Ft. McMurray, Alberta	28 3 43	Landed on rough ice after engine failure
CF-BVU	Fairchild FC-2W2	Fairchild	1930	688	Canadian Airways	23 12 43		DBF at Fort Vermilion, Alberta	25 3 44	Converted to 71C by de Havilland 23/12/43
CF-TCR	Lockheed 14-H2	Lockheed	1939	1503	Yukon Southern Air Transport	17 11 42		Sold in the U.S. as NC 41815		Re-registered as CF-CPC 17/11/42
CF-TCS	Lockheed 14-H2	Lockheed	1939	1504	Yukon Southern Air Transport	17 11 42		Written off at Mt. Cheam, B.C.	20 12 42	Re-registered as CF-CPD 17/11/42

Canadian Pacific Air Lines Aircraft Acquired after July 1, 1942

Table 2

Regn.	Type	Constructor	Year Built	Constr. Number	Acquired From	Date Registered by CPAL	CPAL Fleet Number	Disposition	Disposition Date	Comments
CF-BDL	Waco ZQC-6 Custom	Waco	1937	4593	Fleet Aircraft, Fort Erie, Ontario	28 7 43		W.E. Brett, Chilliwack, B.C.		
CF-BFF	D.H.90 Dragonfly	de Havilland	1937	7543	RCAF	5 12 42		D.H. Aircraft of Canada, Toronto	4 12 45	Served with Quebec Airways
CF-BHU	Noorduyn Norseman V	Canadian Car	1945	N-29-8	Canadian Car	21 12 45	61	Territories Air Service, Edmonton	26 11 49	
CF-BHV	Noorduyn Norseman V	Canadian Car	1945	N-29-10	Canadian Car	13 12 45	62	Territories Air Service, Edmonton	8 11 49	
CF-BHW	Noorduyn Norseman V	Canadian Car	1945	N-29-11	Canadian Car	21 12 45	63	Central Northern Airlines, Winnipeg	14 11 55	
CF-BHX	Noorduyn Norseman V	Canadian Car	1945	N-29-12	Canadian Car	21 12 45	64	Central Northern Airlines, Winnipeg	14 11 55	
CF-BHZ	Noorduyn Norseman V	Canadian Car	1946	N-29-13	Canadian Car	14 3 46	65	F.H. Wheeler, St. Jovite, Quebec	4 1 49	
CF-BQN	Curtiss T-32-C Condor	Curtiss Wright	1932	32	Yukon Southern Air Transport	42		C.H. Babb Inc., Glendale, Calif.	44	Acquired by YSAT 7/8/42
CF-BUA	American Pilgrim 100B	American	1931	6608	Yukon Southern Air Transport	42		T.A.C.A., Honduras	1 44	Acquired by YSAT 7/8/42
CF-BVF	Boeing 247D	Boeing	1933	1706	Yukon Southern Air Transport	27 11 43		C.H. Babb Inc., Glendale, Calif.	7 45	Acquired by YSAT 7/8/42
CF-BVG	Curtiss-Wright D-3 Kingbird	Curtiss-Wright	1931	2016	Yukon Southern Air Transport	43		C.H. Babb Inc., Glendale, Calif.	9 43	Acquired by YSAT 7/8/42
CF-BVT	Boeing 247D	Boeing	1933	1732	RCAF	1 10 43		E.B. Southard, New York City, N.Y.	2 45	Was loaned to YSAT from 5/1/42
CF-BVV	Boeing 247D	Boeing	1933	1725	RCAF	1 10 43		C.H. Babb Inc.	3 45	Was loaned to YSAT from 16/2/42
CF-BVW	Boeing 247D	Boeing	1933	1735	RCAF	1 10 43		C.H. Babb Inc.	4 5 45	Was loaned to Quebec Airways by RCAF from 21/2/42
CF-BVX	Boeing 247D	Boeing	1933	1699	RCAF	1 10 43		E.B. Southard, New York City, N.Y.	1 45	Was loaned to Quebec Airways by RCAF from 1/6/42
CF-BVZ	Boeing 247D	Boeing	1934	1946	RCAF	1 10 43		C.H. Babb Inc.	4 45	Was loaned to Quebec Airways by RCAF from 13/5/42
CF-BXG	Fairchild 71C	Canadian Fairchild	1931	FAC-8	RCAF	9 2 44		DBR at Cliff Lake, Manitoba	13 3 45	Undercarriage collapsed during landing
CF-BXL	Noorduyn Norseman VI	Noorduyn	1944	456	Eldorado Mining & Refining, Toronto	25 3 46	71	DBR at Indin Lake, B.C.	9 12 46	Broke through ice and sank
CF-BZN	Douglas DC-3	Douglas	1943	13845	Doris Yellowknife Gold Mines, Toronto	8 5 46	271	Trans-Labrador Air Lines, Mont Joli, Quebec	19 10 56	
CF-CGV	D.H.82A Tiger Moth	de Havilland	1938	404	Patterson and Hill Aircraft, Toronto	26 6 43		Curtiss Reid Flying Service, Montreal	22 6 44	
CF-CPA	Lockheed Lodestar 18-56A	Lockheed	1943	2177	Lockheed	30 6 43	261	Hollinger Ungava Transport	6 6 50	Allocated to CPAL by the Joint Chiefs of Staff, Washington, D.C.
CF-CPB	Lockheed Lodestar 18-56A	Lockheed	1943	2179	Lockheed	30 6 43	262	F.D. Lundy, Vancouver	2 50	Allocated to CPAL by the Joint Chiefs of Staff, Washington, D.C.
CF-CPC	Lockheed 14-H2	Lockheed	1939	1503	Yukon Southern Air Transport	17 11 42		Sold in U.S. as NC 41815		Acquired by YSAT 31/7/41 from Trans-Canada Airlines as CF-TCR
CF-CPD	Lockheed 14-H2	Lockheed	1939	1504	Yukon Southern Air Transport	17 11 42		Written off Mt. Cheam, B.C.	20 12 42	Acquired by YSAT 4/8/41 from Trans-Canada Airlines as CF-TCS
CF-CPE	Lockheed Lodestar 18-56	Lockheed	1943	2489	Lockheed	5 7 43	263	C.H. Babb Inc., Glendale, Calif.	8 8 50	Ex-42-56016, Allocated to CPAL by the USAAF
CF-CPF	Lockheed Lodestar 18-56	Lockheed	1943	2466	Lockheed	10 7 43	264	C.H. Babb Inc., Glendale, Calif.	5 51	Ex-42-55913, Allocated to CPAL by the USAAF
CF-CPG	Lockheed Lodestar 18-56	Lockheed	1943	2509	Lockheed	29 7 43	265	C.H. Babb Inc., Glendale, Calif.	1 51	Ex-42-56036, Allocated to CPAL by the USAAF
CF-CPH	Lockheed Lodestar 18-14	Lockheed	1943	2403	Lockheed	43				Ex-CF-TDI, Allocated to CPAL by the USAAF
CF-CPI	Lockheed Lodestar 18-08	Lockheed	1943	2464	Lockheed	43				Ex-CF-TDH, Allocated to CPAL by the USAAF
CF-CPJ	Lockheed Lodestar 18-08A	Lockheed	1943	2465	Lockheed	43				Ex-CF-TDG, Allocated to CPAL by the USAAF
CF-CPK	Lockheed Lodestar 18-56	Lockheed	1943	2534	Lockheed	29 7 43	266	Canada Packers, Toronto	22 9 50	Ex-42-56041, Allocated to CPAL by the USAAF
CF-CPL	Noorduyn Norseman VI	Noorduyn	1944	253	Noorduyn	22 3 44				Ex-43-5263, Allocated to CPAL by the Canadian Government
CF-CPM	Noorduyn Norseman VI	Noorduyn	1944	254	Noorduyn	22 3 44	72	Mont Laurier Aviation	6 6 47	Ex-43-5262, Allocated to CPAL by the Canadian Government
CF-CPN	Noorduyn Norseman VI	Noorduyn	1944	255	Noorduyn	22 3 44	73	Mont Laurier Aviation	6 6 47	Ex-43-5264, Allocated to CPAL by the Canadian Government
CF-CPO	Noorduyn Norseman VI	Noorduyn	1944	256	Noorduyn	22 3 44	74	Mont Laurier Aviation	20 2 48	Ex-43-5265, Allocated to CPAL by the Canadian Government
CF-CPP	Noorduyn Norseman VI	Noorduyn	1944	436	Noorduyn	13 4 44	75	Written off	13 11 47	Ex-43-35362
CF-CPQ	Noorduyn Norseman VI	Noorduyn	1944	437	Noorduyn	13 4 44	76			Ex-43-35363

Regn.	Type	Constructor	Year Built	Constr. Number	Acquired From	Date Registered by CPAL	CPAL Fleet Number	Disposition	Disposition Date	Comments
CF-CPR	Noorduyn Norseman VI	Noorduyn	1944	438	Noorduyn	13 4 44	77			Ex-43-35364, Records also show cancelled
CF-CPS	Noorduyn Norseman VI	Noorduyn	1944	439	Noorduyn	13 4 44	78	Ontario Central Airlines	3 2 48	Ex-43-35365, Allocated to CPAL by the Canadian Government
CF-CPT	Lockheed Lodestar 18-56A	Lockheed		2268	United States War Department	24 5 45	267	Remmert Werner Corp., St. Louis	12 10 51	Ex-42-55878
CF-CPU	Lockheed Lodestar 18-56	Lockheed		2492	United States Army Air Force	7 45	268	C.H. Babb Inc., Glendale, California	2 51	
CF-CPV	Douglas DC-3	Douglas	1942	4594	C.H. Babb Inc., Glendale, California	19 1 46	272	Transair, Winnipeg	1 9 57	Ex-41-18502, Subsequently registered as CF-TAR
CF-CPW	Douglas DC-3	Douglas	1942	4666	C.H. Babb Inc., Glendale, California	8 6 46	273	Transair, Winnipeg	28 8 57	Ex-41-18541, Subsequently registered as CF-TAS
CF-CPX	Douglas DC-3	Douglas	1942	6085	C.H. Babb Inc., Glendale, California	7 46	274	Harrison Airways, Vancouver	19 6 69	Ex-41-18679, delivered to Harrison Airways 6 5 69
CF-CPY	Douglas DC-3	Douglas	1942	4665	C.H. Babb Inc., Glendale, California	4 46	275	Connelly-Dawson Airways, Whitehorse	28 4 60	Ex-41-18540
CF-CPZ	Lockheed Lodestar 18-56	Lockheed		2563	United States Army Air Force	24 1 45	269	C.H. Babb Inc., Glendale, California	1 51	Ex-42-56070
CF-CRC	Noorduyn Norseman IV	Noorduyn	1940	25	Royal Canadian Air Force/Crown Assets	11 8 46	43	Central Northern Airways	28 6 47	Ex-692
CF-CRD	Noorduyn Norseman IV	Noorduyn	1940	23	Royal Canadian Air Force/Crown Assets	12 2 46	44	Central Northern Airways	28 6 47	Ex-681
CF-CRE	Noorduyn Norseman IV	Noorduyn	1940	26	Royal Canadian Air Force/Crown Assets	1 2 46	45	Great Northern Airways	13 8 47	Ex-698
CF-CRF	Noorduyn Norseman IV	Noorduyn	1940	37	Royal Canadian Air Force/Crown Assets	1 3 46	46	Central Northern Airways	28 6 47	Ex-2464
CF-CRG	Anson V	Federal Aircraft		MDF 180	Royal Canadian Air Force/Crown Assets	25 4 46	221	Northland Fish Ltd.	29 9 47	Ex-12084
CF-CRH	Anson V	Federal Aircraft		MDF 330	Royal Canadian Air Force/Crown Assets	25 4 46	222	Central Aircraft Ltd.	30 9 55	Ex-12519
CF-CRI	Anson V	Federal Aircraft		MDF 169	Royal Canadian Air Force/Crown Assets	25 4 46	223		23 5 50	Ex-12072
CF-CRJ	Hudson III	Lockheed		6448		15 5 46	241	Photographic Survey	5 49	
CF-CRK	Hudson III	Lockheed		7555			242	Photographic Survey	5 49	
CF-CRL	Hudson III	Lockheed		7546		24 6 46	243	Photographic Survey	5 49	
CF-CRM	Hudson III	Lockheed		7550		25 4 47	244	Photographic Survey	5 49	
CF-CRN	Hudson III	Lockheed					245	Photographic Survey	5 49	
CF-CRO	Hudson III	Lockheed		7547		13 5 47	246	Photographic Survey	5 49	
CF-CRP	PBY-5A Canso A	Canadian Vickers		CV 271	Royal Canadian Air Force/Crown Assets	29 11 45	231	Trans-Labrador Airlines	9 5 57	Ex-9837
CF-CRQ	PBY-5A Canso A	Canadian Vickers		CV 256	Royal Canadian Air Force/Crown Assets	23 3 46	232	Written off at Osiska Lake, Quebec	9 6 49	Ex-9822
CF-CRR	PBY-5A Canso A	Canadian Vickers			Royal Canadian Air Force/Crown Assets	1 4 46	233	Northland Airlines	5 8 60	Ex-9767, Fleet number was also 933
CF-CRS	Noorduyn Norseman IV	Noorduyn	1941	53	Royal Canadian Air Force/Crown Assets	8 5 46	47	Written off	22 4 48	Ex-2480
CF-CRT	Noorduyn Norseman IV	Noorduyn	1937	15	Royal Canadian Air Force/Crown Assets	8 5 46	48	Central Northern Airways	28 6 47	Ex-696, Also Ex-CF-BFR prior to the acquisition by the RCAF 24 2 40
CF-CRU	Noorduyn Norseman IV	Noorduyn	1937	8	Royal Canadian Air Force/Crown Assets	8 5 46	49	Peace River Northern Airlines	13 8 47	Ex-697, Also Ex-CF-BAN
CF-CRV	PBY-5A Canso A	Canadian Vickers			Royal Canadian Air Force/Crown Assets	8 4 46	234	Written off at Prince Rupert	31 12 53	Ex-9755
CF-CRW	Douglas DC-3	Douglas	1943	18958	C.H. Babb Inc., Glendale, California	23 10 46	276	Quebecair	19 12 58	Ex-42-100495, Leased to Quebecair 29/7/58
CF-CRX	Douglas DC-3	Douglas	1943	19276	C.H. Babb Inc., Glendale, California	17 8 46	277	Harrison Airways, Vancouver	23 10 74	Ex-42-100813, CP Air's last DC-3 flight—Abbotsford to Vancouver, July 4 74
CF-CRY	Douglas DC-3	Douglas	1944	20592	C.H. Babb Inc., Glendale, California	29 11 46	278	Steward-Davis, Gardena, California	18 2 58	Ex-43-16126
CF-CRZ	Douglas DC-3	Douglas	1944	20180	United States Army Air Force	30 12 46	279	Harrison Airways, Vancouver	2 5 69	Ex-43-15714
CF-CUA	Douglas DC-3	Douglas	1942	4518	United States Army Air Force	2 2 47	280	Bomb explosion at Forrestville, Quebec	9 9 49	The aircraft involved in the infamous Albert Guay case
CF-CUB	Douglas DC-3	Douglas	1944	12711	C.H. Babb Inc., Glendale, California	2 7 47	281	Steward Davis, Gardena, California	18 2 58	Ex-42-92863
CF-CUC	Douglas DC-3	Douglas	1943	19366	C.H. Babb Inc., Glendale, California	8 11 46	282	Cities Services, Edmonton	28 1 60	Ex-42-100903
CF-CUD	Douglas DC-3	Douglas	1942	6187	C.H. Babb Inc., Glendale, California	26 10 46	283	Quebecair	11 5 59	Ex-NC67136, Re-registered by Quebecair as CF-QBM
CF-CUE	Douglas DC-3	Douglas	1944	12983	C.H. Babb Inc., Glendale, California	17 1 47	284	Department of Transport	1 2 56	Ex-42-93108
CF-CUF	Douglas DC-3	Douglas	1944	12855	C.H. Babb Inc., Glendale, California	21 3 47	286	Written off at Penticton	22 12 50	Ex-42-92993
CF-CUG	Douglas DC-3	Douglas	1943	9891	Peace River Northern Airlines	21 5 47	287	Eldorado Mining and Smelting	13 2 58	Ex-42-24029
CF-CUH	Anson V	Federal Aircraft					228	Central Northern Airways	20 7 49	
CF-CUI	Anson V	Federal Aircraft					229	Central Northern Airways	20 7 49	
CF-DIG	Douglas DC-3	Douglas	1943	11850	Aircraft Industries of Canada	14 2 47	285	Transair, Winnipeg	1 1 60	Ex-42-088, Subsequently registered CF-TAT
CF-EFZ	Anson V	Federal Aircraft		MDF-220	Federal Aircraft	20 5 47	226	Cold Lake Air Services	23 10 53	Ex-12124
CF-ESA	Anson V			431	Aero Photos Ltd.	5 6 47	224	Written off	29 6 49	
CF-ESE	Anson V			BRC-1672	Federal Aircraft	46	225	C.H. Babb, Glendale, California	23 6 49	
CF-ESF	Anson V			432	Federal Aircraft	46	227	Central Aircraft Ltd.	23 5 50	
CF-CPI	Canadair C4-1	Canadair	1949	147	Canadair	5 49	401	Trans-Canada Airlines	27 11 51	*Empress of Sydney*, Re-registered as CF-TFU
CF-CPR	Canadair C4-1	Canadair	1949	148	Canadair	5 49	402	Written off at Tokyo	9 2 50	*Empress of Vancouver*
CF-CPJ	Canadair C4-1	Canadair	1949	149	Canadair	11 7 49	403	Trans-Canada Airlines	5 2 52	*Empress of Auckland*, Re-registered as CF-TFV
CF-CPP	Canadair C4-1	Canadair	1949	150	Canadair	11 7 49	404	Trans-Canada Airlines	31 12 51	*Empress of Hong Kong*, Re-registered as CF-TFW
CF-CPC	Douglas DC-4	Douglas		10327	PanAmerican Ex-N88933	50	411	Disappeared off Alaska, never found	21 7 51	
CF-CPD	Douglas DC-4	Douglas		10412	PanAmerican Ex-N88936	24 10 50	412	Cathay Pacific Airways	8 8 54	Re-registered as VR-HFF
CF-CUJ	Douglas DC-4	Douglas		27261	PanAmerican Ex-N88882	3 11 51	413	Maritime Central Airlines	10 4 57	
CF-CUK	Douglas DC-4	Douglas		10323	PanAmerican Ex-N88932	28 12 51	414	Transocean Air Lines	5 4 54	Re-registered as N9940F
CF-CUL	Douglas DC-4	Douglas		10384	PanAmerican Ex-N88928	20 11 51	415	Transocean Air Lines	5 4 54	Re-registered as N9941F
CF-CUU	Convair 240	Convair		73	Continental Air Lines Ex-N90844	12 12 52	391	Nito Airlines, Japan	23 12 63	Re-registered as JA5125
CF-CUV	Convair 240	Convair		94	Continental Air Lines Ex-N90845	19 3 53	392	All Nippon Air Lines, Japan	19 2 64	Re-registered as JA5126. Resold to TOA Airways, Japan
CF-CUW	Convair 240	Convair		95	Continental Air Lines Ex-N90846	16 2 53	393	All Nippon Air Lines, Japan	9 63	Re-registered as JA5118
CF-CUX	Convair 240	Convair		96	Continental Air Lines Ex-N90847	2 3 53	394	All Nippon Air Lines, Japan	16 9 64	Re-registered as JA5131
CF-CUY	Convair 240	Convair		97	Continental Air Lines Ex-N90848	8 5 53	395	All Nippon Air Lines, Japan	18 6 64	Re-registered as JA5130
CF-CUM	D.H.106 Comet 1A	de Havilland	1953	06013	de Havilland		421	Royal Aircraft Establishment, U.K.	31 12 53	Never acquired by CPAL. Registered as G-ANAV, scrapped 1955
CF-CUN	D.H.106 Comet 1A	de Havilland	1953	06014	de Havilland	1 2 53	422	Written off at Karachi, Pakistan	3 3 53	*Empress of Hawaii*
CF-CZG	Curtiss C-46F	Curtiss	1944	22523	Flying Tiger Line Ex-N67958	28 1 55	251	Carolina Aircraft Corporation	6 63	
CF-CZH	Curtiss C-46F	Curtiss	1944	22515	Flying Tiger Line Ex-N67962	6 2 55	252	Quebecair	15 12 57	
CF-CZI	Curtiss C-46F	Curtiss	1945	22542	Miami Airlines Ex-N1672M	11 2 55	253	Pacific Western Airlines	19 7 59	Converted to Super 46 Cargo in 1958
CF-CZJ	Curtiss C-46F	Curtiss	1945	22574	Miami Airlines Ex-N1679M	10 2 55	254	Pacific Western Airlines	21 7 59	Converted to Super 46 Cargo in 1958
CF-CZK	Curtiss C-46F	Curtiss		22501	American Air Export Ex-N5617V	18 2 55	255	Carolina Aircraft Corporation	19 3 63	
CF-CZL	Curtiss C-46F	Curtiss		22494	Transocean Air Lines Ex-N68967	12 3 55	256	Northern Wings, Mont Joli, Quebec	4 11 57	Leased to Trans-Labrador 9/4/57

Regn.	Type	Constructor	Year Built	Constr. Number	Acquired From	Date Registered by CPAL	CPAL Fleet Number	Disposition	Disposition Date	Comments
CF-CZM	Curtiss C-46	Curtiss	1944	22453	Compania Cubana de Aviacion Ex-N4879V	4 5 55	257	Pacific Western Airlines	21 7 59	Converted to Super 46 to carry 44 passengers in 1958
CF-CZN	Curtiss C-46	Curtiss	1944	22445	Intercontinental Airways Ex-N4878V	9 4 55	258	Pacific Western Airlines	21 7 59	Converted to Super 46 to carry 44 passengers in 1958
CF-CZO	DHC-3 Otter	DHC	1955	71	de Havilland Canada	1 4 55	71	Pacific Western Airlines	23 2 59	
CF-CZP	DHC-3 Otter	DHC	1955	69	de Havilland Canada	1 4 55	72	Pacific Western Airlines	23 2 59	
CF-CUS	Douglas DC-6A	Douglas	1953	44063	Douglas	8 53	435	Aigle Azur, Paris, France	13 4 54	
CF-CUT	Douglas DC-6A	Douglas	1953	44064	Douglas	9 53	436	Northwest Airlines	29 6 54	Re-registered as N566
CF-CZY	Douglas DC-6A	Douglas		45497	Douglas	14 6 58	445	Maritime Central Airways	25 9 58	Traded for CF-CZY DC-6B No. 449 — see below
CF-CZZ	Douglas DC-6A/B	Douglas		45498	Douglas	11 58	446	Pacific Western Airlines	70	Converted to DC-6B by Air-Research, Los Angeles, 17/2/59.
CF-CPB	Douglas DC-6A/B	Douglas		45499	Douglas Ex-N11565	29 7 58	447	Northwest Airlines	20 4 59	Converted to DC-6A/B by Air Research and Airomotive, Burbank
CF-CPC	Douglas DC-6A/B	Douglas		45500	Douglas Ex-N45500	16 9 58	448	World Airways	10 61	*Empress of Santa Maria*
CF-CUO	Douglas DC-6B	Douglas		43842	Douglas	17 1 53	431	UAT, France	3 6 59	*Empress of Lima,* Re-registered as F-BHMR. Lease-purchase
CF-CUP	Douglas DC-6B	Douglas		43843	Douglas	3 2 53	432	Written off at Cold Bay, Alaska	29 8 56	
CF-CUQ	Douglas DC-6B	Douglas		43844	Douglas	26 2 53	433	Bomb explosion at Dog Creek, B.C.	8 7 65	*Empress of Tokyo,* Leased to Trans Caribbean and Cunard Eagle
CF-CUR	Douglas DC-6B	Douglas		44062	Douglas	18 6 53	434	UAT, France	29 4 59	*Empress of Amsterdam*
CF-CZE	Douglas DC-6B	Douglas		44891	Douglas	16 1 56	437	World Airways	15 11 61	*Empress of Toronto,* Re-registered as N45502
CF-CZF	Douglas DC-6B	Douglas		44892	Douglas	2 2 56	438	Trans-Air, Sweden	12 11 61	*Empress of Sydney,* Re-registered as SE-BDH
CF-CZQ	Douglas DC-6B	Douglas		45078	Douglas Ex-OD-ADP G-ARZO	3 10 56	439	Concare Aircraft Leasing Corpn.	20 8 69	*Empress of Hong Kong,* Re-registered as N122M.
CF-CZR	Douglas DC-6B	Douglas		45079	Douglas	25 11 56	440	Trans-Air, Sweden	11 1 62	*Empress of Auckland,* Re-registered as SE-BDI
CF-CZS	Douglas DC-6B/C	Douglas		45326	Douglas	1 5 57	441	Transair, Winnipeg	18 4 69	*Empress of Montreal,* Sent to Santa Monica for conversion to cargo 9/10/61
CF-CZT	Douglas DC-6B	Douglas		45327	Douglas	30 6 57	442	OFC Leasing Corporation	25 8 69	*Empress of Lisbon,* Re-registered as N1228
CF-CZU	Douglas DC-6B	Douglas		45328	Douglas	18 6 57	443	Concare Aircraft Leasing Corpn.	20 8 69	*Empress of Honolulu,* Re-registered as N55CA
CF-CZV	Douglas DC-6B	Douglas		45329	Douglas	15 8 57	444	Trans-Air, Sweden	9 11 61	*Empress of Suva,* Re-registered as SE-BDG
CF-CZY	Douglas DC-6B	Douglas		45505	Maritime Central Airways	25 9 58	449	Trans-Carribean Airways	6 12 60	*Empress of Mexico City,* See above DC-6A CF-CZY No. 445
CF-CUS	Douglas DC-6B	Douglas		45178	Western Air Lines Ex-N93123	26 8 65	450	Western Air Lines	3 12 68	Leased aircraft returned to U.S. as N93123
CF-CZA	Bristol Britannia 314	Bristol	1958	13393	Bristol	1 4 58	521	Air Links Ltd., England	8 7 65	*Empress of Buenos Aires/Hong Kong,* Re-registered as G-ATGD.
CF-CZB	Bristol Britannia 314	Bristol	1958	13394	Bristol	29 4 58	522	Written off at Honolulu	22 7 62	*Empress of Vancouver/Lima*
CF-CZC	Bristol Britannia 314	Bristol	1958	13395	Bristol	30 5 58	523	Transglobe Airways	26 11 65	*Empress of Madrid/Tokyo,* Re-registered as G-ATLE.
CF-CZD	Bristol Britannia 314	Bristol	1958	13396	Bristol	29 6 58	524	Caledonian Airways	24 1 66	*Empress of Buenos Aires,* Re-registered as G-ATNZ.
CF-CZW	Bristol Britannia 314	Bristol	1958	13453	Bristol	6 8 58	525	Caledonian Airways	9 2 66	*Empress of Edmonton/Toronto/Rome,* Re-registered as G-ASTF.
CF-CZX	Bristol Britannia 314	Bristol	1958	13428	Bristol	3 7 58	526	Caledonian Airways	23 12 65	*Empress of Santa Maria/Canada,* Re-registered as G-ATMA.
CF-CPD	Bristol Britannia 324	Bristol	1959	13516	Bristol	16 10 59	527	Cunard Eagle	14 2 61	*Empress of Amsterdam,* Re-registered as G-ARKA. Scrapped July 1971
CF-CPE	Bristol Britannia 324	Bristol	1959	13517	Bristol	12 11 59	528	Cunard Eagle	11 4 61	*Empress of Mexico City,* Re-registered as G-ARKB. Scrapped July 1971
C-FCPF*	Douglas DC-8-43	Douglas	1961	45620	Douglas	22 2 61	601	Aerovias Colombianas	28 11 81	*Empress of Vancouver/Hong Kong/Rome/Santiago*
C-FCPG	Douglas DC-8-43	Douglas	1961	45623	FBA Corp., Apaloka, Florida	15 11 61	602	FBA Corp., Apaloka, Florida	17 3 80	*Empress of Montreal/Rome/Buenos Aires,* First commercial aircraft to exceed Mach 1
C-FCPH	Douglas DC-8-43	Douglas	1961	45621	Douglas	3 3 61	603	FBA Corp., Apaloka, Florida	10 11 80	*Empress of Winnipeg/Tokyo/Lima*
C-FCPI	Douglas DC-8-43	Douglas	1961	45622	Douglas	19 5 61	604	FBA Corp., Apaloka, Florida	24 11 80	*Empress of Calgary/Honolulu/Amsterdam/Toronto/Hong Kong*
C-FCPJ	Douglas DC-8-43	Douglas	1963	45661	Douglas	3 5 63	605	Aerovias Colombianas	12 12 81	*Empress of Toronto/Sydney/Mexico City*
CF-CPK	Douglas DC-8-43	Douglas	1965	45761	Douglas	14 10 65	606	Written off at Tokyo	4 3 66	*Empress of Edmonton/Hong Kong*
C-FCPM	Douglas DC-8-53	Douglas	1966	45809	Douglas	31 5 66	607	Aerovias Colombianas	7 6 82	*Empress of Amsterdam/Lisbon*
C-FCPN	Douglas DC-8-51	Douglas	1958	45252	Trans International Airlines, Atlanta Ex-N8008D	2 10 66	600	Returned to TIA	1 10 67	*Empress of Santiago,* Prototype DC-8, Leased aircraft
C-FCPT	Douglas DC-8-55F	Douglas	1966	45858	Braniff Ex-N1509U	17 11 67	608	International Aviation Services (U.K.)	17 2 78	*Empress of Santiago,* Leased to Flying Tigers 14/9/77-31/1/78
N791SA	Boeing 707-138B	Boeing	1959	17698	Standard Airways	15 10 67	791	Written off at Vancouver	7 2 68	*Empress of Sydney,* Leased aircraft
C-FCPO	Douglas DC-8-63	Douglas	1968	45926	Douglas	17 1 68	801	Worldways, Toronto	28 5 83	*Empress of Tokyo/Quebec*
C-FCPP	Douglas DC-8-63	Douglas	1968	45927	Douglas	31 1 68	802	Worldways, Toronto	9 5 83	*Empress of Honolulu/Alberta,* Leased to UAT 10/3/72-13/3/73 as F-BOLJ
C-FCPQ	Douglas DC-8-63	Douglas	1968	45928	Douglas	24 2 68	803	Worldways, Toronto	9 5 83	*Empress of Hong Kong/Ontario*
C-FCPS	Douglas DC-8-63	Douglas	1968	45929	Douglas	16 6 68	804	Worldways, Toronto	18 6 83	*Empress of Sydney/Fiji/Madrid/British Columbia*
C-FCPL	Douglas DC-8-63	Douglas	1972	46095	Eastern Airlines Ex-N8757	13 11 72	805	Cammacorp	7 4 82	*Empress of Athens/Manitoba,* Converted to Series 73F
C-FCPN	Boeing 727-117	Boeing	1970	20327	Boeing	10 3 70	721	National Aircraft Leasing, Los Angeles	2 5 77	
C-FCPK	Boeing 727-117	Boeing	1970	20328	Boeing	20 4 70	722	National Aircraft Leasing, Los Angeles	6 6 77	
C-FCUR	Boeing 727-117	Boeing	1971	20512	Boeing	11 3 71	723	Boeing Equipment Holding Company	17 3 77	
C-FCUS	Boeing 727-117	Boeing	1971	20513	Boeing	24 4 71	724	National Aircraft Leasing, Los Angeles	24 5 77	
C-GCPA	Boeing 727-217	Boeing	1975	21055	Boeing	15 4 75	771	Dan Air	1 12 83	*Empress of San Francisco,* Leased to Dan Air 30/3/82 prior to sale
C-GCPB	Boeing 727-217	Boeing	1975	21056	Boeing	27 4 75	772	Dan Air	1 3 84	*Empress of Los Angeles,* Leased to Dan Air 1/2/83 prior to sale
C-FCRA	Boeing 747-217B	Boeing	1973	20801	Boeing	16 11 73	741	Pakistan International Airlines	22 9 86	*Empress of Asia/Japan/Italy*
C-FCRB	Boeing 747-217B	Boeing	1973	20802	Boeing	3 12 73	742	Pakistan International Airlines	9 5 86	*Empress of Canada/Japan*
C-FCRD	Boeing 747-217B	Boeing	1974	20927	Boeing	21 11 74	743	Pakistan International Airlines	27 10 86	*Empress of Australia/Japan/Canada,* Leased to Braniff 15/11/78-7/12/78
C-FCRE	Boeing 747-217B	Boeing	1974	20929	Boeing	2 12 74	744	Pakistan International Airlines	18 12 85	*Empress of Italy/Australia*
C-FCPB	Boeing 737-217	Boeing	1968	19884	Boeing	22 10 68	701	People Express	9 11 82	
C-FCPC	Boeing 737-217	Boeing	1968	19885	Boeing	9 11 68	702	People Express	22 11 82	
C-FCPD	Boeing 737-217	Boeing	1968	19886	Boeing	1 12 68	703	People Express	20 12 82	
C-FCPE	Boeing 737-217	Boeing	1968	19887	Boeing	20 12 68	704	People Express	11 3 83	
C-FCPU	Boeing 737-217	Boeing	1968	19888	Boeing	27 12 68	705	People Express	23 5 83	
C-FCPV	Boeing 737-217	Boeing	1969	20196	Boeing	24 3 69	766	In service		*Empress of Vancouver/Expo '86/Vancouver,* Originally No. 706
C-FCPZ	Boeing 737-217	Boeing	1969	20197	Boeing	28 3 69	767	In service		*Empress of Los Angeles,* Originally No. 707
C-GCPM	Boeing 737-217 Advanced	Boeing	1979	21716	Boeing	22 5 79	708	In service		*Empress of San Francisco*
C-GCPN	Boeing 737-217 Advanced	Boeing	1979	21717	Boeing	20 6 79	709	In service		*Empress of Calgary*
C-GCPO	Boeing 737-217 Advanced	Boeing	1979	21718	Boeing	3 7 79	710	In service		*Empress of Edmonton*

* On January 1, 1974, Canada's aircraft registration prefix changed from CF- to C-

Regn.	Type	Constructor	Year Built	Constr. Number	Acquired From	Date Registered by CPAL	CPAL Fleet Number	Disposition	Disposition Date	Comments
C-GCPP	Boeing 737-217 Advanced	Boeing	1980	22255	Boeing	28 5 80	711	In service		*Empress of Winnipeg*
C-GCPQ	Boeing 737-217 Advanced	Boeing	1980	22256	Boeing	18 6 80	712	In service		*Empress of Victoria*
C-GCPS	Boeing 737-217 Advanced	Boeing	1981	22257	Boeing	20 4 81	714	In service		*Empress of Prince George*
C-GCPT	Boeing 737-217 Advanced	Boeing	1981	22258	Boeing	10 6 81	715	In service		*Empress of Fort St. John*
C-GCPU	Boeing 737-217 Advanced	Boeing	1981	22259	Boeing	12 6 81	716	In service		*Empress of Fort Nelson*
C-GCPV	Boeing 737-217 ER	Boeing	1981	22260	Boeing	29 7 81	717	In service		*Empress of Toronto*
C-GCPX	Boeing 737-217 ER	Boeing	1981	22341	Boeing	6 8 81	718	In service		*Empress of Ottawa*
C-GCPY	Boeing 737-217 Advanced	Boeing	1981	22342	Boeing	30 10 81	719	In service		*Empress of Halifax*
C-GCPZ	Boeing 737-217 ER	Boeing	1982	22658	Boeing	13 4 82	720	In service		*Empress of Montreal*
C-GFCP	Boeing 737-217 Advanced	Boeing	1982	22659	Boeing	20 5 82	721	In service		*Empress of Prince Rupert*
C-GJCP	Boeing 737-217 Advanced	Boeing	1982	22728	Boeing	1 10 82	722	In service		*Empress of Terrace*
C-GKCP	Boeing 737-217 Advanced	Boeing	1982	22729	Boeing	1 11 82	723	In service		*Empress of Watson Lake*
C-GMCP	Boeing 737-217 Advanced	Boeing	1983	22864	Boeing	1 3 83	724	In service		*Empress of Whitehorse*
C-GQCP	Boeing 737-217 Advanced	Boeing	1983	22865	Boeing	22 4 83	725	In service		*Empress of Richmond*
C-GRCP	Boeing 737-2K2	Boeing	1978	21397	Leased from Transavia for five years	11 10 85	726	In service		*Empress of Grande Prairie*, Ex-PH-TVP, Transavia
C-GXCP	Boeing 737-204	Boeing	1982	22640	Leased from Britannia for six months	1 11 85	727	Returned to Britannia Airways	28 4 86	*The Hon. C.S. Rolls*, Ex-G-BJCV
C-FACP	Boeing 737-2L9	Boeing	1979	22072	Leased from Air Nauru	17 10 85	728	In service		*Empress of St. John's*, Ex-OY-APO, Maersk Air
C-FHCP	Boeing 737-2T5	Boeing	1980	22024	Leased from Chemical Bank Canada Leasing	3 4 86	729	In service		*Empress of Kittimat*, Ex-G-BGTV
C-FCPM	Boeing 737-2T7	Boeing	1982	22761	Monarch Airlines	31 10 86	730	In service		*Empress of Yukon*, Ex-G-DWHH
C-FCPN	Boeing 737-2T7	Boeing	1982	22762	Monarch Airlines	2 6 86	731	In service		*Empress of Hamilton*, Ex-G-DGDP
C-GQBB	Boeing 737-296	Boeing	1980	22276	Quebecair	20 10 86	732	In service		Leased to Pan American 9/5/83 - 10/5/85
C-GQBH	Boeing 737-296	Boeing	1981	22516	Quebecair	20 10 86	734	In service		Leased to Pan American 29/4/83 - 27/4/85
C-FICP	Boeing 737-2K2	Boeing	1980	22025	Leased from Transavia for six months	1 11 86	780	In service		Ex PH-TVR
C-FCPG	Boeing 737-317	Boeing	1985	23173	Boeing	12 4 85	751	GPA Group, Shannon, Ireland	28 4 86	*Empress of Ontario*
C-FCPI	Boeing 737-317	Boeing	1985	23174	Boeing	26 4 85	752	GPA Group, Shannon, Ireland	3 7 86	*Empress of Nova Scotia*
C-FCPJ	Boeing 737-317	Boeing	1985	23175	Boeing	7 5 85	753	GPA Group, Shannon, Ireland	15 4 86	*Empress of Alberta*
C-FCPK	Boeing 737-317	Boeing	1986	23176	Boeing	3 4 86	754	GPA Group, Shannon, Ireland	15 12 86	*Empress of Manitoba*,
C-FCPL	Boeing 737-317	Boeing	1986	23177	Boeing	10 4 86	755	GPA Group, Shannon, Ireland	22 12 86	*Empress of Quebec*,
N1834U	DC-10-10	McDonnell Douglas	1972	47966	United Air Lines	21 3 83	334	In service		*Empress of Lima*, Leased from United Air Lines until 1987
N1836U	DC-10-10	McDonnell Douglas	1973	47968	United Air Lines	1 7 83	336	In service		*Empress of Santiago/Expo '86*, Leased from United Air Lines until 1987
N1837U	DC-10-10	McDonnell Douglas	1973	47969	United Air Lines	31 4 83	337	In service		*Empress of Fiji*, Leased from United Air Lines until 1987
N1816U	DC-10-10	McDonnell Douglas	1973	46615	United Air Lines	14 7 85		Returned to United Air Lines	8 9 85	Leased for 57 days to cover operations while Nos. 903 and 907 had long range tanks fitted
C-GCPC	DC-10-30	McDonnell Douglas	1979	46540	McDonnell Douglas	27 3 79	901	In service		*Empress of Quebec/Amsterdam*, Leased to Varig 4/4/79-3/4/80
C-GCPD	DC-10-30	McDonnell Douglas	1979	46541	McDonnell Douglas	19 7 79	902	In service		*Empress of Sydney/British Columbia*, Leased to Varig 20/7/79-14/6/80
C-GCPE	DC-10-30 ER	McDonnell Douglas	1979	46542	McDonnell Douglas	2 11 79	903	In service		*Empress of Alberta/Rome/Buenos Aires*
C-GCPF	DC-10-30 ER	McDonnell Douglas	1980	46543	McDonnell Douglas	26 11 80	904	Leased	12 7 83	*Empress of Buenos Aires/Santiago*, Leased to United Air Lines
C-GCPG	DC-10-30 ER	McDonnell Douglas	1981	48285	McDonnell Douglas	27 2 81	905	Leased	5 4 83	*Empress of Fiji*, Leased to United Air Lines
C-GCPH	DC-10-30 ER	McDonnell Douglas	1981	48288	McDonnell Douglas	3 11 81	906	Leased	25 3 83	*Empress of Lima*, Leased to United Air Lines
C-GCPI	DC-10-30 ER	McDonnell Douglas	1982	48296	McDonnell Douglas	19 2 82	907	In service		*Empress of Honolulu/Auckland*
C-GCPJ	DC-10-30	McDonnell Douglas	1981	46991	Singapore Airlines	17 3 82	908	In service		*Empress of Rome*
C-FCRA	DC-10-30	McDonnell Douglas	1974	46931	Pakistan International Airlines	22 9 86	909	In service		*Empress of Hong Kong*, Ex-PK-AXC
C-FCRB	DC-10-30	McDonnell Douglas	1974	46940	Pakistan International Airlines	9 5 86	910	In service		*Empress of Tokyo*, Ex-PK-AXD
C-FCRE	DC-10-30	McDonnell Douglas	1975	47868	Pakistan International Airlines	16 12 85	911	In service		*Empress of Canada*, Ex-PK-BBL
C-FCRD	DC-10-30	McDonnell Douglas	1976	47889	Pakistan International Airlines	27 10 86	912	In service		*Empress of Lisbon*, Ex-PK-AYM

Eastern Provincial Airways Aircraft

Regn.	Type	Constructor	Year Built	Constr. Number	Acquired From	Date Registered by EPA	CPAL Fleet Number	Disposition	Disposition Date	Comments
C-FEPL	Boeing 737-2E1	Boeing	1969	20396	Boeing	25 11 69	201	In service		*Empress of Gander*, Ex-N1785B
C-FEPR	Boeing 737-2E1	Boeing	1969	20397	Boeing	15 12 69	202	In service		*Empress of Saint John*, Ex-N1786B
C-FEPO	Boeing 737-2A3	Boeing	1969	20300	Boeing	17 7 70	203	In service		*Empress of Charlottetown*, Ex-N1788B
C-FEPP	Boeing 737-2E1	Boeing	1973	20681	Boeing	12 3 73	204	In service		*Empress of Fredericton*
C-FEPU	Boeing 737-2E1	Boeing	1973	20776	Boeing	29 10 73	205	In service		*Empress of Cape Breton*
C-GEPA	Boeing 737-2E1	Boeing	1974	20976	Boeing	6 12 74	206	In service		*Empress of Cornerbrook*
C-GEPM	Boeing 737-2T5	Boeing	1981	22395	Leased from International Lease Finance	8 3 85	207	In service		*Empress of Labrador*, Leased until 25 11 88

Air Maritime

Regn.	Type	Constructor	Year Built	Constr. Number	Acquired From	Date Registered by AM	AM Fleet Number	Disposition	Disposition Date	Comments
C-FINE	British Aerospace 748-232	Hawker Siddley	1967	1611	Inexco Oil	1 2 75	301	For disposal		Ex-VP-BCK, Bahamas Airways
C-GDOP	British Aerospace 748-238	Hawker Siddley	1976	1745	Austin Airways	16 4 82	304	For disposal		Ex-YV-46C, LAV
C-GEPB	British Aerospace 748-254	Hawker Siddley	1970	1686	Ghana Airways	3 5 81	303	For disposal		Ex-9G-ABX, Ghana Airways
C-GEPI	British Aerospace 748-227	Hawker Siddley	1966	1594	COPA, Panama	15 5 78	302	For disposal		Ex-HP-432, COPA, Panama

Nordair Aircraft (incorporated into CPAL fleet on January 1, 1987)

Regn.	Type	Constructor	Year Built	Constr. Number	Acquired From	Date Registered by Nordair	CPAL Fleet Number	Disposition	Disposition Date	Comments
C-FNAB	Boeing 737-242C	Boeing	1968	19847	Boeing	27 11 68	701	In service		Ex-N6241
C-FNAH	Boeing 737-242C	Boeing	1969	19848	Boeing	18 4 69	702	In service		Combi
C-FNAQ	Boeing 737-242C	Boeing	1970	20455	Boeing	13 5 70	703	In service		Ex-EI-BOC, Combi
C-FNAP	Boeing 737-242C	Boeing	1970	20496	Boeing	16 6 71	704	In service		Ex-N1788B, Combi
C-GNDL	Boeing 737-242	Boeing	1975	21186	Boeing	12 11 75	705	In service		
C-FNDM	Boeing 737-242	Boeing	1979	22074	Boeing	30 11 79	706	In service		
C-GNDR	Boeing 737-242	Boeing	1980	22075	Boeing	31 1 80	707	In service		Ex-N8536Z
C-GNDC	Boeing 737-242C	Boeing	1979	21728	Boeing	15 6 79	761	In service		Combi
C-GNDU	Boeing 737-242C	Boeing	1982	22877	Boeing	6 6 82	762	In service		Combi
C-GNDS	Boeing 737-2Q8	Boeing	1978	21518	Leased from International Lease Finance	31 12 80	771	In service		Ex-N977MP, International Lease Finance
C-GNDX	Boeing 737-229	Boeing	1974	20911	Sabena	20 20 86		In service		Leased from Sabena Ex OO-SDE
C-FNAI	FH-227E	Fairchild Hiller	1966	505	Fairchild	30 8 71	505	In service		Ex-N7802M, Mohawk
C-FNAJ	FH-227E	Fairchild Hiller	1966	508	Fairchild	24 4 72	508	In service		Ex-N7804M, Mohawk
C-FNAK	FH-227D	Fairchild Hiller	1966	519	Fairchild	22 11 72	519	In service		
C-GNDH	FH-227B	Fairchild Hiller	1966	529	Touraine Air Transport, France	19 9 82	529	In service		Ex-N4220, Ozark Airlines
C-GNDI	FH-227B	Fairchild Hiller	1967	564	Touraine Air Transport, France	82	564	In service		Ex-N4235, Ozark Airlines
C-GNDZ	L-188C Electra	Lockheed	1959	1111	American Jet Industries	8 2 78	111	In service		Ex-N128US, Northwest Orient
C-FNAY	L-188C Electra	Lockheed	1959	1113	Northwest Orient	21 3 72	113	In service		Ex-N130US, Northwest Orient

Bibliography

A complete listing of all the books, journals, magazines and articles that have been read to provide some of the information for this book would be extremely lengthy. The following list comprises those works which were most useful and which are available through libraries, bookstores, etc. Some are out of print and readers may have to revert to larger libraries and used bookstores to obtain copies.

Angelucci, E., *World Encyclopedia of Civil Aircraft*, Crown Publishers, New York, 1982.

Angelucci, E. and Matricardi, P., *World Aircraft 1918 - 1935*, Sampson Low, Maiden head, England, 1977.

Booth, J.M.A., *Canadian Pacific in the Selkirks*, BRMNA, Calgary, 1986.

Bowers, P.M., *Curtiss Aircraft 1907 - 1947*, Putnam, London, 1979.

Casey, L.S. and Batchelor, J., *Seaplanes and Flying Boats*, Phoebus, London, 1980.

Chant, C., *Early Airliners*, Phoebus, London, 1980.

Chant, C., and Batchelor, J., *Jet Airliners*, Phoebus, London, 1979.

Chant, C., and Batchelor, J., *Piston-Engined Airliners*, Phoebus, London, 1980.

Charlebois, P., *Sternwheelers & Sidewheelers — The Romance of Steam-driven Paddleboats in Canada*, NC Press, Toronto, 1978.

Cohen, S., *Yukon River Steamboats — A Pictorial History*, Pictorial Histories Publishing, Missoula, Montana, 1982.

Cooksley, P.G., *Advanced Jetliners*, Phoebus, London, 1980.

Ellis, F.H., *Canada's Flying Heritage*, University of Toronto Press, Toronto, 1954.

Ellis, J.R., *The Canadian Civil Aircraft Register*, Canadian Aviation Historical Association, Willowdale, 1965 - 1975.

Endres, G.G., *World Airline Fleets 1986*, Aviation Data Centre, London, 1986.

Gray, F.O., *Air Canada — The First 40 . . .*, Air Canada, Montreal, 1977.

Gradidge, J.M.G., *The Douglas DC-3 and its predecessors*, Air Britain, Tonbridge, England, 1984.

Green, W. and Pollinger, G., *The Aircraft of the World*, Macdonald, London, Third Edition, 1965.

Green, W. and Swanborough, G., *The World's Airliners*, Arco, New York, 1982.

Grey, C.G. and Bridgman, L., *Jane's All the World Aircraft 1938*, reprinted by David and Charles, Newton Abbot, England, 1972.

Gunston, B., *Early Jetliners*, Phoebus, London, 1980.

Hardy, M., *World Civil Aircraft Since 1945*, Charles Scribner's Sons, New York, 1979.

Hotson, F.W., *The de Havilland Canada Story*, CANAV Books, Toronto, 1983.

Jackson, A.J., *Avro Aircraft Since 1908*, Putnam, London, 1965.

Jackson, A.J., *De Havilland Aircraft Since 1909*, Putnam, London, 1978.

Jerram, M.F. and Barnett, C., *General Aviation*, Phoebus, London, 1980.

Juptner, J.P., *U.S. Civil Aircraft (Volumes 1 - 8)*, Aero Publishers, Fallbrook, California, 1962 - 1981.

Keith, R.A., *Bush Pilot With A Briefcase*, Doubleday, Toronto, 1972.

Lamb, W.K., *History of the Canadian Pacific Railway*, Macmillan, New York, 1977.

McDonough, K., *Atlantic Wings*, Model Aeronautical Press, Hemel Hempstead, England, 1966.

Milberry, L., *Aviation in Canada*, McGraw-Hill Ryerson, Toronto, 1979.

Milberry, L., *The Canadair North Star*, CANAV Books, Toronto, 1982.

Molson, K.M., *Pioneering in Canadian Air Transport*, James Richardson and Sons, Winnipeg, 1974.

Molson, K.M. and Taylor, H.A., *Canadian Aircraft since 1909*, Canada's Wings, Stittsville, Ontario, 1982.

Munson, K., *Airliners Since 1946*, Macmillan, New York, Second Edition, 1975.

Ormes, I. and Ormes, R., *The Sky Masters*, William Kimber, London, 1976.

Powell, G., *Ferryman*, Airlife, Shrewsbury, England, 1982.

Schiff, B.J., *The Boeing 707*, Aero Publishers, Fallbrook, California, Third Printing, 1982.

Smith, P., *It Seems Like Only Yesterday*, McClelland and Stewart, Toronto, 1986.

Solberg, C., *Conquest of the Skies*, Little Brown and Company, Boston and Toronto, 1979.

Stroud, J., *European Transport Aircraft Since 1910*, Putnam, London, 1966.

Stroud, J., *Airliners of the 1930s*, Phoebus, London, 1980.

Sutherland, A.G., *Canada's Aviation Pioneers*, McGraw-Hill Ryerson, Toronto, 1978.

Swanborough, G., *Civil Aircraft of the World*, Charles Scribner's Sons, New York, 1980.

Taylor, J.W.R., *Jane's All The World's Aircraft*, Jane's Publishing Company, London, 1985.

Tomkins, N.M., *Airliner Production List 1980/81*, Airline Publications and Sales, Hounslow, England, 1981.

Tomkins, N.M. and Halliday, R.D., *Airlines Production List 1986*, Aviation Data Centre, London, 1986.

In addition, much information was obtained from the following periodical publications.

The Aeroplane, London, England.

Canadian Aviation Historical Society Journal, Willowdale, Ontario.

Canadian Pacific Air Lines' Annual Reports.

CP Air News, Editor G. McBurnie, Canadian Pacific Air Lines, Vancouver. (Now retitled *Esprit!*)*

Flight International, Sutton, England.

The History of CP Air, compiled by P. Golding, Canadian Pacific Air Lines, Public Relations Department, Vancouver, 1985.*

The Spanner, Canadian Pacific's in-house, staff magazine from October 1947 until replaced by *CP Rail News* in September 1971.*

* In house journals, not available to the public.

Acknowledgements

As is always the case with a work of this type, many friends and acquaintances have provided information, assistance and support. Without their help, kindness, goodwill, patient assistance and encouragement, it could not have been completed.

Special thanks go to Jim McKeachie, the recently retired Director of Public Relations of Canadian Pacific Air Lines, and his former staff for the information they provided. George McBurnie allowed me access to past issues of the CP Air News. Peter Golding was extremely helpful and Gordon Croucher supplied me with many of the necessary photographs. John Duck, Manager Aeronautical Services, was of immeasurable assistance providing data which were incorporated into the aircraft tables at the end of this work. Hank Van Bockhoven, Supervisor Materials Planning, very kindly allowed me free access to his CPAL aircraft roster after he heard of my preparing this work. Richard Benedetti, Canadian Pacific Air Lines Sales Representative in Calgary and Carol Caney, formerly with Canadian Pacific Public Relations in Calgary, located information for me. Nicholas Morant supplied several photographs and, as always, was a source of much information and inspiratation.

Clark Seaborn, George Evens and Gerry Raham of Calgary provided many ideas and suggestions and Phil Lucas, who flew for Canadian Airways, gave me an insight into the hazardous conditions one had to endure flying for Canada's major airline in the 1930s. J.P. (Pat) McDonald, formerly of the Air Historical Branch of the Air Ministry in London, England, forwarded much information and improved my English considerably. As an ex-North Star captain with the RCAF, Pat corrected many points I had misconstrued from my armchair flying. Geoffrey Lester of the University of Alberta prepared the maps. I am especially appreciative of the forewords provided by Donald Carty, President of CPAL and N.R. "Buck" Crump, ex-Chairman and President of Canadian Pacific Limited. Finally, I would like to thank my daughter Susan and Mrs. Katalin Dyke for transposing my handwriting into a typed manuscript. Their labours, outside their normal working hours, are gratefully acknowledged.

This work is dedicated with love, affection and thanks to my wife Carol and to our children Susan, Michael and Nigel. For seven years they suffered my lengthy absences on business trips which totalled approximately half of each year. They did not complain that my work kept me away for so much of the time and understood my preoccupation with trying to catch up with my "book work" when I got home. For their understanding and support, I thank them.

The Author

Donald Bain was born in Scotland, educated at St. Paul's School, London and graduated from the University of Nottingham with an M.Sc. in Geology in 1963. Later that year he came to Canada and in 1964 commenced work with Mobil Oil Canada, Ltd. in Dawson Creek, British Columbia. In 1971, he obtained an M.Sc. in Administrative Studies at The City University, London, England. He left Mobil in 1973 to work for PanCanadian Petroleum where he was Co-ordinator Exploration Administration. In 1979, he joined the Canadian Imperial Bank of Commerce and spent seven years looking after the technical and business development aspects of the Bank's overseas oil and gas loans. He is married with three children and lives in Calgary, Alberta where he is now General Manager of Union Faith (Canada) Limited.